기후변화
국제조약집

Essential Documents in International Climate Change Law

박덕영 편저

박영사

이 편저서는 2016년 대한민국 교육부와 한국연구재단의 지원을 받아 수행된 연구임
(NRF-2016S1A3A2925230)

머리말

우리는 기후변화의 시대에 살고 있다. 기후변화가 인간의 활동으로 초래되었다는 것은 이제 자명한 '사실'로 받아들여지고 있으며, 전 세계가 그 대응을 위해 노력을 기울여야 하는 상황이다. 다행스럽게도 1992년 채택된 기후변화협약(UNFCCC)을 시작으로 1997년 교토의정서가 성립되었고, 2015년에는 파리협정이 채택되었다. 이로써 국제사회는 어렵고 더디게만 보였던 국제적 합의를 계속하여 업그레이드시키는 성과를 거두었다. 비록 미국 트럼프 행정부가 파리협정에 대한 탈퇴를 선언한 바 있지만, 기후변화에 대응하기 위한 국제적 논의와 노력은 계속 이어질 것으로 확신한다.

이 책은 필자가 낸 『국제법 기본조약집』 및 『국제경제법 기본조약집』과 그 맥을 같이 하는 것이다. 그동안 기후변화와 관련된 국제조약들을 한 데 묶어 정리하게 되었다. 우선 법적 구속력은 없지만, 국제적 환경보호에 있어 매우 중요한 의미를 지니는 1972년 스톡홀름 선언과 1992년 환경과 개발에 관한 리우선언을 영한대역으로 구성했다. 이어서 기후변화에 대응하기 위한 국제적 논의의 성과들인 기후변화협약, 교토의정서 및 파리협정을 마찬가지로 영한대역으로 실었다. 더 나아가 기후변화협약 당사국총회의 결정문들 중에서 중요하면서도 자주 인용되고, 파리협정 채택 이후에도 중요한 의미가 있는 것들을 추려 수록하였다. 다만, 이들 결정문은 공식적인 우리말 번역문이 존재하지 않으므로 영어원문만으로 구성하고, 가급적 결정문의 구조를 훼손하지 않기 위해 노력했다.

이 책은 우선 최근 대학들에서 확산되고 있는 기후변화에 대한 관심과 그만큼 늘어난 관련된 강의들에서 활용될 수 있을 것으로 기대된다. 특히 학생들은 영한대역을 통해 우리말과 영어원문을 함께 살펴봄으로써 원어의 의미를 더욱 정확하게 이해하고, 조약용어에 대한 표준적인 우리말 번역을 확인할 수 있을 것이다. 한편 이 책은 조약문뿐 아니라 총회 결정문도 수록함으로써 기후변화협상에 참여하는 우리 정부 대표단을 비롯한 전문가와 실무자들도 쉽게 휴대하고 활용할 수 있는 레퍼런스가 될 것으로 생각된다.

iv

기후변화에 대응하기 위한 국제적 논의는 앞으로도 다이내믹하게 전개될 것이고, 그만큼 다양한 문서들이 생산될 것이다. 앞으로 나오게 될 중요 결정문들 역시 새 판에서 지속적으로 반영할 것을 약속드린다. 아울러 많은 독자들의 제안과 요청에도 귀를 기울이고자 한다.

이 책의 출간을 허락해 주신 박영사 안종만 회장님과 조성호 이사님, 여러 조약들과 결정문들을 정성스럽게 편집해 주신 문선미 과장님께 감사드리며, 책의 발간을 처음부터 끝까지 챙겨준 필자의 제자이자 SSK 기후변화와 국제법 연구센터의 연구교수인 김승민 박사와 이일호 박사에게도 고마움을 전한다.

2017년 6월 기후변화를 실감하는 여름의 문턱에서
편저자 박 덕 영 씀

차례

환경선언

1. Declaration of the United Nations Conference on the Human Environment (1972)

Date : 16 June 1972

Link : www.un.org/documents

The United Nations Conference on the Human Environment,

Having met at Stockholm from 5 to 16 June 1972,

Having considered the need for a common outlook and for common principles to inspire and guide the peoples of the world in the preservation and enhancement of the human environment,

Proclaims that:

1. Man is both creature and moulder of his environment, which gives him physical sustenance and affords him the opportunity for intellectual, moral, social and spiritual growth. In the long and tortuous evolution of the human race on this planet a stage has been reached when, through the rapid acceleration of science and technology, man has acquired the power to transform his environment in countless ways and on an unprecedented scale. Both aspects of man's environment, the natural and the man-made, are essential to his well-being and to the enjoyment of basic human rights-even the right to life itself.

2. The protection and improvement of the human environment is a major issue which affects the well-being of peoples and economic development throughout the world; it is the urgent desire of the peoples of the whole world and the duty of all Governments.

3. Man has constantly to sum up experience and go on discovering, inventing, creating and advancing. In our time, man's capability to transform his surroundings, if used wisely, can bring to all peoples the benefits of development and the opportunity to enhance the quality of life. Wrongly or heedlessly applied, the same power can do incalculable harm to human beings and the human environment. We see around us growing evidence of man-made harm in many regions of the earth: dangerous levels of pollution in water, air, earth and living beings; major and undesirable disturbances to the ecological balance of the biosphere; destruction and depletion of irreplaceable resources; and gross deficiencies, harmful to the physical, mental and social health of man, in the man-made environment, particularly in the living and working environment.

4. In the developing countries most of the environmental problems are caused by under-development. Millions continue to live far below the minimum levels required for a decent human existence, deprived of adequate food and clothing, shelter and education, health and sani-

tation. Therefore, the developing countries must direct their efforts to development, bearing in mind their priorities and the need to safeguard and improve the environment. For the same purpose, the industrialized countries should make efforts to reduce the gap themselves and the developing countries. In the industrialized countries, environmental problems are generally related to industrialization and technological development.

5. The natural growth of population continuously presents problems for the preservation of the environment, and adequate policies and measures should be adopted, as appropriate, to face these problems. Of all things in the world, people are the most precious. It is the people that propel social progress, create social wealth, develop science and technology and, through their hard work, continuously transform the human environment. Along with social progress and the advance of production, science and technology, the capability of man to improve the environment increases with each passing day.

6. A point has been reached in history when we must shape our actions throughout the world with a more prudent care for their environmental consequences. Through ignorance or indifference we can do massive and irreversible harm to the earthly environment on which our life and well-being depend. Conversely, through fuller knowledge and wiser action, we can achieve for ourselves and our posterity a better life in an environment more in keeping with human needs and hopes. There are broad vistas for the enhancement of environmental quality and the creation of a good life. What is needed is an enthusiastic but calm state of mind and intense but orderly work. For the purpose of attaining freedom in the world of nature, man must use knowledge to build, in collaboration with nature, a better environment. To defend and improve the human environment for present and future generations has become an imperative goal for mankind—a goal to be pursued together with, and in harmony with, the established and fundamental goals of peace and of worldwide economic and social development.

7. To achieve this environmental goal will demand the acceptance of responsibility by citizens and communities and by enterprises and institutions at every level; all sharing equitably in common efforts. Individuals in all walks of life as well as organizations in many fields, by their values and the sum of their actions, will shape the world environment of the future.

Local and national governments will bear the greatest burden for large—scale environmental policy and action within their jurisdictions. International co—operation is also needed in order to raise resources to support the developing countries in carrying out their responsibilities in this field. A growing class of environmental problems, because they are regional or global in extent or because they affect the common international realm, will require extensive co-operation among nations and action by international organizations in the common interest.

The Conference calls upon Governments and peoples to exert common efforts for the preservation and improvement of the human environment, for the benefit of all the people and for their posterity.

Principles

States the common conviction that:

Principle 1

Man has the fundamental right to freedom, equality and adequate conditions of life, in an environment of a quality that permits a life of dignity and well-being, and he bears a solemn responsibility to protect and improve the environment for present and future generations. In this respect, policies promoting or perpetuating apartheid, racial segregation, discrimination, colonial and other forms of oppression and foreign domination stand condemned and must be eliminated.

원칙 1

인간은 품위 있고 행복한 생활을 가능하게 하는 환경 속에서 자유, 평등과 적당한 수준의 생활보건을 향유할 기본적 권리를 가지며, 현 세대 및 다음 세대를 위해 환경을 보호, 개선할 엄숙한 책임을 진다. 이 점에서 인권 차별, 인권 분리, 차별대우, 식민정책 및 그 밖의 형태의 억압이나 외국 지배를 영속화하려고 하거나 추구하는 정책은 규탄되어야 하며 배척되어야 한다.

Principle 2

The natural resources of the earth, including the air, water, land, flora and fauna and especially representative samples of natural ecosystems, must be safeguarded for the benefit of present and future generations through careful planning or management, as appropriate.

원칙 2

대기, 물, 토양, 동식물군과 특히 자연생태계의 대표적 표본 종 등을 포함하는 지구상의 천연 자원은 현재 및 장차의 세대를 위하여 세심한 계획, 적절한 관리를 통해 보호되어야 한다.

Principle 3

The capacity of the earth to produce vital renewable resources must be maintained

원칙 3

중요한 재생이 가능한 자원을 생산하는 지구의 능력은 유지되어야 하며, 가능한 한 회복

and, wherever practicable, restored or improved.

또는 개선되어야 한다.

Principle 4

원칙 4

Man has a special responsibility to safeguard and wisely manage the heritage of wildlife and its habitat, which are now gravely imperilled by a combination of adverse factors. Nature conservation, including wildlife, must therefore receive importance in planning for economic development.

인간은 여러 악조건의 복합작용으로 현재 심각한 위기에 처한 야생동물 및 그 서식지를 보호하고 현명하게 관리할 특별한 책임이 있다. 따라서 야생생물을 포함하는 자연의 보존은 경제개발 계획에서 중요한 위치를 정하여야 한다.

Principle 5

원칙 5

The non-renewable resources of the earth must be employed in such a way as to guard against the danger of their future exhaustion and to ensure that benefits from such employment are shared by all mankind.

지구상의 재생이 불가능한 자원은 장래 고갈의 위험에 대처할 수 있는 방법으로 활용되어야 하며 그로부터 얻는 이익은 인류가 공유하여야 한다.

Principle 6

원칙 6

The discharge of toxic substances or of other substances and the release of heat, in such quantities or concentrations as to exceed the capacity of the environment to render them harmless, must be halted in order to ensure that serious or irreversible damage is not inflicted upon ecosystems. The just struggle of the peoples of all countries against pollution should be supported.

환경의 능력을 초과할 정도의 양이나 고농도의 유독 물질 또는 기타 물질의 배출 및 열의 방출은 생태계에 심각하고도 돌이킬 수 없는 피해를 끼치기 않도록 하기 위해서 지양되어야 한다. 모든 국가 국민들의 오염 방지를 위한 정당한 투쟁은 지지를 받아야 한다.

Principle 7

원칙 7

States shall take all possible steps to prevent pollution of the seas by substances

모든 국가들은 인류 건강에 위해를 야기시키고 생물자원과 해양동물에 해독을 끼치며 문

that are liable to create hazards to human health, to harm living resources and marine life, to damage amenities or to interfere with other legitimate uses of the sea.

학적 가치를 손상시키거나 그 밖에 다른 해양의 올바른 활용을 방해하는 물질들에 의한 해양오염을 방지하기 위하여 가능한 모든 조치를 취하지 않으면 안 된다.

Principle 8

Economic and social development is essential for ensuring a favourable living and working environment for man and for creating conditions on earth that are necessary for the improvement of the quality of life.

원칙 8

경제와 사회 개발은 인류의 바람직한 생활 및 노동환경을 유지하기 위하여 불가결한 것이며 또한 생활의 질적 향상에 필요한 제 조건을 지구상에 확보하기 위하여 필수적인 것이다.

Principle 9

Environmental deficiencies generated by the conditions of under-development and natural disasters pose grave problems and can best be remedied by accelerated development through the transfer of substantial quantities of financial and technological assistance as a supplement to the domestic effort of the developing countries and such timely assistance as may be required.

원칙 9

자연의 재해와 저개발상태에서 발생되는 환경상의 결함은 중대한 문제를 제기하고 있으며 이와 같은 결함은 개도국 자체의 국내적인 노력에 대한 보충으로 충실한 재정적, 기술적인 원조제공을 통한 개발의 촉진에 의하여서 가장 잘 시정될 수 있으며 또 이러한 시의 적절한 원조가 필요할 것이다.

Principle 10

For the developing countries, stability of prices and adequate earnings for primary commodities and raw materials are essential to environmental management since economic factors as well as ecological processes must be taken into account.

원칙 10

개도국들을 위해서는 경제적 요소와 생태계학적 과정을 고려하지 않으면 안 되는 까닭에 물가 안정과 일차 생산품 및 원료를 구입할 수 있는 적정 수입이 환경 관리를 위해 필요 불가결하다.

Principle 11

The environmental policies of all States should enhance and not adversely affect

원칙 11

모든 국가의 환경대책은 개발도상국의 현재와 장래의 개발의 가능성을 향상시키는 것이

the present or future development potential of developing countries, nor should they hamper the attainment of better living conditions for all, and appropriate steps should be taken by States and international organizations with a view to reaching agreement on meeting the possible national and international economic consequences resulting from the application of environmental measures.

어야 되며 결코 이에 악영향을 미치거나 모든 사람의 보다 나은 생활 조건의 달성을 방해하여서는 안 된다. 또한 국가 및 국제기구는 환경조치를 적용함으로서 나타날 국내 및 국가 간의 경제적 영향에 대처한 합의에 도달하기 위하여 적당한 조치를 취하지 않으면 안 된다.

Principle 12

Resources should be made available to preserve and improve the environment, taking into account the circumstances and particular requirements of developing countries and any costs which may emanate from their incorporating environmental safeguards into their development planning and the need for making available to them, upon their request, additional international technical and financial assistance for this purpose.

원칙 12

모든 자원은 개도국의 사정과 특수한 필요성 그리고 그들의 개발 계획에 환경 보호조치를 융합시킴으로서 발생되는 비용을 고려에 넣고 환경 보호와 향상을 위해서 제공되어야 하고 또 이 목적을 위하여 개도국의 요구한다면 추가적인 기술과 재정상의 국제원조를 제공할 필요가 있다.

Principle 13

In order to achieve a more rational management of resources and thus to improve the environment, States should adopt an integrated and co-ordinated approach to their development planning so as to ensure that development is compatible with the need to protect and improve environment for the benefit of their population.

원칙 13

보다 합리적인 자원의 관리와 이로 인한 환경의 향상을 기하여 위하여 모든 국가는 그들의 개발계획에 종합적이고 조정된 시책을 적용함으로서 그들 국민의 이익을 위하여 개발과 인간 환경의 보호 및 개선의 필요성간에는 모순됨이 없다는 것을 확실히 하지 않으면 안 된다.

Principle 14

Rational planning constitutes an essential

원칙 14

합리적인 계획은 개발의 필요성과 환경 보호

tool for reconciling any conflict between the needs of development and the need to protect and improve the environment.

및 개선의 필요성간에 모순을 조정하기 위하여 필요 불가결한 수단이다.

Principle 15

원칙 15

Planning must be applied to human settlements and urbanization with a view to avoiding adverse effects on the environment and obtaining maximum social, economic and environmental benefits for all. In this respect, projects which are designed for colonialist and racist domination must be abandoned.

환경에 미치는 악영향을 피하고 모든 국민의 사회적, 경제적 및 환경상의 이익을 최대한 확보하기 위하여 인간 거주 및 도시 계획이 적용되지 않으면 안 된다. 이 점에 있어서 식민주의 및 인권 차별주의를 위해서 계획된 시도는 포기되어야 한다.

Principle 16

원칙 16

Demographic policies which are without prejudice to basic human rights and which are deemed appropriate by Governments concerned should be applied in those regions where the rate of population growth or excessive population concentrations are likely to have adverse effects on the environment of the human environment and impede development.

인구증가율이나 인구과밀화로 인하여 환경상 및 개발에 악영향을 미칠 지역 또는 인구의 감소로 인간 환경의 향상과 개발에 장애를 가져오는 지역들에서는 기본적 인권을 치매한다는 일이 없이 관계 정부에 의해서 적당하다고 인정되는 인구정책이 실시되어야 한다.

Principle 17

원칙 17

Appropriate national institutions must be entrusted with the task of planning, managing or controlling the environmental resources of States with a view to enhancing environmental quality.

환경의 질을 향상시키기 위해 국가의 환경자원을 계획, 관리 또는 규제하는 임무가 그 국가의 적당한 기관에 부과되어야 한다.

Principle 18

원칙 18

Science and technology, as part of their contribution to economic and social devel-

과학과 기술은 경제 및 사회 발전에 공헌함에 있어 환경에 대한 위해를 파악, 회피, 규

opment, must be applied to the identification, avoidance and control of environmental risks and the solution of environmental problems and for the common good of mankind.

제하며, 환경문제 해결과 인류 공동선을 추구하기 위하여 응용되어야만 한다.

Principle 19

원칙 19

Education in environmental matters, for the younger generation as well as adults, giving due consideration to the underprivileged, is essential in order to broaden the basis for an enlightened opinion and responsible conduct by individuals, enterprises and communities in protecting and improving the environment in its full human dimension. It is also essential that mass media of communications avoid contributing to the deterioration of the environment, but, on the contrary, disseminate information of an educational nature on the need to protect and improve the environment in order to enable man to develop in every respect.

환경문제에 대한 교육, 젊은 세대와 함께 성인층을 대상으로 특히 사회의 하류층에 충분한 배려를 하여야 하는 교육은 환경을 완전한 인류의 차원에서 보호 개선함에 있어 개인 기업 및 지역사회가 취해야 할 책임있는 행동과 계몽된 여론의 기반을 확대함에 필요 불가결하다. 통신의 대중수단이 환경악화에 원인이 됨을 피하고 반면에 모든 면에서 인류발전이 가능토록 하기 위하여 환경을 개선하고 보호하는 필요성에서 교육의 성격을 지닌 정보를 전파함이 또한 필요 불가결하다.

Principle 20

원칙 20

Scientific research and development in the context of environmental problems, both national and multinational, must be promoted in all countries, especially the developing countries. In this connexion, the free flow of up-to-date scientific information and transfer of experience must be supported and assisted, to facilitate the solution of environmental problems; environmental technologies should be made available to developing countries on terms which would encourage their wide dissemination without

환경문제에 관한 국가 내 또는 다국가 간의 과학적 연구 개발은 모든 국가에서 장려되어야 하며 특히 개발도상국가에서는 더욱 그러하다. 최신 과학지식, 경험의 자유로운 전파는 환경문제 해결을 용이하게 하기 위하여 지원 및 협조가 있어야 하며 환경에 관한 기술은 개도국에서 경제적 부담 없이 광범하게 보급되는 조건으로 활용할 수 있어야 한다.

constituting an economic burden on the developing countries.

Principle 21

States have, in accordance with the Charter of the United Nations and the principles of international law, the sovereign right to exploit their own resources pursuant to their own environmental policies, and the responsibility to ensure that activities within their jurisdiction or control do not cause damage to the environment of other States or of areas beyond the limits of national jurisdiction.

Principle 22

States shall co-operate to develop further the international law regarding liability and compensation for the victims of pollution and other environmental damage caused by activities within the jurisdiction or control of such States to areas beyond their jurisdiction.

Principle 23

Without prejudice to such criteria as may be agreed upon by the international community, or to standards which will have to be determined nationally, it will be essential in all cases to consider the systems of values prevailing in each country, and the extent of the applicability of standards which are valid for the most advanced countries but which maybe inappropriate and of unwarranted social cost for the developing countries.

원칙 21

모든 국가는 국제연합 헌장 및 국제법의 원칙에 의해 자국의 자원을 그 환경정책에 따라 개발할 주권을 보유함과 동시에 자국의 관할권 내의 활동이나 규제가 타국의 환경이나 자국 관할권 외의 지역에 피해를 야기시키는 일이 없도록 할 책임이 있다.

원칙 22

모든 국가는 자국의 관할권 및 규제권이 미치는 범위 내에서의 활동이 자국 관할권 내의 지역에 미친 오염 기타 환경 피해의 희생자들에 대한 책임 및 보상에 관한 국제성을 보다 진전시키도록 협력하지 않으면 안 된다.

원칙 23

장차 국제사회에서 합의가 이루어질 수 있는 환경기준 또는 국가 별로 결정되어야 할 일반기준에 구애함이 없이 현재 각 국에서 지배적인 가치체계를 고려하고, 또한 선진국에서는 유효하지만 개도국에서는 부적합하거나 부당한 사회적 비용이 될 수 있는 여러 가지 기준을 어느 정도까지 적용할 수 있는가를 항상 고려하는 것이 필요하다.

Principle 24

International matters concerning the protection and improvement of the environment should be handled in a co-operative spirit by all countries, big and small, on an equal footing. Co-operation through multilateral or bilateral arrangements or other appropriate means is essential to effectively control, prevent, reduce and eliminate adverse environmental effects resulting from activities conducted in all spheres, in such a way that due account is taken of the sovereignty and interests of all States.

Principle 25

States shall ensure that international organizations play a co-ordinated, efficient and dynamic role for the protection and improvement of the environment.

Principle 26

Man and his environment must be spared the effects of nuclear weapons and all other means of mass destruction. States must strive to reach prompt agreement, in the relevant international organs, on the elimination and complete destruction of such weapons.

원칙 24

환경보존 및 개선에 관한 국제문제는 대소를 막론하고 모든 국가가 평등한 입장에 입각한 협조정신으로 다루어야만 한다. 양국 간 또는 다국 간의 조정 기타 적절한 조치를 통한 협조는 세계 각처에서 행해진 활동으로 초래된 환경에 대한 악영향을 방지, 제거, 감소시키거나 효과적으로 규제하기 위하여 필요 불가결하다. 이와 같은 협조에는 모든 국가의 주권과 이익을 충분히 고려하여야 한다.

원칙 25

각 국은 국제기구가 환경보호와 개선을 위하여 협조적이고 능률적이며 또한 강력한 역할을 할 수 있도록 보장하여야 한다.

원칙 26

인간과 그의 환경은 핵무기의 영향과 다른 모든 대량 파괴의 수단으로부터 구제되어야 한다. 모든 국가는 국제기구의 테두리 내에서 그러한 무기의 제거와 완전파괴에 신속한 합의가 이루어지도록 노력하지 않으면 안 된다.

2. The Rio Declaration on Environment and Development (1992)

2. 환경과 개발에 관한 리우선언

Date : 14 June 1992
Link : www.un.org/documents

PREAMBLE

전   문

The United Nations Conference on Environment and Development, Having met at Rio de Janeiro from 3 to 14 June 1992,

유엔환경개발회의가 1992년 6월 3일—14일간 리우데자네이로에서 개최되었으며;

Reaffirming the Declaration of the United Nations Conference on the Human Environment, adopted at Stockholm on 16 June 1972, a/and seeking to build upon it,

1972년 스톡홀름에서 채택된 'UN 인간환경회의선언'을 재확인하고 이를 더욱 확고히 할 것을 추구하여;

With the goal of establishing a new and equitable global partnership through the creation of new levels of cooperation among States, key sectors of societies and people,

모든 국가와 사회의 주요 분야, 그리고 모든 사람들 사이의 새로운 차원의 협력을 창조함으로써 새롭고 공평한 범세계적 동반자 관계를 수립할 목적으로;

Working towards international agreements which respect the interests of all and protect the integrity of the global environmental and developmental system,

모두의 이익을 존중하고 또한 지구의 환경 및 개발체제의 통합성을 보호하기 위한 국제협정체결을 위하여 노력하며;

Recognizing the integral and interdependent nature of the Earth, our home,

우리들의 삶의 터전인 지구의 통합적이며 상호의존적인 성격을 인식하면서;

Proclaims that:

다음과 같이 선언한다:

Principle 1

원칙 1

Human beings are at the centre of concerns for sustainable development. They are en-

인간을 중심으로 지속가능한 개발이 논의되어야 한다. 인간은 자연과 조화를 이룬 건강

titled to a healthy and productive life in harmony with nature.

하고 생산적인 삶을 향유하여야 한다.

Principle 2

원칙 2

States have, in accordance with the Charter of the United Nations and the principles of international law, the sovereign right to exploit their own resources pursuant to their own environmental and developmental policies, and the responsibility to ensure that activities within their jurisdiction or control do not cause damage to the environment of other States or of areas beyond the limits of national jurisdiction.

각 국가는 유엔헌장과 국제법 원칙에 조화를 이루면서 자국의 환경 및 개발정책에 따라 자국의 자원을 개발할 수 있는 주권적 권리를 갖고 있으며 자국의 관리구역 또한 통제범위 내에서의 활동이 다른 국가나 관할범위 외부지역의 환경에 피해를 끼치지 않도록 할 책임을 갖고 있다.

Principle 3

원칙 3

The right to development must be fulfilled so as to equitably meet developmental and environmental needs of present and future generations.

개발의 권리는 개발과 환경에 대한 현세대와 차세대의 요구를 공평하게 충족할 수 있도록 실현되어야 한다.

Principle 4

원칙 4

In order to achieve sustainable development, environmental protection shall constitute an integral part of the development process and cannot be considered in isolation from it.

지속가능한 개발을 성취하기 위하여 환경보호는 개발과정의 중요한 일부를 구성하며 개발과정과 분리시켜 고려되어서는 안 된다.

Principle 5

원칙 5

All States and all people shall cooperate in the essential task of eradicating poverty as an indispensable requirement for sustainable development, in order to decrease the disparities in standards of living and better meet the needs of the majority of the people of the world.

모든 국가와 국민은 생활수준의 격차를 줄이고 세계 대다수의 사람들의 기본수요를 충족시키기 위하여 지속가능한 개발의 필수요건인 빈곤의 퇴치라는 중대한 과업을 위해 협력하여야 한다.

Principle 6

The special situation and needs of developing countries, particularly the least developed and those most environmentally vulnerable, shall be given special priority. International actions in the field of environment and development should also address the interests and needs of all countries.

Principle 7

States shall cooperate in a spirit of global partnership to conserve, protect and restore the health and integrity of the Earth's ecosystem. In view of the different contributions to global environmental degradation, States have common but differentiated responsibilities. The developed countries acknowledge the responsibility that they bear in the international pursuit of sustainable development in view of the pressures their societies place on the global environment and of the technologies and financial resources they command.

Principle 8

To achieve sustainable development and a higher quality of life for all people, States should reduce and eliminate unsustainable patterns of production and consumption and promote appropriate demographic policies.

Principle 9

States should cooperate to strengthen endogenous capacity−building for sustainable

원칙 6

개발도상국, 특히 최빈개도국과 환경적으로 침해받기 쉬운 개도국의 특수상황과 환경보전의 필요성은 특별히 우선적으로 고려의 대상이 되어야 한다. 또한 환경과 개발 분야에 있어서의 국제적 활동은 모든 나라의 이익과 요구를 반영하여야 한다.

원칙 7

각 국가는 지구생태계의 건강과 안전성을 보존, 보호 및 회복시키기 위하여 범세계적 동반자의 정신으로 협력하여야 함. 지구의 환경악화에 대한 제각기 다른 책임을 고려하여, 각 국가는 공통된 그러나 차별적인 책임을 가진다. 선진국들은 그들이 지구환경에 끼친 영향과 그들이 소유하고 있는 기술 및 재정적 자원을 고려하여 지속가능한 개발을 추구하기 위한 국제적 노력에 있어서 분담하여야 할 책임을 인식한다.

원칙 8

지속가능한 개발과 모든 사람의 보다 나은 생활의 질을 추구하기 위하여 각 국가는 지속불가능한 생산과 소비 패턴을 줄이고 제거하여야 하며 적절한 인구정책을 촉진하여야 한다.

원칙 9

각 국가는 과학적, 기술적 지식의 교환을 통하여 과학적 이해를 향상시키고 새롭고 혁신

development by improving scientific understanding through exchanges of scientific and technological knowledge, and by enhancing the development, adaptation, diffusion and transfer of technologies, includeing new and innovative technologies.

적인 기술을 포함한 기술의 개발, 적용, 존속, 전파 그리고 이전을 증진시킴으로써 지속가능한 개발을 위한 내재적 능력을 형성, 강화하도록 협력하여야 한다.

Principle 10

Environmental issues are best handled with the participation of all concerned citizens, at the relevant level. At the national level, each individual shall have appropriate access to information concerning the environment that is held by public authorities, including information on hazardous materials and activities in their communities, and the opportunity to participate in decision-making processes. States shall facilitate and encourage public awareness and participation by making information widely available. Effective access to judicial and administrative proceedings, including redress and remedy, shall be provided.

원칙 10

환경문제는 적절한 수준의 모든 관계 시민들의 참여가 있을 때 가장 효과적으로 다루어진다. 국가차원에서 각 개인은 지역사회에서의 유해물질과 처리에 관한 정보를 포함하여 공공기관이 가지고 있는 환경정보에 적절히 접근하고 의사결정과정에 참여할 수 있는 기회를 부여받아야 한다. 각 국가는 정보를 광범위하게 제공함으로써 공동의 인식과 참여를 촉진하고 증진시켜야 한다. 피해의 구제와 배상 등 사법 및 행정적 절차에 효과적으로 접근할 수 있어야 한다.

Principle 11

States shall enact effective environmental legislation. Environmental standards, management objectives and priorities should reflect the environmental and developmental context to which they apply. Standards applied by some countries may be inappropriate and of unwarranted economic and social cost to other countries, in particular developing countries.

원칙 11

각 국가는 효과적인 환경법칙을 규정하여야 한다. 환경기준, 관리목적, 그리고 우선순위는 이들이 적용되는 환경과 개발의 정황이 반영되어야 한다. 어느 한 국가에서 채택된 기준은 다른 국가, 특히 개도국에게 부적당하거나 지나치게 경제·사회적 비용을 초래할 수도 있다.

Principle 12

States should cooperate to promote a sup-

원칙 12

각 국가는 환경악화문제에 적절히 대처하기

portive and open international economic system that would lead to economic growth and sustainable development in all countries, to better address the problems of environmental degradation. Trade policy measures for environmental purposes should not constitute a means of arbitrary or unjustifiable discrimination or a disguised restriction on international trade. Unilateral actions to deal with environmental challenges outside the jurisdiction of the importing country should be avoided. Environmental measures addressing transboundary or global environmental problems should, as far as possible, be based on an international consensus.

위하여, 모든 국가의 경제성장과 지속가능한 개발을 도모함에 있어 도움이 되고 개방적인 국제경제체제를 증진시키도록 협력하여야 한다. 환경적 목적을 위한 무역정책수단은 국제무역에 대하여 자의적 또는 부당한 차별적 조치나 위장된 제한을 포함해서는 안 된다. 수입국 관할지역 밖의 환경적 문제에 대응하기 위한 일방적 조치는 회피되어야 한다. 국경을 초월하거나 지구적 차원의 환경문제에 대처하는 환경적 조치는 가능한 한 국제적 합의에 기초하여야 한다.

Principle 13

States shall develop national law regarding liability and compensation for the victims of pollution and other environmental damage. States shall also cooperate in an expeditious and more determined manner to develop further international law regarding liability and compensation for adverse effects of environmental damage caused by activities within their jurisdiction or control to areas beyond their jurisdiction.

원칙 13

각 국가는 환경오염이나 기타 환경위해의 피해자에 대한 책임과 배상에 관한 국제법을 발전시켜야 한다. 각 국가는 자국의 관할권 또는 통제지역 내에서의 활동이 자국의 관리범위 이외 지역에 초래한 악영향에 대한 책임과 배상에 관한 국제법을 보다 발전시키기 위하여 신속하고 확실한 방법으로 협력하여야 한다.

Principle 14

States should effectively cooperate to discourage or prevent the relocation and transfer to other States of any activities and substances that cause severe environmental degradation or are found to be harmful to human health.

원칙 14

각 국가는 환경악화를 심각하게 초래하거나 인간의 건강에 위해한 것으로 밝혀진 활동이나 물질을 다른 국가로 재배치 또는 이전하는 것을 억제하거나 예방하기 위하여 효율적으로 협력하여야 한다.

Principle 15

In order to protect the environment, the precautionary approach shall be widely applied by States according to their capabilities. Where there are threats of serious or irreversible damage, lack of full scientific certainty shall not be used as a reason for postponing cost—effective measures to prevent environmental degradation.

원칙 15

환경을 보호하기 이하여 각 국가의 능력에 따라 예방적 조치가 널리 실시되어야 한다. 심각한 또는 회복 불가능한 피해의 우려가 있을 경우, 과학적 불확실성이 환경악화를 지양하기 위한 비용/효과적인 조치를 지연시키는 구실로 이용되어서는 안 된다.

Principle 16

National authorities should endeavour to promote the internalization of environmental costs and the use of economic instruments, taking into account the approach that the polluter should, in principle, bear the cost of pollution, with due regard to the public interest and without distorting international trade and investment.

원칙 16

국가 당국은 오염자가 원칙적으로 오염의 비용을 부담하여야 한다는 원칙을 고려하여 환경비용의 내부화와 경제적 수단의 이용을 증진시키도록 노력하여야 한다. 이에 있어서 공공이익을 적절히 고려하여야 하며 국제무역과 투자를 왜곡시키지 않아야 한다.

Principle 17

Environmental impact assessment, as a national instrument, shall be undertaken for proposed activities that are likely to have a significant adverse impact on the environment and are subject to a decision of a competent national authority.

원칙 17

환경에 심각한 악영향을 초래할 가능성이 있으며 관할 국가당국의 의사결정을 필요로 하는 사업계획에 대하여 환경영향평가가 국가적 제도로서 실시되어야 한다.

Principle 18

States shall immediately notify other States of any natural disasters or other emergencies that are likely to produce sudden harmful effects on the environment of those States. Every effort shall be made by the international community to help States so afflicted.

원칙 18

각 국가는 다른 국가의 환경에 급격한 위해를 초래할 수 있는 어떠한 자연재해나 기타의 긴급사태를 상대방 국가에 즉시 통고해야 한다. 국제사회는 이러한 피해를 입은 국가를 돕기 위하여 모든 노력을 기울여야 한다.

Principle 19

States shall provide prior and timely notification and relevant information to potentially affected States on activities that may have a significant adverse transboundary environmental effect and shall consult with those States at an early stage and in good faith.

Principle 20

Women have a vital role in environmental management and development. Their full participation is therefore essential to achieve sustainable development.

Principle 21

The creativity, ideals and courage of the youth of the world should be mobilized to forge a global partnership in order to achieve sustainable development and ensure a better future for all.

Principle 22

Indigenous people and their communities and other local communities have a vital role in environmental management and development because of their knowledge and traditional practices. States should recognize and duly support their identity, culture and interests and enable their effective participation in the achievement of sustainable development.

Principle 23

The environment and natural resources of

원칙 19

각 국가는 국경을 넘어서 환경에 심각한 악영향을 초래할 수 있는 활동에 대하여 피해가 예상되는 국가에게 시기적절한 사전 통고 및 관련 정보를 제공하여야 하며 초기단계에서 성실하게 이들 국가와 협의하여야 한다.

원칙 20

여성은 환경관리 및 개발에 있어서 중대한 역할을 수행한다. 따라서 지속가능한 개발을 달성하기 위해서는 그들의 적극적인 참여가 필수적이다.

원칙 21

지속가능한 개발을 성취하고 모두의 밝은 미래를 보장하기 위하여 전 세계 청년들의 독창성, 이상, 그리고 용기가 결집되어 범세계적 동반자 관계가 구축되어야 한다.

원칙 22

토착민과 그들의 사회, 그리고 기타의 지역사회는 그들의 지식과 전통적 관행으로 인하여 환경관리와 개발에 있어서 중요한 역할을 수행한다. 각 국가는 그들의 존재와 문화 및 이익을 인정하고 적절히 지지하여야 하며, 또한 지속가능한 개발을 성취하기 위하여 그들의 효과적인 참여가 가능하도록 하여야 한다.

원칙 23

압제, 지배 및 점령 하에 있는 국민의 환경과

people under oppression, domination and occupation shall be protected.

자연자원은 보호되어야 한다.

Principle 24

원칙 24

Warfare is inherently destructive of sustainable development. tates shall therefore respect international law providing protection for the environment in times of armed conflict and cooperate in its further development, as necessary.

전쟁은 본질적으로 지속가능한 개발을 파괴한다. 따라서 각 국가는 무력 분쟁시 환경의 보호를 규정하는 국제법을 존중하여야 하며 필요한 경우에는 이의 발전을 위하여 협력하여야 한다.

Principle 25

원칙 25

Peace, development and environmental protection are interdependent and indivisible.

평화, 발전, 환경보호는 상호의존적이며 불가분의 관계에 있다.

Principle 26

원칙 26

States shall resolve all their environmental disputes peacefully and by appropriate means in accordance with the Charter of the United Nations.

국가는 그들의 환경 분쟁을 유엔헌장에 따라 평화적으로 또한 적절한 방법으로 해결하여야 한다.

Principle 27

원칙 27

States and people shall cooperate in good faith and in a spirit of partnership in the fulfilment of the principles embodied in this Declaration and in the further development of international law in the field of sustainable development.

각 국가와 국민들은 이 선언에 구현된 원칙을 준수하고 지속가능한 개발 분야에 있어서의 관련 국제법을 한층 발전시키기 위하여 성실하고 동반자적 정신으로 협력하여야 한다.

기후변화 국제조약

3. United Nations Framework Convention on Climate Change (1992)

3. 기후변화에 관한 국제연합 기본협약

Date : 9 May 1992
In force : 21 March 1994
States Party : 197
Korea : 21 March 1994 (조약 제1213호)
Link : www.unfccc.int

The Parties to this Convention,

이 협약의 당사자는,

Acknowledging that change in the Earth's climate and its adverse effects are a common concern of humankind, Concerned that human activities have been substantially increasing the atmospheric concentrations of greenhouse gases, that these increases enhance the natural greenhouse effect, and that this will result on average in an additional warming of the Earth's surface and atmosphere and may adversely affect natural ecosystems and humankind,

지구의 기후변화와 이로 인한 부정적 효과가 인류의 공통 관심사임을 인정하고, 인간활동이 대기중의 온실가스 농도를 현저히 증가시켜 왔으며, 이로 인해 자연적 온실효과가 증대되고 이것이 평균적으로 지구표면 및 대기를 추가적으로 온난화시켜 자연생태계와 인류에게 부정적 영향을 미칠 수 있음을 우려하며,

Noting that the largest share of historical and current global emissions of greenhouse gases has originated in developed countries, that per capita emissions in developing countries are still relatively low and that the share of global emissions originating in developing countries will grow to meet their social and development needs,

과거와 현재의 지구전체 온실가스의 큰 부분이 선진국에서 배출되었다는 것과 개발도상국의 1인당 배출량은 아직 비교적 적으나 지구전체의 배출에서 차지하는 개발도상국의 배출비율이 그들의 사회적 및 개발의 요구를 충족시키기 위하여 증가할 것임을 주목하고,

Aware of the role and importance in terrestrial and marine ecosystems of sinks and reservoirs of greenhouse gases,

육지와 해양 생태계에서 온실가스의 흡수원과 저장소가 하는 역할과 중요성을 인식하며,

Noting that there are many uncertainties in predictions of climate change, particul-

기후변화에 대한 예측, 특히 그 시기·규모 및 지역적 양태에 대한 예측에 불확실성이

arly with regard to the timing, magnitude and regional patterns thereof,

많음을 주목하고,

Acknowledging that the global nature of climate change calls for the widest possible cooperation by all countries and their participation in an effective and appropriate international response, in accordance with their common but differentiated responsibilities and respective capabilities and their social and economic conditions,

기후변화의 세계적 성격에 대응하기 위하여는 모든 국가가 그들의 공통적이면서도 그 정도에 차이가 나는 책임, 각각의 능력 및 사회적·경제적 여건에 따라 가능한 모든 협력을 다하여 효과적이고 적절한 국제적 대응에 참여하는 것이 필요함을 인정하며,

Recalling the pertinent provisions of the Declaration of the United Nations Conference on the Human Environment, adopted at Stockholm on 16 June 1972,

1972년 6월 16일 스톡홀름에서 채택된 국제연합인간환경회의 선언의 관련규정을 상기하고,

Recalling also that States have, in accordance with the Charter of the United Nations and the principles of international law, the sovereign right to exploit their own resources pursuant to their own environmental and developmental policies, and the responsibility to ensure that activities within their jurisdiction or control do not cause damage to the environment of other States or of areas beyond the limits of national jurisdiction,

국가는 국제연합헌장과 국제법의 원칙에 따라 고유의 환경정책과 개발정책에 입각하여 자기나라의 자원을 개발할 주권적 권리를 가지며, 자기나라의 관할 혹은 통제지역 안의 활동 때문에 다른 국가나 관할권 이원지역의 환경에 피해가 발생하지 아니하도록 보장할 책임이 있음을 또한 상기하며,

Reaffirming the principle of sovereignty of States in international cooperation to address climate change,

기후변화에 대응하기 위한 국제협력에 있어서 국가주권원칙을 재확인하고,

Recognizing that States should enact effective environmental legislation, that environmental standards, management objectives and priorities should reflect the environmental and developmental context to which they apply, and that standards applied by some countries may be inappropriate

국가는 효과적인 환경법령을 제정하여야 하며, 환경기준과 관리의 목적 및 우선순위는 이들이 적용되는 환경 및 개발상황을 반영하여야 하며, 어떠한 국가에 의하여 적용된 기준이 다른 국가, 특히 개발도상국에 대해서는 부적절하며 또한 부당한 경제적·사회적 비용을 유발할 수도 있다는 것을 인식하며,

and of unwarranted economic and social cost to other countries, in particular developing countries,

Recalling the provisions of General Assembly resolution 44/228 of 22 December 1989 on the United Nations Conference on Environment and Development, and resolutions 43/53 of 6 December 1988, 44/207 of 22 December 1989, 45/212 of 21 December 1990 and 46/169 of 19 December 1991 on protection of global climate for present and future generations of mankind,

Recalling also the provisions of General Assembly resolution 44/206 of 22 December 1989 on the possible adverse effects of sea-level rise on islands and coastal areas, particularly low-lying coastal areas and the pertinent provisions of General Assembly resolution 44/172 of 19 December 1989 on the implementation of the Plan of Action to Combat Desertification,

Recalling further the Vienna Convention for the Protection of the Ozone Layer, 1985, and the Montreal Protocol on Substances that Deplete the Ozone Layer, 1987, as adjusted and amended on 29 June 1990,

Noting the Ministerial Declaration of the Second World Climate Conference adopted on 7 November 1990,

Conscious of the valuable analytical work being conducted by many States on climate change and of the important contributions of the World Meteorological Organization, the United Nations Environment Programme

국제연합 환경개발회의에 관한 1989년 12월 22일 총회 결의 44/228호, 인류의 현재 및 미래 세대를 위한 지구기후의 보호에 관한 1988년 12월 6일 결의 43/53호, 1989년 12월 22일 결의 44/207호, 1990년 12월 21일 결의 45/212호 및 1991년 12월 19일 결의 46/169호의 규정을 상기하고,

해수면 상승이 도서 및 해안지역, 특히 저지대 해안지역에 가져올 수 있는 부정적 효과에 관한 1989년 12월 22일 총회결의 44/206호의 규정과 사막화 방지 실천계획의 이행에 관한 1989년 12월 19일의 총회결의 44/172호의 관련규정을 또한 상기하며,

1985년의 오존층보호를위한비엔나협약, 1990년 6월 29일에 개정된 1987년의 오존층파괴물질에관한몬트리올의정서를 또한 상기하고,

1990년 11월 7일 채택된 제2차 세계기후회의 각료선언을 주목하며,

많은 국가가 행한 기후변화에 관한 귀중한 분석작업과 세계기상기구·국제연합환경계획 및 국제연합체제 안의 그 밖의 기구들, 그리고 그 밖의 국제적 및 정부간 기구가 과학연구결과의 교환과 연구의 조정에서 이룩한 중

and other organs, organizations and bodies of the United Nations system, as well as other international and intergovernmental bodies, to the exchange of results of scientific research and the coordination of research,

Recognizing that steps required to understand and address climate change will be environmentally, socially and economically most effective if they are based on relevant scientific, technical and economic considerations and continually re-evaluated in the light of new findings in these areas,

Recognizing that various actions to address climate change can be justified economically in their own right and can also help in solving other environmental problems,

Recognizing also the need for developed countries to take immediate action in a flexible manner on the basis of clear priorities, as a first step towards comprehensive response strategies at the global, national and, where agreed, regional levels that take into account all greenhouse gases, with due consideration of their relative contributions to the enhancement of the greenhouse effect,

Recognizing further that low-lying and other small island countries, countries with low-lying coastal, arid and semiarid areas or areas liable to floods, drought and desertification, and developing countries with fragile mountainous ecosystems are particularly vulnerable to the adverse effects of climate change,

Recognizing the special difficulties of those countries, especially developing countries,

요한 기여를 의식하고,

기후변화를 이해하고 이에 대응하기 위하여 필요한 조치는 관련 과학적·기술적 및 경제적 고려에 바탕을 두고 이러한 분야의 새로운 발견에 비추어 계속적으로 재평가될 경우에 환경적·사회적 및 경제적으로 가장 효과적이라는 것을 인식하며,

기후변화에 대응하기 위한 다양한 조치는 그 자체만으로도 경제적으로 정당화될 수 있으며, 또한 그 밖의 환경문제를 해결하는 데 도움을 줄 수 있음을 인식하고,

선진국이 온실효과의 증대에 대한 자기나라의 상대적 책임을 정당히 고려하여 세계적·국가적 그리고 합의되는 경우 지역적 차원에서의 모든 온실가스에 대한 종합대응전략의 첫 단계로서 명확한 우선순위에 입각하여 신축성 있게 신속한 조치를 취할 필요성을 또한 인식하며,

저지대 국가 및 군소 도서국가, 저지대 연안지역·건조지역·반건조지역 또는 홍수·가뭄 및 사막화에 취약한 지역을 가지고 있는 국가, 그리고 연약한 산악생태계를 가지고 있는 개발도상국이 특별히 기후변화의 부정적 효과에 취약하다는 것을 또한 인식하고,

그 경제가 특별히 화석연료의 생산·사용 및 수출에 의존하고 있는 국가, 특히 개발도상국

whose economies are particularly dependent on fossil fuel production, use and exportation, as a consequence of action taken on limiting greenhouse gas emissions,

Affirming that responses to climate change should be coordinated with social and economic development in an integrated manner with a view to avoiding adverse impacts on he latter, taking into full account the legitimate priority needs of developing countries for the achievement of sustained economic growth and the eradication of poverty,

Recognizing that all countries, especially developing countries, need access to resources required to achieve sustainable social and economic development and that, in order for developing countries to progress towards that goal, their energy consumption will need to grow taking into account the possibilities for achieving greater energy efficiency and for controlling greenhouse gas emissions in general, including through the application of new technologies on terms which make such an application economically and socially beneficial,

Determined to protect the climate system for present and future generations,

Have agreed as follows:

Article 1
Definitions

For the purposes of this Convention:

1. "Adverse effects of climate change"

이 온실가스 배출을 제한하기 위하여 취한 조치로 인해 겪을 특별한 어려움을 인식하며,

기후변화에 대한 대응은 사회적 및 경제적 발전에 대한 부정적인 영향을 피하기 위하여, 특히 개발도상국의 지속적인 경제성장 달성과 빈곤퇴치를 위한 정당하고 우선적인 요구를 충분히 고려하여 사회적 및 경제적 발전과 통합적인 방식으로 조정되어야 한다는 것을 확인하고,

모든 국가, 특히 개발도상국은 지속가능한 사회적 및 경제적 발전을 달성하는 데 필요한 자원에의 접근을 필요로 하며, 개발도상국이 이러한 목적을 달성하기 위해서는, 경제적 및 사회적으로 유리한 조건의 신기술의 적용 등을 통하여 더 높은 에너지 효율성을 달성하고 온실가스 배출량을 전반적으로 통제할 수 있으리라는 가능성을 고려하는 한편, 개발도상국의 에너지 소비가 증가할 필요가 있을 것임을 인식하며,

현재와 미래의 세대를 위하여 기후체계를 보호할 것을 결의하여,

다음과 같이 합의하였다.

제1조
정 의

이 협약의 목적상,

1. "기후변화의 부정적 효과"라 함은 기후변

means changes in the physical environment or biota resulting from climate change which have significant deleterious effects on the composition, resilience or productivity of natural and managed ecosystems or on the operation of socio-economic systems or on human health and welfare.

2. "Climate change" means a change of climate which is attributed directly or indirectly to human activity that alters the composition of the global atmosphere and which is in addition to natural climate variability observed over comparable time periods.

3. "Climate system" means the totality of the atmosphere, hydrosphere, biosphere and geosphere and their interactions.

4. "Emissions" means the release of greenhouse gases and/or their precursors into the atmosphere over a specified area and period of time.

5. "Greenhouse gases" means those gaseous constituents of the atmosphere, both natural and anthropogenic, that absorb and re-emit infrared radiation.

6. "Regional economic integration organization" means an organization constituted by sovereign States of a given region which has competence in respect of matters governed by this Convention or its protocols and has been duly authorized, in accordance with its internal procedures, to sign, ratify, accept, approve or accede to the instruments concerned.

화에 기인한 물리적 환경 또는 생물상의 변화로서 자연적 생태계 및 관리되는 생태계의 구성·회복력 또는 생산성, 사회경제체제의 운용 또는 인간의 건강과 복지에 대하여 현저히 해로운 효과를 야기하는 것을 말한다.

2. "기후변화"라 함은 인간활동에 직접 또는 간접으로 기인하여 지구대기의 구성을 변화시키는 상당한 기간 동안 관측된 자연적 기후 가변성에 추가하여 일어나는 기후의 변화를 말한다.

3. "기후체계"라 함은 대기권, 수권, 생물권과 지리권 그리고 이들의 상호작용의 총체를 말한다.

4. "배출"이라 함은 특정지역에 특정기간 동안 온실가스 및/또는 그 전구물질을 대기중으로 방출하는 것을 말한다.

5. "온실가스"라 함은 적외선을 흡수하여 재방출하는 천연 및 인공의 기체성의 대기구성물을 말한다.

6. "지역경제통합기구"라 함은 이 협약 및 부속의정서가 규율하는 사항에 관하여 권한을 가지며, 또한 내부절차에 따라 정당하게 권한을 위임받아 관련문서에 서명·비준·수락·승인 또는 가입할 수 있는 특정지역의 주권국가들로 구성된 기구를 말한다.

7. "Reservoir" means a component or components of the climate system where a greenhouse gas or a precursor of a greenhouse gas is stored.

8. "Sink" means any process, activity or mechanism which removes a greenhouse gas, an aerosol or a precursor of a greenhouse gas from the atmosphere.

9. "Source" means any process or activity which releases a greenhouse gas, an aerosol or a precursor of a greenhouse gas into the atmosphere.

Article 2
Objective

The ultimate objective of this Convention and any related legal instruments that the Conference of the Parties may adopt is to achieve, in accordance with the relevant provisions of the Convention, stabilization of greenhouse gas concentrations in the atmosphere at a level that would prevent dangerous anthropogenic interference with the climate system. Such a level should be achieved within a time-frame sufficient to allow ecosystems to adapt naturally to climate change, to ensure that food production is not threatened and to enable economic development to proceed in a sustainable manner.

Article 3
Principles

In their actions to achieve the objective of the Convention and to implement its pro-

---

7. "저장소"라 함은 온실가스 또는 그 전구물질이 저장되는 기후 체계의 하나 또는 그 이상의 구성요소들을 말한다.

8. "흡수원"이라 함은 대기로부터 온실가스, 그 연무질 또는 전구물질을 제거하는 모든 과정·활동 또는 체계를 말한다.

9. "배출원"이라 함은 대기중으로 온실가스, 그 연무질 또는 전구물질을 방출하는 모든 과정 또는 활동을 말한다.

제 2 조
목   적

이 협약과 당사국총회가 채택하는 모든 관련 법적 문서의 궁극적 목적은, 협약의 관련규정에 따라, 기후체계가 위험한 인위적 간섭을 받지 않는 수준으로 대기중 온실가스 농도의 안정화를 달성하는 것이다. 그러한 수준은 생태계가 자연적으로 기후변화에 적응하고 식량생산이 위협받지 않으며 경제개발이 지속가능한 방식으로 진행되도록 할 수 있기에 충분한 기간 내에 달성되어야 한다.

제 3 조
원   칙

협약의 목적을 달성하고 그 규정을 이행하기 위한 행동에 있어서, 당사자는 무엇보다도 다

visions, the Parties shall be guided, inter alia, by the following:

1. The Parties should protect the climate system for the benefit of present and future generations of humankind, on the basis of equity and in accordance with their common but differentiated responsibilities and respective capabilities. Accordingly, the developed country Parties should take the lead in combating climate change and the adverse effects thereof.

2. The specific needs and special circumstances of developing country Parties, especially those that are particularly vulnerable to the adverse effects of climate change, and of those Parties, especially developing country Parties, that would have to bear a disproportionate or abnormal burden under the Convention, should be given full consideration.

3. The Parties should take precautionary measures to anticipate, prevent or minimize the causes of climate change and mitigate its adverse effects. Where there are threats of serious or irreversible damage, lack of full scientific certainty should not be used as a reason for postponing such measures, taking into account that policies and measures to deal with climate change should be cost—effective so as to ensure global benefits at the lowest possible cost. To achieve this, such policies and measures should take into account different socio—economic contexts, be comprehensive, cover all relevant sources, sinks and reservoirs

음 원칙에 따른다.

1. 당사자는 형평에 입각하고 공통적이면서도 그 정도에 차이가 나는 책임과 각각의 능력에 따라 인류의 현재 및 미래 세대의 이익을 위하여 기후체계를 보호해야 한다. 따라서, 선진국인 당사자는 기후변화 및 그 부정적 효과에 대처하는 데 있어 선도적 역할을 해야 한다.

2. 기후변화의 부정적 효과에 특별히 취약한 국가 등 개발도상국인 당사자와, 개발도상국인 당사자를 포함하여 이 협약에 따라 불균형적이며 지나친 부담을 지게 되는 당사자의 특수한 필요와 특별한 상황은 충분히 고려되어야 한다.

3. 당사자는 기후변화의 원인을 예견·방지 및 최소화하고 그 부정적 효과를 완화하기 위한 예방조치를 취하여야 한다. 심각하거나 회복할 수 없는 손상의 위협이 있는 경우, 충분한 과학적 확실성이 없다는 이유로 이러한 조치를 연기하여서는 아니되며, 기후변화를 다루는 정책과 조치는 최저비용으로 세계적 이익을 보장할 수 있도록 비용효과적이어야 한다. 이 목적을 달성하기 위하여, 이러한 정책과 조치는 서로 다른 사회경제적 상황을 고려하여야 하고, 종합적이어야 하며, 온실가스의 모든 관련 배출원·흡수원 및 저장소 그리고 적응 조치를 포함하여야 하며, 모든 경제분야를 포괄하여야 한다. 기후변화에 대한 대응노

of greenhouse gases and adaptation, and comprise all economic sectors. Efforts to address climate change may be carried out cooperatively by interested Parties.

4. The Parties have a right to, and should, promote sustainable development. Policies and measures to protect the climate system against human-induced change should be appropriate for the specific conditions of each Party and should be integrated with national development programmes, taking into account that economic development is essential for adopting measures to address climate change.

5. The Parties should cooperate to promote a supportive and open international economic system that would lead to sustainable economic growth and development in all Parties, particularly developing country Parties, thus enabling them better to address the problems of climate change. Measures taken to combat climate change, including unilateral ones, should not constitute a means of arbitrary or unjustifiable discrimination or a disguised restriction on international trade.

Article 4
Commitments

1. All Parties, taking into account their common but differentiated responsibilities and their specific national and regional development priorities, objectives and circumstances, shall:

(a) Develop, periodically update, publish

력은 이해 당사자가 협동하여 수행할 수 있다.

4. 당사자는 지속가능한 발전을 증진할 권리를 보유하며 또한 증진하여야 한다. 경제발전이 기후변화에 대응하는 조치를 취하는 데 필수적임을 고려하여, 인간활동으로 야기된 기후변화로부터 기후체계를 보호하기 위한 정책과 조치는 각 당사자의 특수한 상황에 적절하여야 하며 국가개발계획과 통합되어야 한다.

5. 당사자는 모든 당사자, 특히 개발도상국인 당사자가 지속적 경제 성장과 발전을 이룩하고 그럼으로써 기후변화문제에 더 잘 대응할 수 있도록 하는 지지적이며 개방적인 국제경제체제를 촉진하기 위하여 협력한다. 일방적 조치를 포함하여 기후변화에 대처하기 위하여 취한 조치는 국제무역에 대한 자의적 또는 정당화할 수 없는 차별수단이나 위장된 제한수단이 되어서는 아니된다.

제4조
공   약

1. 모든 당사자는 공통적이면서도 그 정도에 차이가 나는 책임과 자기나라의 특수한 국가적, 지역적 개발우선순위·목적 및 상황을 고려하여 다음 사항을 수행한다.

가. 당사국총회가 합의하는 비교가능한 방법

and make available to the Conference of the Parties, in accordance with Article 12, national inventories of anthropogenic emissions by sources and removals by sinks of all greenhouse gases not controlled by the Montreal Protocol, using comparable methodologies to be agreed upon by the Conference of the Parties;

(b) Formulate, implement, publish and regularly update national and, where appropriate, regional programmes containing measures to mitigate climate change by addressing anthropogenic emissions by sources and removals by sinks of all greenhouse gases not controlled by the Montreal Protocol, and measures to facilitate adequate adaptation to climate change;

(c) Promote and cooperate in the development, application and diffusion, including transfer, of technologies, practices and processes that control, reduce or prevent anthropogenic emissions of greenhouse gases not controlled by the Montreal Protocol in all relevant sectors, including the energy, transport, industry, agriculture, forestry and waste management sectors;

(d) Promote sustainable management, and promote and cooperate in the conservation and enhancement, as appropriate, of sinks and reservoirs of all greenhouse gases not controlled by the Montreal Protocol, including biomass, forests and oceans as well as other terrestrial, coastal and marine ecosystems;

(e) Cooperate in preparing for adaptation to the impacts of climate change; de-

론을 사용하여, 몬트리올의정서에 의하여 규제되지 않는 모든 온실가스의 배출원에 따른 인위적 배출과 흡수원에 따른 제거에 관한 국가통계를 제12조에 따라 작성, 정기적으로 갱신 및 공표하고 당사국총회에 통보한다.

나. 몬트리올의정서에 의하여 규제되지 않는 모든 온실가스의 배출원에 따른 인위적 배출의 방지와 흡수원에 따른 제거를 통하여 기후변화를 완화하는 조치와 기후변화에 충분한 적응을 용이하게 하는 조치를 포함한 국가적 및 적절한 경우 지역적 계획을 수립·실시·공표하고 정기적으로 갱신한다.

다. 에너지·수송·산업·농업·임업 그리고 폐기물관리분야를 포함한 모든 관련분야에서 몬트리올의정서에 의하여 규제되지 않는 온실가스의 인위적 배출을 규제·감축 또는 방지하는 기술·관행 및 공정을 개발·적용하고, 이전을 포함하여 확산시키는 것을 촉진하고 협력한다.

라. 생물자원·산림·해양과 그 밖의 육상·연안 및 해양 생태계 등 몬트리올의정서에 의하여 규제되지 않는 온실가스의 흡수원과 저장소의 지속가능한 관리를 촉진하고 또한 적절한 보존 및 강화를 촉진하며 이를 위해 협력한다.

마. 기후변화의 영향에 대한 적응을 준비하는 데 협력한다. 즉, 연안관리·수자원 및 농

velop and elaborate appropriate and integrated plans for coastal zone management, water resources and agriculture,
and for the protection and rehabilitation of areas, particularly in Africa, affected by drought and desertification,
as well as floods;

(f) Take climate change considerations
into account, to the extent feasible, in
their relevant social, economic and environmental policies and actions, and
employ appropriate methods, for exam-
ple impact assessments, formulated
and determined nationally, with a view
to minimizing adverse effects on the
economy, on public health and on the
quality of the environment, of projects
or measures undertaken by them to
mitigate or adapt to climate change;

(g) Promote and cooperate in scientific,
technological, technical, socio—economic
and other research, systematic observation and development of data archives
related to the climate system and intended to further the understanding
and to reduce or eliminate the remaining uncertainties regarding the causes,
effects, magnitude and timing of climate
change and the economic and social
consequences of various response strategies;

(h) Promote and cooperate in the full, open
and prompt exchange of relevant scientific, technological, technical, socio-
economic and legal information related
to the climate system and climate
change, and to the economic and social
consequences of various response strategies;

업을 위한 계획 그리고 특히 아프리카 등
가뭄·사막화 및 홍수에 의하여 영향받는
지역의 보호와 복구를 위한 적절한 통합
계획을 개발하고 발전시킨다.

바. 관련 사회·경제 및 환경정책과 조치에서
가능한 한 기후 변화를 고려하며, 기후변
화를 완화하고 이에 적응하기 위하여 채
택한 사업과 조치가 경제·공중보건 및
환경의 질에 미치는 부정적 효과를 최소
화할 수 있도록, 예를 들어 영향평가와
같은, 국가적으로 입안되고 결정된 적절
한 방법을 사용한다.

사. 기후변화의 원인·결과·규모·시기 및
여러 대응전략의 경제적·사회적 결과에
관한 이해를 증진시키고 또한 이에 관한
잔존 불확실성을 축소·제거하기 위하여
기후체계와 관련된 과학적·기술적·기
능적·사회경제적 및 그 밖의 조사, 체계
적 관측 그리고 자료보관소의 설치를 촉
진하고 협력한다.

아. 기후체계와 기후변화, 그리고 여러 대응
전략의 경제적·사회적 결과와 관련된 과
학적·기술적·기능적·사회 경제적 및
법률적 정보의 포괄적, 공개적 그리고 신
속한 교환을 촉진하고 협력한다.

(i) Promote and cooperate in education, training and public awareness related to climate change and encourage the widest participation in this process, including that of non-governmental organizations; and

자. 기후변화에 관한 교육, 훈련 및 홍보를 촉진하고 협력하며, 이러한 과정에 비정부간기구 등의 광범위한 참여를 장려한다.

(j) Communicate to the Conference of the Parties information related to implementation, in accordance with Article 12.

차. 제12조에 따라 이행관련 정보를 당사국총회에 통보한다.

2. The developed country Parties and other Parties included in Annex I commit themselves specifically as provided for in the following:

2. 부속서 1에 포함된, 선진국인 당사자와 그 밖의 당사자는 특히 다음에 규정된 사항을 수행할 것에 합의한다.

(a) Each of these Parties shall adopt national policies and take corresponding measures on the mitigation of climate change, by limiting its anthropogenic emissions of greenhouse gases and protecting and enhancing its greenhouse gas sinks and reservoirs. These policies and measures will demonstrate that developed countries are taking the lead in modifying longer-term trends in anthropogenic emissions consistent with the objective of the Convention, recognizing that the return by the end of the present decade to earlier levels of anthropogenic emissions of carbon dioxide and other greenhouse gases not controlled by the Montreal Protocol would contribute to such modification, and taking into account the differences in these Parties' starting points and approaches, economic structures and resource bases, the need to maintain strong and sustainable economic growth, available technologies and other indivi-

가. 당사자는 온실가스의 인위적 배출을 제한하고 온실가스의 흡수원과 저장소를 보호·강화함으로써 기후변화의 완화에 관한 국가정책을 채택하고 이에 상응하는 조치를 취한다. 이러한 정책과 조치를 취함으로써 선진국은 이 협약의 목적에 부합하도록 인위적 배출의 장기적 추세를 수정하는데 선도적 역할을 수행함을 증명한다. 선진국은 이러한 역할을 수행함에 있어 이산화탄소와 몬트리올의정서에 의하여 규제되지 않는 그 밖의 온실가스의 인위적 배출을 1990년대 말까지 종전 수준으로 회복시키는 것이 그러한 수정에 기여함을 인식하고 각 당사자의 출발점 및 접근 방법·경제구조 그리고 자원기반의 차이, 강력하고 지속 가능한 경제성장을 유지할 필요성, 가용기술 그리고 여타 개별적 상황, 아울러 이 목적에 대한 세계적 노력에 각 당사자가 공평하고 적절하게 기여할 필요성을 고려한다. 선진국인 당사자는 그 밖의 당사자와 이러한 정책과 조치를 공동으로 이행할 수

dual circumstances, as well as the need for equitable and appropriate contributions by each of these Parties to the global effort regarding that objective. These Parties may implement such policies and measures jointly with other Parties and may assist other Parties in contributing to the achievement of the objective of the Convention and, in particular, that of this subparagraph;

(b) In order to promote progress to this end, each of these Parties shall communicate, within six months of the entry into force of the Convention for it and periodically thereafter, and in accordance with Article 12, detailed information on its policies and measures referred to in subparagraph (a) above, as well as on its resulting projected anthropogenic emissions by sources and removals by sinks of greenhouse gases not controlled by the Montreal Protocol for the period referred to in subparagraph (a), with the aim of returning individually or jointly to their 1990 levels these anthropogenic emissions of carbon dioxide and other greenhouse gases not controlled by the Montreal Protocol. This information will be reviewed by the Conference of the Parties, at its first session and periodically thereafter, in accordance with Article 7;

(c) Calculations of emissions by sources and removals by sinks of greenhouse gases for the purposes of subparagraph (b) above should take into account the best available scientific knowledge, including of the effective capa-

있으며, 또한 그 밖의 당사자가 협약의 목적, 특히 본호의 목적을 달성하는데 기여하도록 지원할 수 있다.

나. 이러한 목적달성을 촉진하기 위하여 당사자는 이산화탄소와 몬트리올의정서에 의하여 규제되지 않는 그 밖의 온실가스의 인위적 배출을 개별적 또는 공동으로 1990년 수준으로 회복시키기 위한 목적으로, 가호에 언급된 정책 및 조치에 관한 상세한 정보와, 가호에 언급된 기간동안에 이러한 정책과 조치의 결과로 나타나는 몬트리올의정서에 의하여 규제되지 않는 온실가스의 배출원에 따른 인위적 배출과 흡수원에 따른 제거에 관한 상세한 정보를 협약이 자기나라에 대하여 발효한 후 6월 이내에, 또한 그 이후에는 정기적으로 제12조에 따라 통보한다. 당사국총회는 제7조에 따라 제1차 회기에서, 또한 그 이후에는 정기적으로 이러한 정보를 검토한다.

다. 나호의 목적상 온실가스의 배출원에 따른 배출과 흡수원에 따른 제거에 관한 계산은 흡수원의 유효용량 및 기후변화에 대한 가스종별 기여도를 포함하는 최대한으로 이용가능한 과학적 지식을 고려하여야 한다. 당사국총회는 제1차 회기에서

city of sinks and the respective contributions of such gases to climate
change. The Conference of the Parties
shall consider and agree on methodologies for these calculations at its first
session and review them regularly
thereafter;

(d) The Conference of the Parties shall, at
its first session, review the adequacy
of subparagraphs (a) and (b) above.
Such review shall be carried out in the
light of the best available scientific
information and assessment on climate
change and its impacts, as well as relevant technical, social and economic
information. Based on this review, the
Conference of the Parties shall take
appropriate action, which may include
the adoption of amendments to the commitments in subparagraphs (a) and (b)
above. The Conference of the Parties,
at its first session, shall also take decisions regarding criteria for joint implementation as indicated in subparagraph
(a) above. A second review of subparagraphs (a) and (b) shall take place
not later than 31 December 1998, and
thereafter at regular intervals determined by the Conference of the Parties,
until the objective of the Convention is
met;

(e) Each of these Parties shall :
  (i) Coordinate as appropriate with other
      such Parties, relevant economic and
      administrative instruments deve-
      loped to achieve the objective of
      the Convention; and
  (ii) Identify and periodically review its
       own policies and practices which

이러한 계산방식에 대해 심의, 합의하고
그 이후에는 정기적으로 이를 검토한다.

라. 당사국총회는 제1차 회기에서 가호와 나
호의 조치가 충분한 지를 검토한다. 이러
한 검토는 기후변화와 그 영향에 대한 최
대한으로 이용가능한 과학적 정보 및 평
가와 아울러 관련 기술적·사회적 및 경
제적 정보를 고려하여 수행한다. 이러한
검토에 입각하여 당사국총회는 적절한
조치를 취하며, 이에는 가호 및 나호의
공약에 대한 개정의 채택이 포함될 수 있
다. 당사국총회는 제1차 회기에서 가호에
규정된 공동이행에 관한 기준을 또한 결
정한다. 가호와 나호에 대한 제2차 검토
는 1998년 12월 31일 이전에 실시하며,
그 이후에는 이 협약의 목적이 달성될 때
까지 당사국총회가 결정하는 일정한 간
격으로 실시한다.

마. 당사자는 다음을 수행한다.
  (i) 협약의 목적을 달성하기 위하여 개발
      된 관련 경제적 및 행정적 수단들을
      적절히 그 밖의 당사자와 조정한다.

  (ii) 몬트리올의정서에 의하여 규제되지
       않는 온실가스의 인위적 배출수준의

encourage activities that lead to greater levels of anthropogenic emissions of greenhouse gases not controlled by the Montreal Protocol than would otherwise occur;

(f) The Conference of the Parties shall review, not later than 31 December 1998, available information with a view to taking decisions regarding such amendments to the lists in Annexes I and II as may be appropriate, with the approval of the Party concerned;

(g) Any Party not included in Annex I may, in its instrument of ratification, acceptance, approval or accession, or at any time thereafter, notify the Depositary that it intends to be bound by subparagraphs (a) and (b) above. The Depositary shall inform the other signatories and Parties of any such notification.

3. The developed country Parties and other developed Parties included in Annex II shall provide new and additional financial resources to meet the agreed full costs incurred by developing country Parties in complying with their obligations under Article 12, paragraph 1. They shall also provide such financial resources, including for the transfer of technology, needed by the developing country Parties to meet the agreed full incremental costs of implementing measures that are covered by paragraph 1 of this Article and that are agreed between a developing country Party and the international entity or entities referred to in Article 11, in accordance

증가를 초래하는 활동을 조장하는 정책과 관행을 찾아내어 정기적으로 검토한다.

바. 당사국총회는 관련 당사자의 승인을 얻어 부속서 1·2의 명단을 적절히 수정할지를 결정하기 위하여 1998년 12월 31일 이전에 이용 가능한 정보를 검토한다.

사. 부속서 1에 포함되지 않은 당사자는 비준서·수락서·승인서 또는 가입서에서, 그리고 그 이후에는 언제든지 가호와 나호에 구속받고자 하는 의사를 수탁자에게 통고할 수 있다. 수탁자는 그러한 통고를 서명자 또는 당사자에게 통보한다.

3. 부속서 2에 포함된, 선진국인 당사자와 그 밖의 선진당사자는 개발도상국이 제12조 제1항에 따른 공약을 이행하는 데에서 부담하는 합의된 만큼의 모든 비용을 충족시키기 위하여 새로운 추가적 재원을 제공한다. 이러한 당사자는 또한 기술이전을 위한 비용을 포함하여, 본조 제1항에 규정된 것으로서 개발도상국이 제11조에 언급된 국제기구 또는 국제기구들과 합의한 조치를 이행하는 데에서 발생하는, 합의된 만큼의 모든 부가비용을 충족시키기 위하여 제11조에 따라 개발도상국인 당사자가 필요로 하는 새로운 추가적 재원을 제공한다. 이러한 공약의 이행에는 자금 흐름의 충분성과 예측 가능성 및 선진국인 당사자간의 적절한 부

with that Article. The implementation of these commitments shall take into account the need for adequacy and predictability in the flow of funds and the importance of appropriate burden sharing among the developed country Parties.

4. The developed country Parties and other developed Parties included in Annex II shall also assist the developing country Parties that are particularly vulnerable to the adverse effects of climate change in meeting costs of adaptation to those adverse effects.

5. The developed country Parties and other developed Parties included in Annex II shall take all practicable steps to promote, facilitate and finance, as appropriate, the transfer of, or access to, environmentally sound technologies and knowhow to other Parties, particularly developing country Parties, to enable them to implement the provisions of the Convention. In this process, the developed country Parties shall support the development and enhancement of endogenous capacities and technologies of developing country Parties. Other Parties and organizations in a position to do so may also assist in facilitating the transfer of such technologies.

6. In the implementation of their commitments under paragraph 2 above, a certain degree of flexibility shall be allowed by the Conference of the Parties to the Parties included in Annex I undergoing the process of transition to a market

담배분의 중요성을 고려한다.

4. 부속서 2에 포함된, 선진국인 당사자와 그 밖의 선진당사자는 또한 기후변화의 부정적 효과에 특히 취약한 개발도상국인 당사자가 이러한 부정적 효과에 적응하는 비용을 부담할 수 있도록 지원한다.

5. 부속서 2에 포함된, 선진국인 당사자와 그 밖의 선진당사자는 다른 당사자, 특히 개발도상국인 당사자가 이 협약의 규정을 이행할 수 있도록 환경적으로 건전한 기술과 노우하우의 이전 또는 이에 대한 접근을 적절히 증진·촉진하며, 그리고 이에 필요한 재원을 제공하기 위한 모든 실행 가능한 조치를 취한다. 이러한 과정에서 선진국인 당사자는 개발도상국인 당사자의 내생적 능력과 기술의 개발 및 향상을 지원한다. 지원할 수 있는 위치에 있는 그 밖의 당사자와 기구도 이러한 기술이전을 용이하게 하도록 지원할 수 있다.

6. 제2항의 공약을 이행하는 데 있어, 부속서 1에 포함된 당사자로서 시장경제로의 이행과정에 있는 당사자에 대해서는 기후변화에 대응하는 능력을 향상시키도록 당사국총회로부터 어느 정도의 융통성이 허용되며, 이에는 기준으로 선정된 몬트리올의

economy, in order to enhance the ability of these Parties to address climate change, including with regard to the historical level of anthropogenic emissions of greenhouse gases not controlled by the Montreal Protocol chosen as a reference.

7. The extent to which developing country Parties will effectively implement their commitments under the Convention will depend on the effective implementation by developed country Parties of their commitments under the Convention related to financial resources and transfer of technology and will take fully into account that economic and social development and poverty eradication are the first and overriding priorities of the developing country Parties.

8. In the implementation of the commitments in this Article, the Parties shall give full consideration to what actions are necessary under the Convention, including actions related to funding, insurance and the transfer of technology, to meet the specific needs and concerns of developing country Parties arising from the adverse effects of climate change and/or the impact of the implementation of response measures, especially on:

(a) Small island countries;
(b) Countries with low—lying coastal areas;
(c) Countries with arid and semi—arid areas, forested areas and areas liable to forest decay;
(d) Countries with areas prone to natural disasters;

정서에 의해 규제되지 않는 온실가스의 과거 인위적 배출수준에 관한 사항이 포함된다.

7. 개발도상국인 당사자의 협약에 따른 공약의 효과적 이행정도는 선진국인 당사자가 재원 및 기술이전에 관한 협약상의 공약을 얼마나 효과적으로 이행할 지에 달려있으며, 경제적·사회적 개발과 빈곤 퇴치가 개발도상국의 제1차적이며 가장 앞서는 우선순위임을 충분히 고려한다.

8. 본조의 공약을 이행하는 데 있어, 당사자는 특히 다음에 열거한 각 지역에 대한 기후변화의 부정적 효과 그리고/또는 대응조치의 이행에 따른 영향으로부터 발생하는 개발도상국인 당사자의 특수한 필요와 관심을 충족시키기 위하여 재원제공, 보험 그리고 기술이전과 관련된 조치를 포함하여 이 협약에 따라 어떠한 조치가 필요한 지를 충분히 고려한다.

가. 소도서국가
나. 저지대 연안을 보유한 국가
다. 건조·반건조지역, 산림지역 및 산림황폐에 취약한 지역을 보유한 국가

라. 자연재해에 취약한 지역을 보유한 국가

(e) Countries with areas liable to drought and desertification;

(f) Countries with areas of high urban atmospheric pollution;

(g) Countries with areas with fragile ecosystems, including mountainous ecosystems;

(h) Countries whose economies are highly dependent on income generated from the production, processing and export, and/or on consumption of fossil fuels and associated energy-intensive products; and

(i) Land-locked and transit countries. Further, the Conference of the Parties may take actions, as appropriate, with respect to this paragraph.

9. The Parties shall take full account of the specific needs and special situations of the least developed countries in their actions with regard to funding and transfer of technology.

10. The Parties shall, in accordance with Article 10, take into consideration in the implementation of the commitments of the Convention the situation of Parties, particularly developing country Parties, with economies that are vulnerable to the adverse effects of the implementation of measures to respond to climate change. This applies notably to Parties with economies that are highly dependent on income generated from the production, processing and export, and/or consumption of fossil fuels and associated energy-intensive products and/or the use of fossil fuels for which such

마. 가뭄과 사막화에 취약한 지역을 보유한 국가

바. 도시대기가 고도로 오염된 지역을 보유한 국가

사. 산악 생태계를 포함하여 연약한 생태계 지역을 보유한 국가

아. 화석연료와 이에 연관된 에너지 집약적 생산품의 생산·가공 및 수출로부터 얻는 소득에, 그리고/또는 화석연료와 이에 연관된 에너지 집약적 생산품의 소비에 크게 의존하는 경제를 보유한 국가

자. 내륙국과 경유국 또한, 당사국총회는 본 항과 관련하여 적절한 조치를 취할 수 있다.

9. 당사자는 재원제공 및 기술이전과 관련된 조치에서 최빈국의 특수한 필요와 특별한 상황을 충분히 고려한다.

10. 당사자는, 협약의 공약을 이행함에 있어, 기후변화에 대응하기 위한 조치의 이행에 따라 발생하는 부정적 효과에 취약한 경제를 가진 당사자, 특히 개발도상국인 당사자의 여건을 제10조에 따라 고려한다. 이는 화석연료와 이에 연관된 에너지 집약적 생산품의 생산·가공 및 수출로부터 발생하는 소득에 크게 의존하는, 그리고/또는 화석연료와 이에 연관된 에너지 집약적 생산품의 소비에 크게 의존하는, 그리고/또는 다른 대체에너지로 전환하는 데 심각한 어려움을 갖고 있어 화석 연료 사용에 크게 의존하는 경제를 보유한 당사자에게 특히 적용된다.

Parties have serious difficulties in switching to alternatives.

Article 5
Research and systematic observation

In carrying out their commitments under Article 4, paragraph 1(g), the Parties shall:

(a) Support and further develop, as appropriate, international and intergovernmental programmes and networks or organizations aimed at defining, conducting, assessing and financing research, data collection and systematic observation, taking into account the need to minimize duplication of effort;

(b) Support international and intergovernmental efforts to strengthen systematic observation and national scientific and technical research capacities and capabilities, particularly in developing countries, and to promote access to, and the exchange of, data and analyses thereof obtained from areas beyond national jurisdiction; and

(c) Take into account the particular concerns and needs of developing countries and cooperate in improving their endogenous capacities and capabilities to participate in the efforts referred to in subparagraphs (a) and (b) above.

Article 6
Education, training and public awareness

In carrying out their commitments under Article 4, paragraph 1(i), the Parties shall:

(a) Promote and facilitate at the national

제 5 조
조사 및 체계적 관측

제4조 제1항 사호의 공약을 이행함에 있어, 당사자는 다음과 같이 한다.

가. 노력의 중복을 최소화할 필요성을 고려하여 조사·자료 수집 및 체계적 관측에 관한 정의수립·실시·평가 및 경비지원을 목적으로 하는 국제적 및 정부간 계획·조직 또는 기구를 적절히 지원하고 더욱 발전시킨다.

나. 특히 개발도상국에 있어서 체계적 관측과 국가의 과학·기술 조사역량과 능력을 강화하며, 국가관할권 이원지역에서 획득된 자료 및 그 분석결과에의 접근 및 교환을 촉진하는 국제적 및 정부간 노력을 지원한다.

다. 개발도상국의 특별한 관심과 필요를 고려하며, 가호 및 나호에 언급된 노력에 참여하기 위한 개발도상국의 내생적 역량과 능력을 향상시키는 데 협력한다.

제 6 조
교육, 훈련 및 홍보

제4조 제1항 자호의 공약을 이행함에 있어, 당사자는 다음과 같이 한다.

가. 국내적 차원 및 적절한 경우 소지역적 및

and, as appropriate, subregional and regional levels, and in accordance with national laws and regulations, and within their respective capacities

(i) The development and implementation of educational and public awareness programmes on climate change and its effects;

(ii) Public access to information on climate change and its effects;

(iii) Public participation in addressing climate change and its effects and developing adequate responses; and

(iv) Training of scientific, technical and managerial personnel.

(b) Cooperate in and promote, at the international level, and, where appropriate, using existing bodies:

(i) The development and exchange of educational and public awareness material on climate change and its effects; and

(ii) The development and implementation of education and training programmes, including the strengthening of national institutions and the exchange or secondment of personnel to train experts in this field, in particular for developing countries.

Article 7
Conference of the Parties

1. A Conference of the Parties is hereby established.

2. The Conference of the Parties, as the supreme body of this Convention, shall

지역적 차원에서 국내법령에 따라, 또한 각자의 능력 안에서 다음 사항을 촉진하고 장려한다.

(i) 기후변화와 그 효과에 관한 교육 및 홍보계획의 개발과 실시

(ii) 기후변화와 그 효과에 관한 정보에의 공공의 접근

(iii) 기후변화와 그 효과에 대응하고 적절한 대응책을 개발하는 데 대한 공공의 참여

(iv) 과학·기술 및 관리요원의 양성

나. 국제적 차원에서 그리고 적절한 경우 기존기구를 이용하여 다음 사항에서 협력하고 이를 촉진한다.

(i) 기후변화와 그 효과에 관한 교육 및 홍보 자료의 개발과 교환

(ii) 특히 개발도상국을 위하여 이 분야의 전문가를 양성할 국내기관의 강화와 요원의 교류 또는 파견을 포함하는 교육·훈련계획의 개발과 실시

제 7 조
당사국총회

1. 당사국총회를 이에 설치한다.

2. 당사국총회는 협약의 최고기구로서 협약 및 당사국총회가 채택하는 관련 법적 문서

keep under regular review the implementation of the Convention and any
related legal instruments that the Conference of the Parties may adopt, and
shall make, within its mandate, the decisions necessary to promote the effective
implementation of the Convention. To
this end, it shall:

(a) Periodically examine the obligations of
the Parties and the institutional arrangements under the Convention, in the light
of the objective of the Convention, the
experience gained in its implementation and the evolution of scientific and
technological knowledge;

(b) Promote and facilitate the exchange of
information on measures adopted by
the Parties to address climate change
and its effects, taking into account the
differing circumstances, responsibilities
and capabilities of the Parties and their
respective commitments under the Convention;

(c) Facilitate, at the request of two or more
Parties, the coordination of measures
adopted by them to address climate
change and its effects, taking into account the differing circumstances, responsibilities and capabilities of the
Parties and their respective commitments under the Convention;

(d) Promote and guide, in accordance with
the objective and provisions of the Convention, the development and periodic
refinement of comparable methodologies, to be agreed on by the Conference
of the Parties, inter alia, for preparing
inventories of greenhouse gas emis-

의 이행상황을 정기적으로 검토하며, 권한
의 범위 안에서 협약의 효과적 이행 촉진
에 필요한 결정을 한다. 이를 위하여 당사
국총회는 다음을 수행한다.

가. 협약의 목적, 협약의 이행과정에서 얻은
경험 및 과학·기술지식의 발전에 비추어
협약에 따른 당사자의 공약과 제도적 장
치를 정기적으로 검토한다.

나. 당사자의 서로 다른 여건·책임 및 능력
과 협약상의 각자의 공약을 고려하여, 기
후변화와 그 효과에 대응하기 위하여 당
사자가 채택한 조치에 관한 정보의 교환
을 촉진하고 용이하게 한다.

다. 둘 또는 그 이상의 당사자의 요청이 있는
경우, 당사자의 서로 다른 여건·책임 및
능력과 협약에 따른 각자의 공약을 고려
하여, 기후변화 및 그 효과에 대응하기
위하여 당사자가 채택한 조치의 조정을
용이하게 한다.

라. 협약의 목적과 규정에 따라, 특히 온실
가스의 배출원에 따른 배출 및 흡수원에
따른 제거에 관한 목록을 작성하고, 온
실가스의 배출을 제한하고 제거를 강화
하는 조치의 유효성을 평가하기 위한,
당사국총회에서 합의될 비교 가능한 방
법론의 개발 및 정기적 개선을 촉진하고

sions by sources and removals by sinks, and for evaluating the effectiveness of measures to limit the emissions and enhance the removals of these gases;

(e) Assess, on the basis of all information made available to it in accordance with the provisions of the Convention, the implementation of the Convention by the Parties, the overall effects of the measures taken pursuant to the Convention, in particular environmental, economic and social effects as well as their cumulative impacts and the extent to which progress towards the objective of the Convention is being achieved;

(f) Consider and adopt regular reports on the implementation of the Convention and ensure their publication;

(g) Make recommendations on any matters necessary for the implementation of the Convention;

(h) Seek to mobilize financial resources in accordance with Article 4, paragraphs 3, 4 and 5, and Article 11;

(i) Establish such subsidiary bodies as are deemed necessary for the implementation of the Convention;

(j) Review reports submitted by its subsidiary bodies and provide guidance to them;

(k) Agree upon and adopt, by consensus, rules of procedure and financial rules for itself and for any subsidiary bodies;

(l) Seek and utilize, where appropriate, the services and cooperation of, and information provided by, competent international organizations and intergovernmental and non-governmental bod-

지도한다.

마. 협약의 규정에 따라 제공된 모든 정보에 입각하여 당사자의 협약 이행상황, 협약에 따라 취한 조치의 전반적 효과, 특히 누적적 효과를 포함한 환경적·경제적·사회적 효과 및 협약의 목적 성취도를 평가한다.

바. 협약의 이행에 관한 정기보고서를 심의, 채택하고 공표한다.

사. 협약의 이행에 필요한 모든 사항에 대하여 권고한다.

아. 제4조 제3항·제4항·제5항 및 제11조에 따라 재원의 동원을 추구한다.

자. 협약의 이행에 필요하다고 판단되는 보조기관을 설치한다.

차. 보조기관이 제출하는 보고서를 검토하고 지침을 준다.

카. 총회 및 보조기관의 의사규칙 및 재정규칙을 콘센서스로 합의하여 채택한다.

타. 적절한 경우, 권한있는 국제기구·정부간기구 및 비정부간 기구의 지원과 협력 및 이들 기구에 의해 제공되는 정보를 입수하여 이용한다.

ies; and

(m) Exercise such other functions as are required for the achievement of the objective of the Convention as well as all other functions assigned to it under the Convention.

3. The Conference of the Parties shall, at its first session, adopt its own rules of procedure as well as those of the subsidiary bodies established by the Convention, which shall include decision—making procedures for matters not already covered by decision—making procedures stipulated in the Convention. Such procedures may include specified majorities required for the adoption of particular decisions.

4. The first session of the Conference of the Parties shall be convened by the interim secretariat referred to in Article 21 and shall take place not later than one year after the date of entry into force of the Convention. Thereafter, ordinary sessions of the Conference of the Parties shall be held every year unless otherwise decided by the Conference of the Parties.

5. Extraordinary sessions of the Conference of the Parties shall be held at such other times as may be deemed necessary by the Conference, or at the written request of any Party, provided that, within six months of the request being communicated to the Parties by the secretariat, it is supported by at least one third of the Parties.

파. 협약에 따라 부여된 모든 기능과 협약의 목적달성을 위하여 요구되는 그 밖의 기능을 수행한다.

3. 당사국총회는 제1차 회기에서 총회 및 협약에 의하여 설치되는 보조기관의 의사규칙을 채택하며, 이 의사규칙은 협약에 규정된 의사 결정절차에서 다루지 않는 문제에 관한 의사결정절차를 포함한다. 이 절차에는 특별한 결정의 채택에 필요한 특정 의결정족수를 포함할 수 있다.

4. 당사국총회 제1차 회기는 제21조에 규정된 임시사무국이 소집하며 협약 발효 후 1년 이내에 개최한다. 그 이후에는 당사국총회가 달리 결정하지 아니하는 한, 당사국총회 정기회기는 매년 개최된다.

5. 당사국총회 특별회기는 총회가 필요하다고 인정하는 때에 또는 당사자의 서면요청에 의하여 개최한다. 다만, 이러한 서면요청은 사무국이 이를 당사자에게 통보한 후 6월 이내에 최소한 당사자 3분의 1의 지지를 받아야 한다.

6. The United Nations, its specialized agencies and the International Atomic Energy Agency, as well as any State member thereof or observers thereto not Party to the Convention, may be represented at sessions of the Conference of the Parties as observers. Any body or agency, whether national or international, governmental or non-governmental, which is qualified in matters covered by the Convention, and which has informed the secretariat of its wish to be represented at a session of the Conference of the Parties as an observer, may be so admitted unless at least one third of the Parties present object. The admission and participation of observers shall be subject to the rules of procedure adopted by the Conference of the Parties.

Article 8
Secretariat

1. A secretariat is hereby established.

2. The functions of the secretariat shall be:

(a) To make arrangements for sessions of the Conference of the Parties and its subsidiary bodies established under the Convention and to provide them with services as required;
(b) To compile and transmit reports submitted to it;
(c) Tofacilitate assistance to the Parties, particularly developing country Parties, on request, in the compilation and communication of information required in accordance with the provisions of the

6. 국제연합·국제연합전문기구·국제원자력기구 및 이들 기구의 회원국 또는 옵서버인 비당사자는 당사국총회 회기에 옵서버로 참석할 수 있다. 협약과 관련된 분야에서 자격을 갖춘 국내적 또는 국제적 기구나 기관 및 정부간 또는 비정부간 기구나 기관이 당사국총회 회기에 옵서버로서 참석할 희망을 사무국에 통보한 경우, 최소한 출석 당사자 3분의 1이 반대하지 아니하는 한 참석이 허용될 수 있다. 옵서버의 참석허용 및 회의참가는 당사국총회가 채택한 의사규칙에 따른다.

제8조
사 무 국

1. 사무국을 이에 설치한다.

2. 사무국의 기능은 다음과 같다.

가. 당사국총회 및 협약에 따라 설치되는 총회 보조기관의 회의준비와 이에 필요한 지원 제공

나. 사무국에 제출된 보고서의 취합 및 전달

다. 요청이 있을 경우, 당사자 특히 개발도상국인 당사자가 협약규정에 따라 요구되는 정보를 취합, 통보하는 데 있어 이에 대한 지원 촉진

Convention;

(d) To prepare reports on its activities and present them to the Conference of the Parties;

(e) To ensure the necessary coordination with the secretariats of other relevant international bodies;

(f) To enter, under the overall guidance of the Conference of the Parties, into such administrative and contractual arrangements as may be required for the effective discharge of its functions; and

(g) To perform the other secretariat functions specified in the Convention and in any of its protocols and such other functions as may be determined by the Conference of the Parties.

3. The Conference of the Parties, at its first session, shall designate a permanent secretariat and make arrangements for its functioning.

라. 활동보고서의 작성 및 당사국총회에 대한 제출

마. 다른 유관 국제기구 사무국과의 필요한 협조 확보

바. 당사국총회의 전반적인 지침에 따라 효과적인 기능 수행에 필요한 행정적·계약적 약정 체결

사. 협약과 부속의정서에 규정된 그 밖의 사무국 기능과 당사국총회가 결정하는 그 밖의 기능 수행

3. 당사국총회는 제1차 회기에서 상설사무국을 지정하고 그 기능 수행에 필요한 준비를 한다.

Article 9
Subsidiary body for scientific and technological advice

1. A subsidiary body for scientific and technological advice is hereby established to provide the Conference of the Parties and, as appropriate, its other subsidiary bodies with timely information and advice on scientific and technological matters relating to the Convention. This body shall be open to participation by all Parties and shall be multidisciplinary. It shall comprise government representatives competent in the relevant field of

제9조
과학·기술자문 보조기관

1. 당사국총회와 적절한 경우 그 밖의 보조기관에 협약과 관련된 과학·기술문제에 관한 시의적절한 정보와 자문을 제공하기 위하여 과학·기술자문 보조기관을 이에 설치한다. 이 기관은 모든 당사자의 참여에 개방되며 여러 전문분야로 이루어진다. 이 기관은 유관 전문 분야의 권한있는 정부대표로 구성된다. 이 기관은 모든 작업상황에 관하여 당사국총회에 정기적으로 보고한다.

expertise. It shall report regularly to the Conference of the Parties on all aspects of its work.

2. Under the guidance of the Conference of the Parties, and drawing upon existing competent international bodies, this body shall:

(a) Provide assessments of the state of scientific knowledge relating to climate change and its effects;

(b) Prepare scientific assessments on the effects of measures taken in the implementation of the Convention;

(c) Identify innovative, efficient and state—of—the—art technologies and know—how and advise on the ways and means of promoting development and/or transferring such technologies;

(d) Provide advice on scientific programmes, international cooperation in research and development related to climate change, as well as on ways and means of supporting endogenous capacity building in developing countries; and

(e) Respond to scientific, technological and methodological questions that the Conference of the Parties and its subsidiary bodies may put to the body.

3. The functions and terms of reference of this body may be further elaborated by the Conference of the Parties.

Article 10
Subsidiary body for implementation

1. A subsidiary body for implementation is

2. 당사국총회의 시침에 따라, 그리고 권한있는 국제기구의 협력을 얻어 이 기관은 다음 사항을 수행한다.

가. 기후변화와 그 효과에 관한 과학지식의 현황에 대한 평가를 제공한다.

나. 협약의 이행과정에서 취한 조치의 효과에 대한 과학적 평가를 준비한다.

다. 혁신적·효율적인 첨단기술과 노우하우를 파악하고 그러한 기술의 개발 및/또는 이전을 촉진하는 방법과 수단에 관하여 자문한다.

라. 기후변화와 관련된 과학계획 및 연구개발을 위한 국제협력에 관한 자문과 개발도상국의 내생적 역량 형성을 지원하는 방법 및 수단에 관한 자문을 제공한다.

마. 당사국총회와 그 보조기관이 제기하는 과학적·기술적 및 방법론적 질문에 답변한다.

3. 이 기관의 기능과 권한은 당사국총회에서 더 구체화할 수 있다.

제 10 조
이행을 위한 보조기관

1. 당사국총회가 협약의 효과적 이행상황을

hereby established to assist the Conference of the Parties in the assessment and review of the effective implementation of the Convention. This body shall be open to participation by all Parties and comprise government representatives who are experts on matters related to climate change. It shall report regularly to the Conference of the Parties on all aspects of its work.

2. Under the guidance of the Conference of the Parties, this body shall:

(a) Consider the information communicated in accordance with Article 12, paragraph 1, to assess the overall aggregated effect of the steps taken by the Parties in the light of the latest scientific assessments concerning climate change;

(b) Consider the information communicated in accordance with Article 12, paragraph 2, in order to assist the Conference of the Parties in carrying out the reviews required by Article 4, paragraph 2(d); and

(c) Assist the Conference of the Parties, as appropriate, in the preparation and implementation of its decisions.

Article 11
Financial mechanism

1. A mechanism for the provision of financial resources on a grant or concessional basis, including for the transfer of technology, is hereby defined. It shall function under the guidance of and be accoun-

평가하고 검토하는 것을 지원하기 위하여 이행을 위한 보조기관을 이에 설치한다. 이 기관은 모든 당사자의 참여에 개방되며 기후변화 분야의 전문가인 정부대표로 구성된다. 이 기관은 모든 작업상황에 관하여 당사자 총회에 정기적으로 보고한다.

2. 당사국총회의 지침에 따라, 이 기관은 다음 사항을 수행한다.

가. 당사자가 취한 조치의 전반적인 종합적 효과를 평가하기 위하여, 제12조 제1항에 따라 통보된 정보를 기후변화에 관한 최신의 과학적 평가에 비추어 심의한다.

나. 당사국총회가 제4조 제2항 나호에 규정된 검토를 수행하는 것을 지원하기 위하여, 제12조 제2항에 따라 통보된 정보를 심의한다.

다. 적절한 경우, 당사국총회가 결의를 준비하고 이행하는 데 있어 이를 지원한다.

제 11 조
재정지원체제

1. 기술이전을 포함하여 무상 또는 양허성 조건의 재원제공을 위한 지원체제를 이에 규정한다. 이 지원체제는 협약에 관련되는 정책, 계획의 우선순위 및 자격기준을 결정하는 당사국총회의 지침에 따라 기능을

table to the Conference of the Parties, which shall decide on its policies, programme priorities and eligibility criteria related to this Convention. Its operation shall be entrusted to one or more existing international entities.

2. The financial mechanism shall have an equitable and balanced representation of all Parties within a transparent system of governance.

3. The Conference of the Parties and the entity or entities entrusted with the operation of the financial mechanism shall agree upon arrangements to give effect to the above paragraphs, which shall include the following:

(a) Modalities to ensure that the funded projects to address climate change are in conformity with the policies, programme priorities and eligibility criteria established by the Conference of the Parties;

(b) Modalities by which a particular funding decision may be reconsidered in light of these policies, programme priorities and eligibility criteria;

(c) Provision by the entity or entities of regular reports to the Conference of the Parties on its funding operations, which is consistent with the requirement for accountability set out in paragraph 1 above; and

(d) Determination in a predictable and identifiable manner of the amount of funding necessary and available for the implementation of this Convention and the conditions under which that amount

수행하고 총회에 책임을 진다. 그 운영은 하나 또는 그 이상의 기존 국제기구에 위탁된다.

2. 재정지원체제는 투명한 관리제도 안에서 모든 당사자가 공평하고 균형있는 대표성을 갖는다.

3. 당사국총회와 재정지원체제의 운영을 위탁받은 기구는 상기 두 항에 효력을 부여하기 위하여 다음 사항을 포함하는 운영요령에 합의한다.

가. 기후변화를 다루기 위한 재원제공사업이 당사국총회가 마련한 정책, 계획의 우선순위 및 자격기준에 부합하도록 보장하는 방식

나. 특정 재원제공 결정을 이러한 정책, 계획의 우선순위 및 자격기준에 비추어 재심의하는 방식

다. 제1항에 규정된 책임요건과 부합하게, 운영을 맡은 기구가 재원제공활동에 관한 정기보고서를 당사국총회에 제출하는 것

라. 예측 가능하고 확인 가능한 방식으로 협약이행에 필요한 이용 가능한 재원제공액을 결정하고, 이 금액을 정기적으로 검토하는 조건에 관해 결정하는 것

shall be periodically reviewed.

4. The Conference of the Parties shall make arrangements to implement the above-mentioned provisions at its first session, reviewing and taking into account the interim arrangements referred to in Article 21, paragraph 3, and shall decide whether these interim arrangements shall be maintained. Within four years thereafter, the Conference of the Parties shall review the financial mechanism and take appropriate measures.

5. The developed country Parties may also provide and developing country Parties avail themselves of, financial resources related to the implementation of the Convention through bilateral, regional and other multilateral channels.

Article 12
Communication of information
related to implementation

1. In accordance with Article 4, paragraph 1, each Party shall communicate to the Conference of the Parties, through the secretariat, the following elements of information:

(a) A national inventory of anthropogenic emissions by sources and removals by sinks of all greenhouse gases not controlled by the Montreal Protocol, to the extent its capacities permit, using comparable methodologies to be promoted and agreed upon by the Conference of the Parties;

(b) A general description of steps taken or envisaged by the Party to implement

4. 당사국총회는 제21조 제3항에 언급된 임시조치를 검토, 심의하여 제1차 회기에서 상기 규정의 이행을 위한 준비를 하고 임시조치의 유지여부를 결정한다. 그로부터 4년이내에 당사국총회는 재정지원체제에 대해 검토하고 적절한 조치를 취한다.

5. 선진국인 당사자는 또한 협약이행과 관련된 재원을 양자적, 지역적 및 그 밖의 다자적 경로를 통하여 제공하고, 개발도상국인 당사자는 이를 이용할 수 있다.

제12조
이행관련 정보의 통보

1. 제4조 제1항에 따라, 당사자는 사무국을 통하여 다음 사항의 정보를 당사국총회에 통보한다.

가. 당사국총회에서 지지·합의할 비교 가능한 방법론을 이용하여 능력이 허용하는 한도 내에서 작성한 몬트리올의정서에 의해 규제되지 않는 모든 온실가스의 배출원에 따른 인위적 배출과 흡수원에 따른 제거에 관한 국가통계

나. 협약이행을 위하여 당사자가 취했거나 계획중인 조치의 일반적인 서술

the Convention; and

(c) Any other information that the Party considers relevant to the achievement of the objective of the Convention and suitable for inclusion in its communication, including, if feasible, material relevant for calculations of global emission trends.

2. Each developed country Party and each other Party included in Annex I shall incorporate in its communication the following elements of information:

(a) A detailed description of the policies and measures that it has adopted to implement its commitment under Article 4, paragraphs 2(a) and 2(b); and

(b) A specific estimate of the effects that the policies and measures referred to in subparagraph (a) immediately above will have on anthropogenic emissions by its sources and removals by its sinks of greenhouse gases during the period referred to in Article 4, paragraph 2 (a).

3. In addition, each developed country Party and each other developed Party included in Annex II shall incorporate details of measures taken in accordance with Article 4, paragraphs 3, 4 and 5.

4. Developing country Parties may, on a voluntary basis, propose projects for financing, including specific technologies, materials, equipment, techniques or practices that would be needed to implement such projects, along with, if possible, an estimate of all incremental costs, of the reductions of emissions and in-

다. 당사자가 협약 목적의 달성에 관련되고 통보에 포함시키는 것이 적합하다고 판단하는 그 밖의 정보. 이는 가능한 경우 세계적 배출추세 산출에 관련되는 자료를 포함함.

2. 부속서 1에 포함된, 선진국인 당사자와 그 밖의 당사자는 통보에 다음 사항의 정보를 포함한다.

가. 제4조 제2항 가호·나호의 공약이행을 위하여 채택한 정책 및 조치의 상세한 서술

나. 상기 가호에 언급된 정책 및 조치가 제4조 제2항 가호에 언급된 기간 동안 온실가스의 배출원에 따른 인위적 배출 및 흡수원에 따른 제거에 미치는 효과에 대한 상세한 평가

3. 또한 부속서 2에 포함된, 선진국인 당사자와 그 밖의 선진 당사자는 제4조 제3항·제4항 및 제5항에 따라 취한 조치의 상세 내용을 포함한다.

4. 개발도상국인 당사자는 자발적으로 사업이행에 필요한 특정 기술·재료·장비·공법 또는 관행을 포함하는 재원제공사업을 제안할 수 있으며, 이러한 제안에는 가능한 경우 모든 부가비용에 대한 견적, 온실가스의 배출저감 및 제거증가에 대한 견적, 그리고 이로 인한 이익에 대한 평가를

crements of removals of greenhouse gases, as well as an estimate of the consequent benefits.

5. Each developed country Party and each other Party included in Annex I shall make its initial communication within six months of the entry into force of the Convention for that Party. Each Party not so listed shall make its initial communication within three years of the entry into force of the Convention for that Party, or of the availability of financial resources in accordance with Article 4, paragraph 3. Parties that are least developed countries may make their initial communication at their discretion. The frequency of subsequent communications by all Parties shall be determined by the Conference of the Parties, taking into account the differentiated timetable set by this paragraph.

6. Information communicated by Parties under this Article shall be transmitted by the secretariat as soon as possible to the Conference of the Parties and to any subsidiary bodies concerned. If necessary, the procedures for the communication of information may be further considered by the Conference of the Parties.

7. From its first session, the Conference of the Parties shall arrange for the provision to developing country Parties of technical and financial support, on request, in compiling and communicating information under this Article, as well as in identifying the technical and fi-

포함한다.

5. 부속서 1에 포함된, 선진국인 당사자와 그 밖의 당사자는 그 당사자에 대하여 협약이 발효한 후 6월 이내에 최초의 통보를 행한다. 그 밖의 당사자는 그 당사자에 대한 협약발효 후 3년 이내에, 또는 제4조 제3항에 따른 재원을 이용할 수 있는 때로부터 3년 이내에 최초의 통보를 행한다. 최빈국인 당사자는 자신의 재량에 따라 최초의 통보를 행한다. 모든 당사자의 그 후의 통보의 빈도는 당사국총회가 결정하며, 이에는 이 항에 규정된 차등적 일정을 고려한다.

6. 사무국은 본조에 따라 당사자가 통보한 정보를 당사국총회와 유관 보조기관에 가급적 신속히 전달한다. 필요하다면, 당사국총회는 정보의 통보절차를 추가로 심의할 수 있다.

7. 당사국총회는 제1차 회기부터 개발도상국인 당사자가 본조에 따라 정보를 취합 및 통보하고 제4조에 따른 제안사업 및 대응조치와 연관된 기술적·재정적 소요를 판단하는 데 필요한 기술·재정지원을 요청에 따라 개발도상국인 당사자에게 제공하는 것을 주선한다. 그 밖의 당사자, 권한있

nancial needs associated with proposed projects and response measures under Article 4. Such support may be provided by other Parties, by competent international organizations and by the secretariat, as appropriate.

8. Any group of Parties may, subject to guidelines adopted by the Conference of the Parties, and to prior notification to the Conference of the Parties, make a joint communication in fulfilment of their obligations under this Article, provided that such a communication includes information on the fulfilment by each of these Parties of its individual obligations under the Convention.

9. Information received by the secretariat that is designated by a Party as confidential, in accordance with criteria to be established by the Conference of the Parties, shall be aggregated by the secretariat to protect its confidentiality before being made available to any of the bodies involved in the communication and review of information.

10. Subject to paragraph 9 above, and without prejudice to the ability of any Party to make public its communication at any time, the secretariat shall make communications by Parties under this Article publicly available at the time they are submitted to the Conference of the Parties.

는 국제기구 및 사무국은 적절한 경우 이러한 지원을 제공할 수 있다.

8. 당사자로 구성된 집단은 당사국총회가 채택한 지침에 따르고 당사국총회에 사전통고하는 조건으로, 본조에 따른 공약을 이행하기 위하여 공동으로 통보를 행할 수 있다. 단, 이러한 통보에는 협약에 따른 각 당사자의 개별적 공약이행에 관한 정보가 포함되는 것을 조건으로 한다.

9. 사무국이 접수한 정보중 당사자가 당사국총회에 의해 설정되는 기준에 따라 비밀로 지정한 정보는 정보통보와 검토에 관여하는 기관에 제공되기 전에 비밀보호를 위하여 사무국이 취합한다.

10. 제9항에 따를 것을 조건으로, 그리고 통보한 정보를 언제든지 공표할 수 있는 당사자의 능력에 영향을 미치지 아니하고, 사무국은 본조에 따라 당사자가 통보한 정보가 당사국총회에 제출되는 시점에 공개적 이용이 가능하도록 한다.

Article 13
Resolution of questions regarding implementation

The Conference of the Parties shall, at its first session, consider the establishment of a multilateral consultative process, available to Parties on their request, for the resolution of questions regarding the implementation of the Convention.

Article 14
Settlement of disputes

1. In the event of a dispute between any two or more Parties concerning the interpretation or application of the Convention, the Parties concerned shall seek a settlement of the dispute through negotiation or any other peaceful means of their own choice.

2. When ratifying, accepting, approving or acceding to the Convention, or at any time thereafter, a Party which is not a regional economic integration organization may declare in a written instrument submitted to the Depositary that, in respect of any dispute concerning the interpretation or application of the Convention, it recognizes as compulsory ipso facto and without special agreement, in relation to any Party accepting the same obligation:

(a) Submission of the dispute to the International Court of Justice, and/or
(b) Arbitration in accordance with procedures to be adopted by the Conference of the Parties as soon as practicable,

제 13 조
이행관련 문제의 해결

당사국총회는 제1차 회기에서 이 협약의 이행관련 문제의 해결을 위하여, 당사자의 요청으로 이용가능한, 다자간 협의절차의 수립을 심의한다.

제 14 조
분쟁해결

1. 이 협약의 해석 또는 적용에 관하여 둘 또는 그 이상의 당사자간에 분쟁이 있는 경우, 관련 당사자는 교섭 또는 스스로 선택하는 그 밖의 평화적 방법을 통하여 분쟁의 해결을 모색한다.

2. 이 협약의 비준·수락·승인 또는 가입시, 그리고 그 후 언제든지, 지역경제통합기구가 아닌 당사자는 협약의 해석이나 적용에 관한 분쟁에 있어서 동일한 의무를 수락하는 당사자와의 관계에서 다음을 특별한 합의없이, 선언하였다는 사실만으로, 의무적인 것으로 인정함을 수탁자에게 서면으로 선언할 수 있다.

가. 분쟁의 국제사법재판소 회부 그리고/또는

나. 당사국총회가 가능한 한 신속히 중재에 관한 부속서 형태로 채택할 절차에 따른 중재지역경제통합기구인 당사자는 나호

in an annex on arbitration. A Party which is a regional economic integration organization may make a declaration with like effect in relation to arbitration in accordance with the procedures referred to in subparagraph (b) above.

3. A declaration made under paragraph 2 above shall remain in force until it expires in accordance with its terms or until three months after written notice of its revocation has been deposited with the Depositary.

4. A new declaration, a notice of revocation or the expiry of a declaration shall not in any way affect proceedings pending before the International Court of Justice or the arbitral tribunal, unless the parties to the dispute otherwise agree.

5. Subject to the operation of paragraph 2 above, if after twelve months following notification by one Party to another that a dispute exists between them, the Parties concerned have not been able to settle their dispute through the means mentioned in paragraph 1 above, the dispute shall be submitted, at the request of any of the parties to the dispute, to conciliation.

6. A conciliation commission shall be created upon the request of one of the parties to the dispute. The commission shall be composed of an equal number of members appointed by each party concerned and a chairman chosen jointly by the members appointed by each party. The commission shall render a recom-

에서 언급된 절차에 따른 중재와 관련하여 유사한 효력을 가지는 선언을 행할 수 있다.

3. 제2항에 따라 행해진 선언은 선언의 조건에 따라 기한이 만료될 때까지, 또는 서면 철회통고가 수탁자에게 기탁된 후 3월까지 유효하다.

4. 새로운 선언, 선언의 철회통고 또는 선언의 기한만료는 분쟁 당사자가 달리 합의하지 아니하는 한, 국제사법재판소 또는 중재재판소에서 진행중인 소송에 대하여 어떠한 영향도 미치지 아니한다.

5. 제2항의 운용에 따를 것을 조건으로, 일방당사자가 타방 당사자에게 그들간에 분쟁이 존재하고 있음을 통고한 후 12월 동안 분쟁당사자가 제1항에 언급된 수단을 통하여 분쟁을 해결하지 못한 경우, 그 분쟁은 분쟁당사자 일방의 요청에 의하여 조정에 회부된다.

6. 조정위원회는 분쟁당사자 일방의 요청에 따라 설치된다. 위원회는 관련당사자 각각에 의하여 임명된 동수의 위원과 각 당사자에 의해 임명된 위원들이 공동으로 선출한 의장으로 구성된다. 위원회는 권고적 판정을 내리고, 당사자는 이를 성실히 고려한다.

mendatory award, which the parties shall consider in good faith.

7. Additional procedures relating to conciliation shall be adopted by the Conference of the Parties, as soon as practicable, in an annex on conciliation.

8. The provisions of this Article shall apply to any related legal instrument which the Conference of the Parties may adopt, unless the instrument provides otherwise.

Article 15
Amendments to the convention

1. Any Party may propose amendments to the Convention.

2. Amendments to the Convention shall be adopted at an ordinary session of the Conference of the Parties. The text of any proposed amendment to the Convention shall be communicated to the Parties by the secretariat at least six months before the meeting at which it is proposed for adoption. The secretariat shall also communicate proposed amendments to the signatories to the Convention and, for information, to the Depositary.

3. The Parties shall make every effort to reach agreement on any proposed amendment to the Convention by consensus. If all efforts at consensus have been exhausted, and no agreement reached, the amendment shall as a last resort be adopted by a three-fourths

---

7. 당사국총회는 가능한 한 신속히 조정에 관한 부속서 형태로 조정과 관련된 추가절차를 채택한다.

8. 본조의 규정은 해당문서가 달리 규정하지 아니하는 한, 당사국총회가 채택하는 모든 관련 법적 문서에 적용된다.

제 15 조
협약의 개정

1. 모든 당사자는 협약의 개정안을 제안할 수 있다.

2. 협약 개정안은 당사국총회의 정기회기에서 채택된다. 사무국은 제안된 협약개정안을 늦어도 채택회의가 개최되기 6월 전에 당사자에게 통보한다. 또한 사무국은 제안된 개정안을 이 협약 서명자 그리고 참고로 수탁자에게도 통보한다.

3. 당사자는 제안된 협약 개정안이 콘센서스에 의하여 합의에 도달하도록 모든 노력을 다한다. 콘센서스를 위한 모든 노력을 다하였으나 합의에 도달하지 못한 경우, 개정안은 최종적으로 회의에 출석·투표한 당사자 4분의 3의 다수결로 채택된다. 사무국은 채택된 개정안을 수탁자에게 통보

majority vote of the Parties present and voting at the meeting. The adopted amendment shall be communicated by the secretariat to the Depositary, who shall circulate it to all Parties for their acceptance.

4. Instruments of acceptance in respect of an amendment shall be deposited with the Depositary. An amendment adopted in accordance with paragraph 3 above shall enter into force for those Parties having accepted it on the ninetieth day after the date of receipt by the Depositary of an instrument of acceptance by at least three fourths of the Parties to the Convention.

5. The amendment shall enter into force for any other Party on the ninetieth day after the date on which that Party deposits with the Depositary its instrument of acceptance of the said amendment.

6. For the purposes of this Article, "Parties present and voting" means Parties present and casting an affirmative or negative vote.

Article 16
Adoption and amendment of annexes to the convention

1. Annexes to the Convention shall form an integral part thereof and, unless otherwise expressly provided, a reference to the Convention constitutes at the same time a reference to any annexes thereto. Without prejudice to the provisions

하며, 수탁자는 수락을 위하여 이를 모든 당사자에게 배포한다.

4. 개정안에 대한 수락서는 수탁자에게 기탁된다. 제3항에 따라 채택된 개정안은 최소한 협약당사자 4분의 3의 수락서가 수탁자에게 접수된 후 90일째 되는 날부터 수락한 당사자에 대하여 발효한다.

5. 그 밖의 당사자가 그 후에 수탁자에게 수락서를 기탁하는 경우, 개정안은 기탁일 후 90일째 되는 날부터 그 당사자에 대하여 발효한다.

6. 본조의 목적상 "출석 · 투표한 당사자"라 함은 회의에 출석하여 찬성 또는 반대 투표를 한 당사자를 말한다.

제 16 조
부속서의 채택 및 개정

1. 협약의 부속서는 협약의 불가분의 일부를 구성하며, 협약이 언급되는 경우 명시적으로 달리 규정하지 아니하는 한, 이는 동시에 부속서도 언급하는 것으로 본다. 이러한 부속서는 제14조 제2항 나호 및 제7항의 규정에 영향을 미치지 아니하고, 목록 ·

of Article 14, paragraphs 2(b) and 7, such annexes shall be restricted to lists, forms and any other material of a descriptive nature that is of a scientific, technical, procedural or administrative character.

2. Annexes to the Convention shall be proposed and adopted in accordance with the procedure set forth in Article 15, paragraphs 2, 3 and 4.

3. An annex that has been adopted in accordance with paragraph 2 above shall enter into force for all Parties to the Convention six months after the date of the communication by the Depositary to such Parties of the adoption of the annex, except for those Parties that have notified the Depositary, in writing, within that period of their non-acceptance of the annex. The annex shall enter into force for Parties which withdraw their notification of non-acceptance on the ninetieth day after the date on which withdrawal of such notification has been received by the Depositary.

4. The proposal, adoption and entry into force of amendments to annexes to the Convention shall be subject to the same procedure as that for the proposal, adoption and entry into force of annexes to the Convention in accordance with paragraphs 2 and 3 above.

5. If the adoption of an annex or an amendment to an annex involves an amendment to the Convention, that annex or amendment to an annex shall not enter

양식 및 과학적·기술적·절차적 또는 행정적 특성을 가진 서술적 성격의 그 밖의 자료에 제한된다.

2. 협약의 부속서는 제15조 제2항·제3항 및 제4항에 규정된 절차에 따라 제안되고 채택된다.

3. 제2항에 따라 채택된 부속서는, 수탁자가 부속서의 채택을 당사국에 통보한 날부터 6월 후에, 동 기간 내에 부속서를 수락하지 않음을 수탁자에게 서면으로 통고한 당사자를 제외한 모든 당사자에 대하여 발효한다. 부속서는 불수락 통고를 철회한 당사자에 대하여는 수탁자의 통고철회 접수일 후 90일째 되는 날부터 발효한다.

4. 협약 부속서의 개정안의 제안·채택 및 발효는 제2항 및 제3항에 따른 협약 부속서의 제안·채택 및 발효와 동일한 절차를 따른다.

5. 부속서 또는 부속서 개정안의 채택이 협약의 개정을 수반하는 경우, 협약의 개정안이 발효할 때까지 부속서 또는 부속서 개정안은 발효하지 아니한다.

into force until such time as the amendment to the Convention enters into force.

Article 17
Protocols

1. The Conference of the Parties may, at any ordinary session, adopt protocols to the Convention.

2. The text of any proposed protocol shall be communicated to the Parties by the secretariat at least six months before such a session.

3. The requirements for the entry into force of any protocol shall be established by that instrument.

4. Only Parties to the Convention may be Parties to a protocol.

5. Decisions under any protocol shall be taken only by the Parties to the protocol concerned.

Article 18
Right to vote

1. Each Party to the Convention shall have one vote, except as provided for in paragraph 2 below.

2. Regional economic integration organizations, in matters within their competence, shall exercise their right to vote with a number of votes equal to the number of their member States that are Parties to the Convention. Such an organization shall not exercise its right to vote if any of its member States

제 17 조
의 정 서

1. 당사국총회는 정기회기에서 협약에 대한 의정서를 채택할 수 있다.

2. 사무국은 제안된 의정서의 문안을 늦어도 회기가 개최되기 6월 전에 당사자에게 통보한다.

3. 의정서의 발효요건은 그 문서에 규정한다.

4. 협약의 당사자만이 의정서의 당사자가 될 수 있다.

5. 의정서에 따른 결정은 관련 의정서의 당사자만이 할 수 있다.

제 18 조
투 표 권

1. 협약의 당사자는 제2항에 규정된 경우를 제외하고는 하나의 투표권을 가진다.

2. 지역경제통합기구는 그 기구의 권한사항에 대하여 협약의 당사자인 기구 회원국의 수와 동수의 투표권을 행사한다. 기구 회원국의 어느 한 나라라도 투표권을 행사하는 경우, 기구는 투표권을 행사할 수 없으며 그 반대의 경우도 또한 같다.

exercises its right, and vice versa.

Article 19
Depositary

The Secretary-General of the United Nations shall be the Depositary of the Convention and of protocols adopted in accordance with Article 17.

Article 20
Signature

This Convention shall be open for signature by States Members of the United Nations or of any of its specialized agencies or that are Parties to the Statute of the International Court of Justice and by regional economic integration organizations at Rio de Janeiro, during the United Nations Conference on Environment and Development, and thereafter at United Nations Headquarters in New York from 20 June 1992 to 19 June 1993.

Article 21
Interim arrangements

1. The secretariat functions referred to in Article 8 will be carried out on an interim basis by the secretariat established by the General Assembly of the United Nations in its resolution 45/212 of 21 December 1990, until the completion of the first session of the Conference of the Parties.

2. The head of the interim secretariat referred to in paragraph 1 above will cooperate closely with the Intergovern-

제19조
수 탁 자

국제연합사무총장은 이 협약과 협약 제17조에 따라 채택되는 의정서의 수탁자가 된다.

제20조
서   명

이 협약은 국제연합 환경개발회의 기간 중에는 리우데자네이로에서, 1992년 6월 20일부터 1993년 6월 19일까지는 뉴욕의 국제연합본부에서 국제연합 또는 그 전문기구의 회원국, 국제사법재판소 규정 당사자 및 지역경제통합기구의 서명을 위하여 개방된다.

제21조
임시조치

1. 제8조에 언급된 사무국의 기능은 당사국총회의 제1차 회기 종료시까지는 1990년 12월 21일 국제연합총회결의 45/212호에 의해 설립된 사무국에 의하여 임시로 수행된다.

2. 제1항에 언급된 임시사무국의 장은 기후변화에 관한 정부간 협의체가 객관적인 과학적·기술적 자문의 요구에 따를 수 있도

mental Panel on Climate Change to ensure that the Panel can respond to the need for objective scientific and technical advice. Other relevant scientific bodies could also be consulted.

3. The Global Environment Facility of the United Nations Development Programme, the United Nations Environment Programme and the International Bank for Reconstruction and Development shall be the international entity entrusted with the operation of the financial mechanism referred to in Article 11 on an interim basis. In this connection, the Global Environment Facility should be appropriately restructured and its membership made universal to enable it to fulfil the requirements of Article 11.

Article 22
Ratification, acceptance, approval or accession

1. The Convention shall be subject to ratification, acceptance, approval or accession by States and by regional economic integration organizations. It shall be open for accession from the day after the date on which the Convention is closed for signature. Instruments of ratification, acceptance, approval or accession shall be deposited with the Depositary.

2. Any regional economic integration organization which becomes a Party to the Convention without any of its member States being a Party shall be bound by all the obligations under the Convention. In the case of such organizations, one

록 하기 위하여 협의체와 긴밀히 협력한다. 다른 관련 과학기구들과도 또한 협의할 수 있다.

3. 국제연합개발계획, 국제연합환경계획 및 국제부흥개발은행에 의하여 운영되고 있는 지구환경기금은 임시적으로 제11조에 언급된 재정지원체제의 운영을 위탁받는 국제기구가 된다. 이와 관련, 지구 환경기금은 제11조의 요건을 충족할 수 있도록 적절히 재구성되어야 하고 그 회원자격을 보편화하여야 한다.

제 22 조
비준·수락·승인 또는 가입

1. 협약은 국가 및 지역경제통합기구에 의해 비준·수락·승인 또는 가입된다. 협약은 서명기간이 종료된 다음 날부터 가입을 위하여 개방된다. 비준서·수락서·승인서 또는 가입서는 수탁자에게 기탁된다.

2. 협약의 당사자가 되는 지역경제통합기구는, 기구 회원국 중 어느 한 국가도 협약의 당사자가 아닌 경우, 협약에 따른 모든 의무에 구속된다. 기구의 하나 또는 그 이상의 회원국이 협약의 당사자인 경우, 기

or more of whose member States is a Party to the Convention, the organization and its member States shall decide on their respective responsibilities for the performance of their obligations under the Convention. In such cases, the organization and the member States shall not be entitled to exercise rights under the Convention concurrently.

3. In their instruments of ratification, acceptance, approval or accession, regional economic integration organizations shall declare the extent of their competence with respect to the matters governed by the Convention. These organizations shall also inform the Depositary, who shall in turn inform the Parties, of any substantial modification in the extent of their competence.

Article 23
Entry into force

1. The Convention shall enter into force on the ninetieth day after the date of deposit of the fiftieth instrument of ratification, acceptance, approval or accession.

2. For each State or regional economic integration organization that ratifies, accepts or approves the Convention or accedes thereto after the deposit of the fiftieth instrument of ratification, acceptance, approval or accession, the Convention shall enter into force on the ninetieth day after the date of deposit by such State or regional economic integration organization of its instrument of ratification, acceptance, approval or accession.

구와 기구 회원국은 협약에 따른 의무를 수행하기 위한 각각의 책임을 결정한다. 이러한 경우, 기구와 기구회원국은 협약에 따른 권리를 동시에 행사할 수는 없다.

3. 지역경제통합기구는 그 비준서·수락서·승인서 또는 가입서에 협약이 규율하는 사항에 관한 기구의 권한범위를 선언한다. 또한 기구는 권한범위의 실질적 변동에 관하여 수탁자에게 통보하며, 수탁자는 이를 당사자에게 통보한다.

제 23 조
발 효

1. 협약은 50번째의 비준서·수락서·승인서 또는 가입서의 기탁일 후 90일째 되는 날부터 발효한다.

2. 50번째의 비준서·수락서·승인서 또는 가입서가 기탁된 후 협약을 비준·수락·승인 또는 가입하는 국가 또는 지역경제통합 기구에 대하여, 협약은 그 국가 또는 지역경제통합기구의 비준서·수락서·승인서 또는 가입서 기탁일 후 90일째 되는 날부터 발효한다.

3. For the purposes of paragraphs 1 and 2 above, any instrument deposited by a regional economic integration organization shall not be counted as additional to those deposited by States members of the organization.

Article 24
Reservations

No reservations may be made to the Convention.

Article 25
Withdrawal

1. At any time after three years from the date on which the Convention has entered into force for a Party, that Party may withdraw from the Convention by giving written notification to the Depositary.

2. Any such withdrawal shall take effect upon expiry of one year from the date of receipt by the Depositary of the notification of withdrawal, or on such later date as may be specified in the notification of withdrawal.

3. Any Party that withdraws from the Convention shall be considered as also having withdrawn from any protocol to which it is a Party.

Article 26
Authentic texts

The original of this Convention, of which the Arabic, Chinese, English, French, Russian and Spanish texts are equally authentic,

3. 제1항 및 제2항의 목적상 지역경제통합기구가 기탁하는 문서는 기구 회원국이 기탁하는 문서에 추가되는 것으로 보지 아니한다.

제24조
유   보

협약에 대하여는 어떤 유보도 행할 수 없다.

제25조
탈   퇴

1. 당사자는 협약이 자기나라에 대하여 발효한 날부터 3년이 경과한 후에는 언제든지 수탁자에게 서면통고를 함으로써 협약으로부터 탈퇴할 수 있다.

2. 탈퇴는 수탁자가 탈퇴통고를 접수한 날부터 1년의 기한 만료일 또는 탈퇴통고서에 더 늦은 날짜가 명시된 경우에는 그 늦은 날에 발효한다.

3. 협약으로부터 탈퇴한 당사자는 당사자가 되어 있는 모든 의정서로부터도 탈퇴한 것으로 본다.

제26조
정   본

아랍어·중국어·영어·불어·러시아어 및 서반아어본이 동등하게 정본인 이 협약의 원본은 국제연합사무총장에게 기탁된다.

shall be deposited with the Secretary-General of the United Nations.

IN WITNESS WHEREOF the undersigned, being duly authorized to that effect, have signed this Convention.

DONE AT New York this ninth day of May one thousand nine hundred and ninety-two.

이상의 증거로 정당하게 권한을 위임받은 아래 서명자가 협약에 서명하였다.

일천구백구십이년 오월 구일 뉴욕에서 작성하였다.

Annex I

Australia	Austria	Belarus[a]
Belgium	Bulgaria[a]	Canada
Croatia[a]*	Czech Republic[a]*	Denmark
European Economic Community		Estonia[a]
Finland	France	Germany
Greece	Hungary[a]	Iceland
Ireland	Italy	Japan
Latvia[a]	Liechtenstein*	Lithuaniaa
Luxembourg	Monaco*	Netherlands
New Zealand	Norway	Poland[a]
Portugal	Romania[a]	Russian Federation[a]
Slovakia[a]*	Slovenia[a]*	Spain
Sweden	Switzerland	Turkey
Ukraine[a]	United Kingdom	United States

[a] Countries that are undergoing the process of transition to a market economy.

* Publisher's note : Countries added to Annex I by an amendment that entered into force on 13 August 1998, pursuant to decision 4/CP.3 adopted at COP.3.

Annex II

Australia	Austria	Belgium
Canada	Denmark	European Economic Community
Finland	France	Germany
Greece	Iceland	Ireland
Italy	Japan	Luxembourg
Netherlands	New Zealand	Norway
Portugal	Spain	Sweden
Switzerland	United Kingdom	United States

* Publisher's note: Turkey was deleted from Annex II by an amendment that entered into force 28 June 2002, pursuant to decision 26/CP.7 adopted at COP.7.

4. Kyoto Protocol to the United Nations Framework Convention on Climate Change (1997)

4. 기후변화에 관한 국제연합 기본협약에 대한 교토의정서

Date : 11 December 1997
In force : 16 February 2005
States Party : 192
Korea : 16 February 2005 (조약 제1706호)
Link : www.unfccc.int

The Parties to this Protocol,

이 의정서의 당사자는,

Being Parties to the United Nations Framework Convention on Climate Change, hereinafter referred to as "the Convention",

기후변화에 관한 국제연합 기본협약(이하 "협약"이라 한다)의 당사자로서,

In pursuit of the ultimate objective of the Convention as stated in its Article 2,

협약 제2조에 규정된 협약의 궁극적 목적을 추구하고,

Recalling the provisions of the Convention,

협약의 규정을 상기하며,

Being guided by Article 3 of the Convention,

협약 제3조와,

Pursuant to the Berlin Mandate adopted by decision 1/CP.1 of the Conference of the Parties to the Convention at its first session,

협약의 규정에 의한 당사국총회 제1차 회기에서 결정 1/CP.1호로 채택된 베를린위임에 따라,

Have agreed as follows:

다음과 같이 합의하였다.

Article 1

제 1 조

For the purposes of this Protocol, the definitions contained in Article 1 of the Convention shall apply. In addition:

이 의정서의 목적상, 협약 제1조의 정의규정이 적용된다. 추가로,

1. "Conference of the Parties" means the

1. "당사국총회"라 함은 협약의 규정에 의한

Conference of the Parties to the Convention.

2. "Convention" means the United Nations Framework Convention on Climate Change, adopted in New York on 9 May 1992.

3. "Intergovernmental Panel on Climate Change" means the Intergovernmental Panel on Climate Change established in 1988 jointly by the World Meteorological Organization and the Nations Environment Programme.

4. "Montreal Protocol" means the Montreal Protocol on Substances that Deplete the Ozone Layer, adopted in Montreal on 16 September 1987 and as subsequently adjusted and amended.

5. "Parties present and voting" means Parties present and casting an affirmative or negative vote.

6. "Party" means, unless the context otherwise indicates, a Party to this Protocol.

7. "Party included in Annex I" means a Party included in Annex I to the Convention, as may be amended, or a Party which has made a notification under Article 4, paragraph 2(g), of the Convention.

Article 2

1. Each Party included in Annex I, in achieving its quantified emission limitation and reduction commitments under

당사국총회를 말한다.

2. "협약"이라 함은 1992년 5월 9일 뉴욕에서 채택된 기후변화에 관한 국제연합 기본협약을 말한다.

3. "기후변화에 관한 정부간 패널"이라 함은 세계기상기구 및 국제연합 환경계획이 1988년에 공동으로 설립한 기후변화에 관한 정부간 패널을 말한다.

4. "몬트리올의정서"라 함은 1987년 9월 16일 몬트리올에서 채택되고 그 이후 조정·개정된 오존층파괴물질에 관한 몬트리올의정서를 말한다.

5. "출석하여 투표하는 당사자"라 함은 회의에 출석하여 찬성이나 반대투표를 하는 당사자를 말한다.

6. "당사자"라 함은 문맥상 다른 의미로 사용되지 아니하는 한, 이 의정서의 당사자를 말한다.

7. "부속서 1의 당사자"라 함은 협약의 부속서 1(당해 부속서가 개정되는 경우에는 그 개정부속서를 말한다)에 포함된 당사자 및 협약 제4조 제2항 사목에 의하여 통고한 당사자를 말한다.

제2조

1. 부속서 1의 당사자는 제3조의 규정에 의한 수량적 배출량의 제한·감축을 위한 공약을 달성함에 있어 지속가능한 개발을

Article 3, in order to promote sustainable development, shall:

(a) Implement and/or further elaborate policies and measures in accordance with its national circumstances, such as:

   (i) Enhancement of energy efficiency in relevant sectors of the national economy;

   (ii) Protection and enhancement of sinks and reservoirs of greenhouse gases not controlled by the Montreal Protocol, taking into account its commitments under relevant international environmental agreements; promotion of sustainable forest management practices, afforestation and

   (iii) Promotion of sustainable forms of agriculture in light of climate change considerations;

   (iv) Research on, and promotion, development and increased use of, new and renewable forms of energy, of carbon dioxide sequestration technologies and of advanced and innovative environmentally sound technologies;

   (v) Progressive reduction or phasing out of market imperfections, fiscal incentives, tax and duty exemptions and subsidies in all greenhouse gas sectors that run counter to the objective of the Convention application of market instruments;

   (vi) Encouragement of appropriate reforms in relevant sectors aimed at promoting policies and measures which limit or reduce emissions of

촉진하기 위하여 다음 각목의 사항을 수행한다.

가. 자국의 여건에 따라 다음과 같은 정책·조치를 이행하고/이행하거나 더욱 발전시킨다.

   (1) 자국 경제의 관련 부문에서 에너지의 효율성을 향상시킬 것

   (2) 관련 국제환경협정상 자국의 공약을 고려하면서, 온실가스(몬트리올의정서에 의하여 규제되는 것을 제외한다)의 흡수원 및 저장소를 보호·강화하고, 지속가능한 산림관리 작업과 신규조림 및 재조림을 촉진할 것

   (3) 기후변화요소를 고려한 지속가능한 형태의 농업을 촉진할 것

   (4) 신규 및 재생 가능한 형태의 에너지와 이산화탄소의 격리기술 및 선진적·혁신적이며 환경적으로 건전한 기술에 대한 연구·촉진·개발 및 그 이용을 증진할 것

   (5) 모든 온실가스의 배출부문에 있어서 협약의 목적에 위배되는 시장의 불완전성, 재정적 유인, 세금·관세의 면제 및 보조금 등을 점진적으로 감축하거나 단계적으로 폐지하며, 시장적 기제를 적용할 것

   (6) 온실가스(몬트리올의정서에 의하여 규제되는 것을 제외한다)의 배출량을 제한·감축하는 정책 및 조치를

greenhouse gases not controlled by the Montreal Protocol;

(vii) Measures to limit and/or reduce emissions of greenhouse gases not controlled by the Montreal Protocol in the transport sector;

(viii) Limitation and/or reduction of methane emissions through recovery and in waste management, as well as in the production, transport and distribution of energy;

(b) Cooperate with other such Parties to enhance the individual and combined effectiveness of their policies and measures adopted under this Article, pursuant to Article 4, paragraph 2(e) (i), of the Convention. To this end, these Parties shall take steps to share their experience and exchange information on such policies and measures, including developing ways of improving their comparability, transparency and effectiveness. The Conference of the Parties serving as the meeting of the Parties to this Protocol shall, at its first session or as soon as practicable thereafter, consider ways to facilitate such cooperation, taking into account relevant information.

2. The Parties included in Annex I shall pursue limitation or reduction of emissions of greenhouse gases not controlled by the Montreal Protocol from aviation and marine bunker fuels, working through the International Civil Aviation Organization and the International Maritime Organization, respectively.

촉진하기 위하여 관련 부문의 적절한 개선을 장려할 것

(7) 수송부문에서 온실가스(몬트리올의정서에 의하여 규제되는 것을 제외한다)의 배출량을 제한 및/또는 감축하는 조치를 취할 것

(8) 폐기물의 관리와 에너지의 생산·수송·분배 과정에서의 회수 및 사용을 통하여 메탄의 배출량을 제한 및/또는 감축할 것

나. 이 조에서 채택되는 정책 및 조치의 개별적·복합적 효과를 증대하기 위하여 협약 제4조 제2항 마목(1)에 따라 다른 부속서 1의 당사자들과 협력한다. 이를 위하여, 이들 당사자는 이러한 정책 및 조치에 관한 경험을 공유하고 정보를 교환하기 위한 조치를 이행하되, 이에는 정책 및 조치의 비교가능성·투명성 및 그 효과를 개선하기 위한 방안의 개발이 포함된다. 이 의정서의 당사자회의의 역할을 수행하는 당사국총회는 제1차 회기 또는 그 이후에 가능한 한 신속히 모든 관련 정보를 고려하여, 이러한 협력을 촉진하기 위한 방안을 검토한다.

2. 부속서 1의 당사자는 국제민간항공기구 및 국제해사기구에서의 활동을 통하여, 항공기용 및 선박용 연료로부터 각각 발생하는 온실가스(몬트리올의정서에 의하여 규제되는 것을 제외한다) 배출량의 제한·감축을 추구한다.

3. The Parties included in Annex I shall strive to implement policies and measures under this Article in such a way as to minimize adverse effects, including the adverse effects of climate change, effects on international trade, and social, environmental and economic impacts on other Parties, especially developing country Parties and in particular those identified in Article 4, paragraphs 8 and 9, of the Convention, taking into account Article 3 of the Convention. The Conference of the Parties serving as the meeting of the Parties to this Protocol may take further action, as appropriate, to promote the implementation of the provisions of this paragraph.

4. The Conference of the Parties serving as the meeting of the Parties to this Protocol, if it decides that it would be beneficial to coordinate any of the policies and measures in paragraph 1(a) above, taking into account different national circumstances and potential effects, shall consider ways and means to elaborate the coordination of such policies and measures.

Article 3

1. The Parties included in Annex I shall, individually or jointly, ensure that their aggregate carbon dioxide equivalent emissions of the greenhouse gases listed in A do not exceed their assigned amounts, calculated pursuant to their quantified emission limitation and reduction commitments inscribed in Annex

3. 부속서 1의 당사자는 이 조의 규정에 의한 정책 및 조치를 이행하기 위하여 노력하되, 협약 제3조를 고려하여 기후변화의 부정적 효과, 국제통상에 미치는 영향, 다른 당사자들, 특히 개발도상국인 당사자들과 그 중에서도 협약 제4조 제8항 및 제9항에 규정된 당사자들에 대한 사회적·환경적·경제적 영향 등을 포함한 부정적 영향을 최소화하는 방식으로 이행하기 위하여 노력한다. 이 의정서의 당사자회의의 역할을 수행하는 당사국총회는 이 항의 이행을 촉진하기 위하여 적절한 경우 추가적 조치를 취할 수 있다.

4. 이 의정서의 당사자회의의 역할을 수행하는 당사국총회는, 각국의 상이한 여건과 잠재적 영향을 고려하여 제1항 가목의 정책 및 조치를 조정하는 것이 유익하다고 결정하는 경우에는, 이러한 정책 및 조치를 조정하기 위한 방안 및 수단을 검토한다.

제3조

1. 부속서 1의 당사자는, 이들 당사자에 의한 부속서 가에 규정된 온실가스의 총 인위적 배출량을 이산화탄소를 기준으로 환산한 배출량에 대하여 이를 2008년부터 2012년까지의 공약기간 동안 1990년도 수준의 5퍼센트 이상 감축하기 위하여, 이러한 총 배출량이 이 조 및 부속서 나에 규정된 이들 당사자의 수량적 배출량의 제한·감축

B and in accordance with the provisions of this Article, with a view to reducing their overall emissions of such gases by at least 5 per cent below 1990 levels in the commitment period 2008 to 2012.

2. Each Party included in Annex I shall, by 2005, have made demonstrable progress in achieving its commitments under this Protocol.

3. The net changes in greenhouse gas emissions by sources and removals by sinks resulting from direct humaninduced land-use change and forestry activities, limited to afforestation, reforestation and deforestation since 1990, measured as verifiable changes in carbon stocks in each commitment period, shall be used to meet the commitments under this Article of each Party included in Annex I. The greenhouse gas emissions by sources and removals by sinks associated with those activities shall be reported in a transparent and verifiable manner and reviewed in accordance with Articles 7 and 8.

4. Prior to the first session of the Conference of the Parties serving as the meeting of the Parties to this Protocol, each Party included in Annex I shall provide, for consideration by the Subsidiary Body for Scientific and Technological Advice, data to establish its level of carbon stocks in 1990 and to enable an estimate to be made of its changes in carbon stocks in subsequent years. The Conference of the Parties serving as the meeting of the Parties to

을 위한 공약에 따라 계산되는 배출허용량을 초과하지 아니하도록 개별 또는 공동으로 보장한다.

2. 부속서 1의 당사자는 2005년까지 이 의정서상의 공약을 달성하는 데 따른 가시적 진전을 제시하여야 한다.

3. 인위적·직접적인 토지이용의 변화와 임업활동(1990년 이후의 신규조림·재조림 및 산림전용에 한한다)에 기인하는 온실가스의 배출원에 의한 배출량과 흡수원에 의한 제거량간의 순변화량은 각 공약기간마다 탄소저장량의 검증가능한 변화량으로 측정되며, 부속서 1의 당사자가 이 조의 공약을 달성하는데 사용된다. 이러한 활동과 연관되는 온실가스의 배출원에 의한 배출량 및 흡수원에 의한 제거량은 투명하고 검증가능한 방식으로 보고되며, 제7조 및 제8조에 따라 검토된다.

4. 이 의정서의 당사자회의의 역할을 수행하는 당사국총회의 제1차 회기 전에 부속서 1의 당사자는 과학·기술자문 보조기관의 검토를 위하여 자국의 1990년도 탄소저장량의 수준을 설정하고, 다음 연도의 탄소저장량의 변화에 대한 추산을 가능하게 하는 자료를 제공한다. 이 의정서의 당사자회의의 역할을 수행하는 당사국총회는 제1차 회기 또는 그 이후에 가능한 한 조속히 농지·토지이용변화 및 임업부문에서 온실가스의 배출원에 의한 배출량 및 흡수

this Protocol shall, at its first session or as soon as practicable thereafter, decide upon modalities, rules and guidelines as to how, and which, additional humaninduced activities related to changes in greenhouse gas emissions by sources and removals by sinks in the agricultural soil sand the land-use change and forestry categories shall be added to, or subtracted from, the assigned amounts for Parties included in Annex I, taking into account uncertainties, transparency in reporting, verifiability, the methodological work of the Intergovernmental Panel on Climate Change, the advice provided by the Subsidiary Body for Scientific and Technological Advice in accordance with Article 5 and the decisions of the Conference of the Parties. Such a decision shall apply in the second and subsequent commitment periods. A Party may choose to apply such a decision on these additional humaninduced activities for its first commitment period, provided that these activities have taken place since 1990.

5. The Parties included in Annex I undergoing the process of transition to a market economy whose base year or period was established pursuant to decision 9/CP.2 of the Conference of the Parties at its second session shall use that base year or period for the implementation of their commitments under this Article. Any other Party included in Annex Iundergoing the process of transition to a market economy which has not yet submitted its first national

원에 의한 제거량의 변화와 관련된 추가적인 인위적 활동 중 어느 활동을 어떤 방법으로 부속서 1의 당사자의 배출허용량에 추가하거나 공제할 것인지에 관한 방식·규칙 및 지침을 결정한다. 이러한 결정을 함에 있어서는 불확실성, 보고의 투명성, 검증가능성, 기후변화에 관한 정부간 패널의 방법론적 작업, 제5조에 따른 과학·기술자문 보조기관의 자문 및 당사국총회의 결정들이 고려되며, 동 결정은 제2차 공약기간 및 후속의 공약기간에 대하여 적용된다. 당사자는 추가적인 인위적 활동이 1990년 이후에 이루어진 경우에는, 위의 결정을 제1차 공약기간에 대하여 적용하는 것을 선택할 수 있다.

5. 시장경제로의 이행과정에 있는 부속서 1의 당사자로서 당사국총회 제2차 회기의 결정 9/CP.2에 따라 그 이행의 기준연도 또는 기간이 설정된 당사자는 이 조에 따른 공약을 이행함에 있어 그 기준연도 또는 기간을 사용한다. 시장경제로의 이행과정에 있는 부속서 1의 당사자로서 협약 제12조에 따른 제1차 국가보고서를 제출하지 아니한 그 밖의 당사자는 이 조에 따른 공약을 이행함에 있어 1990년도 이외의 역사적 기준연도 또는 기간을 사용할 의사

communication under Article 12 of the Convention may also notify the Conference of the Parties serving as the meeting of the Parties to this Protocol that it intends to use an historical base year or period other than 1990 for the implementation of its commitments under this Article. The Conference of the Parties serving as the meeting of the Parties to this Protocol shall decide on the acceptance of such notification.

6. Taking into account Article 4, paragraph 6, of the Convention, in the implementation of their commitments under this Protocol other than those under this Article, a certain degree of flexibility shall be allowed by the Conference of the Parties serving as the meeting of the Parties to this Protocol to the Parties included in Annex I undergoing the process of transition to a market economy.

7. In the first quantified emission limitation and reduction commitment period, from 2008 to 2012, the assigned amount for each Party included in Annex I shall be equal to the percentage inscribed for it in Annex B of its aggregate anthropogenic carbon dioxide equivalent emissions of the greenhouse gases listed in Annex A in 1990, or the base year or period determined in accordance with paragraph 5 above, multiplied by five. Those Parties included in Annex I for whom land-use change and forestry constituted a net source of greenhouse gas emissions in 1990 shall

가 있음을 이 의정서의 당사자회의의 역할을 수행하는 당사국총회에 통고할 수 있다. 동 당사국총회는 이러한 통고의 수락 여부를 결정한다.

6. 이 의정서의 당사자회의의 역할을 수행하는 당사국총회는 협약 제4조 제6항을 고려하여, 시장경제로의 이행과정에 있는 부속서 1의 당사자에 대하여 이 의정서상의 공약(이 조에 따른 공약을 제외한다)을 이행함에 있어 일정한 융통성을 허용한다.

7. 제1차 수량적 배출량의 제한·감축을 위한 공약기간인 2008년부터 2012년까지 부속서 1의 당사자별 배출허용량은 1990년도나 제5항에 따라 결정된 기준연도 또는 기간에 당해 당사자가 배출한 부속서 가에 규정된 온실가스의 총 인위적 배출량을 이산화탄소를 기준으로 환산한 배출량에 부속서 나에 규정된 당사자별 백분율을 곱한 후 다시 5를 곱하여 산정한다. 토지이용변화와 임업이 1990년도에 온실가스의 순 배출원을 구성한 부속서 1의 당사자는 자국의 배출허용량을 산정함에 있어서 1990년도의 토지이용변화에 기인한, 배출원에 의한 총 인위적 배출량을 이

include in their 1990 emissions base year or period the aggregate anthropogenic carbon dioxide equivalent emissions by sources minus removals by sinks in 1990 from land-use change for the purposes of calculating their assigned amount.

8. Any Party included in Annex I may use 1995 as its base year for hydrofluoro-carbons, perfluorocarbons and sulphur hexafluoride, for the purposes of the calculation referred to in paragraph 7 above.

9. Commitments for subsequent periods for Parties included in Annex I shall be established in amendments to Annex B to this Protocol, which shall be adopted in accordance with the provisions of Article 21, paragraph 7. The Conference of the Parties serving as the meeting of the Parties to this Protocol shall initiate the consideration of such commitments at least seven years before the end of the first commitment period referred to in paragraph 1 above.

10. Any emission reduction units, or any part of an assigned amount, which a Party acquires from another Party in accordance with the provisions of Article 6 or of Article 17 shall be added to the assigned amount for the acquiring Party.

11. Any emission reduction units, or any part of an assigned amount, which a Party transfers to another Party in accordance with the provisions of Article 6 or of Article 17 shall be subtracted from the assigned amount for the trans-

산화탄소를 기준으로 환산한 배출량에서 흡수원에 의한 제거량을 공제한 양을 자국의 1990년도나 기준연도 또는 기간의 배출량에 포함시킨다.

8. 부속서 1의 당사자는 제7항에 규정된 계산을 위하여 수소불화탄소·과불화탄소 및 육불화황에 대하여 1995년도를 기준연도로 사용할 수 있다.

9. 후속기간에 대한 부속서 1의 당사자의 공약은 제21조 제7항에 따라 채택되는 이 의정서 부속서 나의 개정을 통하여 정하여지며, 이 의정서의 당사자회의의 역할을 수행하는 당사국총회는 제1항에 규정된 제1차 공약기간이 종료하기 최소 7년 전에 이러한 공약에 대한 검토를 개시한다.

10. 제6조 또는 제17조의 규정에 따라 일방당사자가 타방당사자로부터 취득하는 배출량의 감축단위 또는 배출허용량의 일부는 이를 취득하는 당사자의 배출허용량에 추가된다.

11. 제6조 또는 제17조의 규정에 따라 일방당사자가 타방당사자에게 이전하는 배출량의 감축단위 또는 배출허용량의 일부는 이를 이전하는 당사자의 배출허용량에서 공제된다.

ferring Party.

12. Any certified emission reductions which a Party acquires from another Party in accordance with the provisions of Article 12 shall be added to the assigned amount for the acquiring Party.

13. If the emissions of a Party included in Annex I in a commitment period are less than its assigned amount under this Article, this difference shall, on request of that Party, be added to the assigned amount for that Party for subsequent commitment periods.

14. Each Party included in Annex I shall strive to implement the commitments mentioned in paragraph 1 above in such a way as to minimize adverse social, environmental and economic impacts on developing country Parties, particularly those identified in Article 4, paragraphs 8 and 9, of the Convention. In line with relevant decisions of the Conference of the Parties on the implementation of those paragraphs, the Conference of the Parties serving as the meeting of the Parties to this Protocol shall, at its first session, consider what actions are necessary to minimize the adverse effects of climate change and/or the impacts of response on Parties referred to in those paragraphs. Among the issues to be considered shall be the establishment of funding, insurance and transfer of technology.

12. 제12조의 규정에 따라 일방당사자가 타방당사자로부터 취득하는 인증받은 배출감축량은 이를 취득하는 당사자의 배출허용량에 추가된다.

13. 일정 공약기간 동안 부속서 1의 당사자의 배출량이 이 조에 따른 배출허용량보다 적을 경우, 그 차이는 당해 당사자의 요청에 따라 동 당사자의 후속 공약기간의 배출허용량에 추가된다.

14. 부속서 1의 당사자는 제1항에 규정된 공약을 이행함에 있어서 개발도상국인 당사자들, 특히 협약 제4조 제8항 및 제9항에 규정된 당사자들에게 미치는 사회적·환경적·경제적인 부정적 영향을 최소화하는 방식으로 이행하기 위하여 노력하여야 한다. 협약 제4조 제8항 및 제9항의 이행에 관한 당사국총회의 관련 결정들에 따라, 이 의정서의 당사자회의의 역할을 수행하는 당사국총회는 제1차 회기에서 협약 제4조 제8항 및 제9항에 규정된 당사자들에 대하여 기후변화의 부정적 효과 및/또는 대응조치의 영향을 최소화하기 위하여 어떠한 조치가 필요한지를 검토하며, 그 검토사항에는 기금의 설립, 보험 및 기술이전이 포함된다.

Article 4

1. Any Parties included in Annex I that have reached an agreement to fulfil their commitments under Article 3 jointly, shall be deemed to have met those commitments provided that their total combined aggregate anthropogenic carbon dioxide equivalent emissions of the greenhouse gases listed in Annex A do not exceed their assigned amounts calculated pursuant to their quantified emission limitation and reduction commitments inscribed in Annex B and in accordance with the provisions of Article 3. The respective emission level allocated to each of the Parties to the agreement shall be set out in that agreement.

2. The Parties to any such agreement shall notify the secretariat of the terms of the agreement on the date of deposit of their instruments of ratification, acceptance or approval of this Protocol, or accession thereto. The secretariat shall in turn inform the Parties and signatories to the Convention of the terms of the agreement.

3. Any such agreement shall remain in operation for the duration of the commitment period specified in Article 3, paragraph 7.

4. If Parties acting jointly do so in the framework of, and together with, a regional economic integration organization, any alteration in the composition of the organization after adoption of this Protocol shall not affect existing com-

제4조

1. 제3조상의 공약을 공동으로 이행하기로 합의한 부속서 1의 당사자들은, 이들 당사자에 의한 부속서 가에 규정된 온실가스의 총 인위적 배출량을 이산화탄소 기준으로 환산하여 합산한 총 배출량이 제3조 및 부속서 나에 규정된 수량적 배출량의 제한·감축을 위한 공약에 따라 계산된 그들의 배출허용량을 초과하지 아니하는 경우에는, 당해 공약을 이행한 것으로 간주된다. 그러한 합의를 한 각 당사자의 배출허용량의 수준은 그 합의에서 정하여진다.

2. 그러한 합의를 한 당사자들은 이 의정서의 비준서·수락서·승인서 또는 가입서의 기탁일에 합의된 내용을 사무국에 통고한다. 사무국은 협약의 당사자 및 서명자에게 그 합의된 내용을 통보한다.

3. 그러한 합의는 제3조 제7항에 명시된 공약기간 동안에만 유효하다.

4. 공동으로 공약을 이행하는 당사자들이 지역경제통합기구의 틀 안에서 동 기구와 함께 공약을 이행하는 경우, 이 의정서의 채택 이후에 이루어지는 동 기구 구성상의 변동은 동 의정서상의 기존 공약에 아무런 영향을 미치지 아니한다. 지역경제통합기

mitments under this Protocol. Any alter-ation in the composition of the organi-zation shall only apply for the purposes of those commitments under Article 3 that are adopted subsequent to that al-teration.

5. In the event of failure by the Parties to such an agreement to achieve their total combined level of emission reductions, each Party to that agreement shall be responsible for its level of emissions set out in the agreement.

6. If Parties acting jointly do so in the framework of, and together with, a re-gional economic integration organization which is itself a Party to this Protocol, each member State of that regional ec-onomic integration organization indivi-dually, and together with the regional economic integration organization acting in accordance with Article 24, shall, in the event of failure to achieve the total combined level of emission reductions, be responsible for its level of emissions as notified in accordance with this Ar-ticle.

Article 5

1. Each Party included in Annex I shall have in place, no later than one year prior to the start of the first commi-tment period, a national system for the estimation of anthropogenic emissions by sources and removals by sinks of all greenhouse gases not controlled by the Montreal Protocol. Guidelines for such national systems, which shall incorporate

구의 구성상의 모든 변동은 그 변동 이후에 채택되는 제3조상의 공약에 대하여만 적용된다.

5. 그러한 합의의 당사자들이 그들 각각의 배출감축량을 합산한 감축량수준을 달성하지 못하는 때에는, 그러한 합의를 한 각 당사자는 그 합의에서 정하여진 자국의 배출량 수준에 대하여 책임을 진다.

6. 공동으로 공약을 이행하는 당사자들이 이 의정서의 당사자인 지역경제통합기구의 틀 안에서 동 기구와 함께 공약을 이행하는 경우, 그들 각각의 배출감축량을 합산한 감축량 수준을 달성하지 못하는 때에는, 지역경제통합기구의 각 회원국은 개별적으로, 또한 제24조에 따라 행동하는 지역경제통합기구와 함께, 이 조에 따라 통고된 자국의 배출량 수준에 대하여 책임을 진다.

제 5 조

1. 부속서 1의 당사자는 늦어도 제1차 공약 기간이 개시되기 일년 전까지 모든 온실가스(몬트리올의정서에 의하여 규제되는 것을 제외한다)의 배출원에 의한 인위적 배출량과 흡수원에 의한 제거량을 추산하기 위한 국가제도를 마련한다. 이 의정서의 당사자회의의 역할을 수행하는 당사국총회는 제1차 회기에서 제2항에 규정된 방

the methodologies specified in paragraph 2 below, shall be decided upon by the Conference of theserving as the meeting of the Parties to this Protocol at its first session.

2. Methodologies for estimating anthropogenic emissions by sources and removals by sinks of all greenhouse gases not controlled by the Montreal Protocol shall be those accepted by the Intergovernmental Panel on Climate Change and agreed upon by the Conference of the Parties at its third session. Where such methodologies are not used, appropriate adjustments shall be applied according to methodologies agreed upon by the Conference of the Parties serving as the meeting of the Parties to this Protocol at its first session. Based on the work of, inter alia, the Intergovernmental Panel on Climate Change and advice provided by the Subsidiary Body for Scientific and Technological Advice, the Conference of the Parties serving as the meeting of the Parties to this Protocol shall regularly review and, as appropriate, revise such methodologies and adjustments, taking fully into account any relevant decisions by the Conference of the Parties. Any revision to methodologies or adjustments shall be used only for the purposes of ascertaining compliance with commitments under Article 3 in respect of any commitment period adopted subsequent to that revision.

3. The global warming potentials used to calculate the carbon dioxide equivalence

법론이 반영된 국가제도에 관한 지침을 결정한다.

2. 모든 온실가스(몬트리올의정서에 의하여 규제되는 것을 제외한다)의 배출원에 의한 인위적 배출량과 흡수원에 의한 제거량을 추산하기 위한 방법론은 기후변화에 관한 정부간 패널이 수락하고 당사국총회가 제3차 회기에서 합의한 것으로 한다. 이러한 방법론이 사용되지 아니하는 경우에는, 이 의정서의 당사자회의의 역할을 수행하는 당사국총회가 제1차 회기에서 합의한 방법론에 따른 적절한 조정이 적용된다. 이 의정서의 당사자회의의 역할을 수행하는 당사국총회는, 특히 기후변화에 관한 정부간 패널의 작업과 과학·기술자문 보조기관의 자문에 기초하고 당사국총회의 관련 결정들을 충분히 고려하여, 이러한 방법론과 조정을 정기적으로 검토하고 적절한 경우에는 이를 수정한다. 이러한 방법론과 조정에 대한 수정은 그러한 수정 이후에 채택되는 제3조상의 공약의 준수를 확인하기 위하여만 사용된다.

3. 부속서 가에 규정된 온실가스의 배출원에 의한 인위적 배출량과 흡수원에 의한 제거

of anthropogenic emissions by sources and removals by sinks of greenhouse gases listed in Annex A shall be those accepted by the Intergovernmental Panel on Climate Change and agreed upon by the Conference of the Parties at its third session. Based on the work of, inter alia, the Intergovernmental Panel on Climate Change and advice provided by the Subsidiary Body for Scientific and Technological Advice, the Conference of the Parties serving as the meeting of the Parties to this Protocol shall regularly review and, as appropriate, revise the global warming potential of each such greenhouse gas, taking fully into account any relevant decisions by the Conference of the Parties. Any revision to a global warming potential shall apply only to commitments under Article 3 in respect of any commitment period adopted subsequent to that revision.

량에 대하여 이산화탄소를 기준으로 한 환산치를 계산하는 데 사용되는 지구온난화지수는 기후변화에 관한 정부간 패널이 수락하고 당사국총회가 제3차 회기에서 합의한 것으로 한다. 이 의정서의 당사자회의의 역할을 수행하는 당사국총회는, 특히 기후변화에 관한 정부간 패널의 작업과 과학·기술자문 보조기관의 자문에 기초하고 당사국총회의 관련 결정들을 충분히 고려하여, 각 온실가스의 지구온난화지수를 정기적으로 검토하고 적절한 경우에는 이를 수정한다. 지구온난화지수에 대한 수정은 그러한 수정 이후에 채택되는 제3조상의 공약에 대하여만 적용된다.

Article 6

1. For the purpose of meeting its commitments under Article 3, any Party included in Annex I may transfer to, or acquire from, any other such Party emission reduction units resulting from projects aimed at reducing anthropogenic emissions by sources or enhancing anthropogenic removals by sinks of greenhouse gases in any sector of the economy, provided that:

(a) Any such project has the approval of the Parties involved;

(b) Any such project provides a reduction in emissions by sources, or an en-

제 6 조

1. 부속서 1의 당사자는 제3조상의 공약을 이행하기 위하여, 모든 경제 부문에서 온실가스의 배출원에 의한 인위적 배출량의 감축이나 흡수원에 의한 인위적 제거량의 증대를 목표로 하는 사업으로부터 발생하는 배출량의 감축단위를 다른 부속서 1의 당사자에게 이전하거나 그들로부터 취득할 수 있다. 이 경우, 다음 각목의 요건을 충족하여야 한다.

가. 이러한 사업에 대하여 관련 당사자들의 승인이 있을 것

나. 이러한 사업은 그 사업이 시행되지 아니하는 경우와 대비하여, 배출원에 의한 배

hancement of removals by sinks, that is additional to any that would other-wise occur;

(c) It does not acquire any emission re-duction units if it is not in compliance with its obligations under Articles 5 and 7; and

(d) The acquisition of emission reduction units shall be supplemental to dome-stic actions for the purposes of meeting commitments under Article 3.

2. The Conference of the Parties serving as the meeting of the Parties to this Protocol may, at its first session or as soon as practicable thereafter, further elaborate guidelines for the implement-ation of this Article, including for verifi-cation and reporting.

3. A Party included in Annex I may au-thorize legal entities to participate, under its responsibility, in actions leading to the generation, transfer or acquisition under this Article of emission reduction units.

4. If a question of implementation by a Party included in Annex I of the re-quirements referred to in this Article is identified in accordance with the relevant provisions of Article 8, transfers and acquisitions of emission reduction units may continue to be made after the ques-tion has been identified, provided that any such units may not be used by a Party to meet its commitments under Article 3 until any issue of compliance is resolved.

출량의 추가적 감축이나 흡수원에 의한 제거량의 추가적 증대를 제공할 것

다. 당사자가 제5조 및 제7조상의 의무를 준수하지 아니하는 경우, 그 당사자는 배출량의 감축단위를 취득하지 못하도록 할 것

라. 배출량의 감축단위의 취득은 제3조상의 공약의 이행을 위한 국내 조치의 보조수단으로 활용되어야 할 것

2. 이 의정서의 당사자회의의 역할을 수행하는 당사국총회는 제1차 회기 또는 그 이후에 가능한 한 조속히 이 조의 검증·보고 및 이행을 위한 지침을 더욱 발전시킬 수 있다.

3. 부속서 1의 당사자는 자국의 책임 하에 법인이 이 조의 규정에 의한 배출량의 감축단위의 발생·이전 및 취득을 초래하는 활동에 참여하는 것을 허가할 수 있다.

4. 부속서 1의 당사자에 의한 이 조에 규정된 요건의 이행문제가 제8조의 관련 규정에 따라 확인되는 경우, 배출량의 감축단위의 이전과 취득은 그러한 문제가 확인된 이후에도 계속 이루어질 수 있다. 다만, 당사자는 준수에 관한 모든 문제가 해결될 때까지는 이러한 감축단위를 제3조상의 공약을 이행하는 데 사용할 수 없다.

Article 7

1. Each Party included in Annex I shall incorporate in its annual inventory of anthropogenic emissions by sources and removals by sinks of greenhouse gases not controlled by the Montreal Protocol, submitted in accordance with the relevant decisions of the Conference of the Parties, the necessary supplementary information for the purposes of ensuring compliance with Article 3, to be determined in accordance with paragraph 4 below.

2. Each Party included in Annex I shall incorporate in its national communication, submitted under Article 12 of the Convention, the supplementary information necessary to demonstrate compliance with its commitments under this Protocol, to be determined in accordance with paragraph 4 below.

3. Each Party included in Annex I shall submit the information required under paragraph 1 above annually, beginning with the first inventory due under the Convention for the first year of the commitment period after this Protocol has entered into force for that Party. Each such Party shall submit the information required under paragraph 2 above as part of the first national communication due under the Convention after this Protocol has entered into force for it and after the adoption of guidelines as provided for in paragraph 4 below. The frequency of subsequent submission of information required under

제7조

1. 부속서 1의 당사자는 당사국총회의 관련 결정에 따라 제출하는 온실가스(몬트리올 의정서에 의하여 규제되는 것을 제외한다)의 배출원에 의한 인위적 배출량과 흡수원에 의한 제거량에 관한 자국의 연례통계목록에, 제3조의 준수를 보장하기 위하여 필요한 보충정보로서 제4항에 따라 결정되는 것을 포함시킨다.

2. 부속서 1의 당사자는 협약 제12조에 따라 제출하는 자국의 국가보고서에, 이 의정서상의 공약의 준수를 증명하기 위하여 필요한 보충정보로서 제4항에 따라 결정되는 것을 포함시킨다.

3. 부속서 1의 당사자는 이 의정서가 자국에 대하여 발효한 이후의 공약기간의 첫째 연도에 대하여 협약상 제출하여야 하는 제1차 통계목록을 시작으로 제1항에서 요구하는 정보를 매년 제출한다. 동 당사자는 이 의정서가 자국에 대하여 발효하고 제4항에 규정된 지침이 채택된 이후에, 협약상 제출하여야 하는 제1차 국가보고서의 일부로서 제2항에서 요구하는 정보를 제출한다. 이 조에서 요구하는 정보의 후속 제출빈도는 당사국총회에서 결정되는 국가보고서의 제출일정을 고려하여, 이 의정서의 당사자회의의 역할을 수행하는 당사국총회가 결정한다.

this Article shall be determined by the Conference of the Parties serving as the meeting of the Parties to this Protocol, taking into account any timetable for the submission of national communications decided upon by the Conference of the Parties.

4. The Conference of the Parties serving as the meeting of the Parties to this Protocol shall adopt at its first session, and review periodically thereafter, guidelines for the preparation of the information required under this Article, taking into account guidelines for the preparation of national communications by Parties included in Annex I adopted by the Conference of the Parties. The Conference of the Parties serving as the meeting of the Parties to this Protocol shall also, prior to the first commitment period, decide upon modalities for the of assigned amounts.

Article 8

1. The information submitted under Article 7 by each Party included in Annex I shall be reviewed by expert review teams pursuant to the relevant decisions of the Conference of the Parties and in accordance with guidelines adopted for this purpose by the Conference of the Parties serving as the meeting of the Parties to this Protocol under paragraph 4 below. The information submitted under Article 7, paragraph 1, by each Party included in Annex I shall be reviewed as part of the annual compilation and accounting of emissions inventories and

4. 이 의정서의 당사자회의의 역할을 수행하는 당사국총회는 제1차 회기에서, 당사국총회에서 채택되는 부속서 1의 당사자의 국가보고서 작성을 위한 지침을 고려하여, 이 조에서 요구하는 정보의 작성지침을 채택하고, 그 후 정기적으로 이를 검토한다. 또한 이 의정서의 당사자회의의 역할을 수행하는 당사국총회는 제1차 공약기간 이전에 배출허용량의 계산방식을 결정한다.

제 8 조

1. 부속서 1의 당사자가 제7조에 따라 제출하는 정보에 대하여는 당사국총회의 관련 결정들과 이 의정서의 당사자회의의 역할을 수행하는 당사국총회가 제4항의 규정에 의하여 그 목적을 위하여 채택한 지침에 따라 전문가 검토반이 이를 검토한다. 부속서 1의 당사자가 제7조 제1항에 따라 제출하는 정보는 배출량의 통계목록과 배출허용량의 연례 취합 및 계산의 일부로서 검토된다. 추가적으로, 부속서 1의 당사자가 제7조 제2항에 따라 제출하는 정보는 보고서 검토의 일부로서 검토된다.

assigned amounts. Additionally, the information submitted under Article 7, paragraph 2, by each Party included in Annex I shall be reviewed as part of the review of communications.

2. Expert review teams shall be coordinated by the secretariat and shall be composed of experts selected from those nominated by Parties to the Convention and, as appropriate, by intergovernmental organizations, in accordance with guidance provided for this purpose by the of the Parties.

3. The review process shall provide a thorough and comprehensive technical assessment of all aspects of the implementation by a Party of this Protocol. The expert review teams shall prepare a report to the Conference of the Parties serving as the meeting of the Parties to this Protocol, assessing the implementation of the commitments of the Party and identifying any potential problems in, and factors influencing, the fulfillment of commitments. Such reports shall be circulated by the secretariat to all Parties to the Convention. The secretariat shall list those questions of implementation indicated in such reports for further consideration by the Conference of the Parties serving as the meeting of the Parties to this Protocol.

4. The Conference of the Parties serving as the meeting of the Parties to this Protocol shall adopt at its first session, and review periodically thereafter, guidelines for the review of implementation

2. 전문가 검토반은, 당사국총회가 정한 방침에 따라, 사무국에 의하여 조정되며, 협약의 당사자가, 적절한 경우에는 정부간 기구가, 지명하는 인사 중에서 선정되는 전문가로 구성된다.

3. 검토과정에서는 이 의정서의 당사자에 의한 이행의 모든 측면에 대하여 철저하고 포괄적인 기술적 평가가 이루어진다. 전문가 검토반은 당사자의 공약이행을 평가하고, 그 이행과정에 있어서의 모든 잠재적 문제점과 공약의 이행에 영향을 미치는 모든 요소들을 확인하여, 이 의정서의 당사자회의의 역할을 수행하는 당사국총회에 제출할 보고서를 작성한다. 사무국은 이러한 보고서를 협약의 모든 당사자에게 배포하는 한편, 이 의정서의 당사자회의의 역할을 수행하는 당사국총회가 보다 심층적으로 이를 검토할 수 있도록 그 보고서에서 지적된 이행상의 문제점을 목록화 한다.

4. 이 의정서의 당사자회의의 역할을 수행하는 당사국총회는 제1차 회기에서, 당사국총회의 관련 결정들을 고려하여, 전문가 검토반이 이 의정서의 이행을 검토하기 위한 지침을 채택하고 그 후 정기적으로 이

of this Protocol by expert review teams taking into account the relevant decisions of the Conference of the Parties.

를 검토한다.

5. The Conference of the Parties serving as the meeting of the Parties to this Protocol shall, with the assistance of the Subsidiary Body for Implementation and, as appropriate, the Subsidiary Body for Scientific and Technological Advice, consider:

5. 이 의정서의 당사자회의의 역할을 수행하는 당사국총회는 이행보조기관, 적절한 경우에는 과학·기술자문 보조기관의 지원을 받아 다음 사항을 검토한다.

(a) The information submitted by Parties under Article 7 and the reports of the expert reviews thereon conducted under this Article; and

가. 당사자가 제7조에 따라 제출한 정보 및 이 조의 규정에 의하여 그 정보에 대하여 행하여진 전문가의 검토보고서

(b) Those questions of implementation listed by the secretariat under paragraph 3 above, as well as any questions raised by Parties.

나. 사무국이 제3항에 따라 목록화한 이행상의 문제점 및 당사자가 제기한 모든 문제점

6. Pursuant to its consideration of the information referred to in paragraph 5 above, the Conference of the Parties serving as the meeting of the Parties to this Protocol shall take decisions on any matter required for the implementation of this Protocol.

6. 이 의정서의 당사자회의의 역할을 수행하는 당사국총회는 제5항에 규정된 정보에 대한 검토에 따라 이 의정서의 이행을 위하여 필요한 모든 사항에 관하여 결정한다.

Article 9

제9조

1. The Conference of the Parties serving as the meeting of the Parties to this Protocol shall periodically review this Protocol in the light of the best available scientific information and assessments on climate change and its impacts, as well as relevant technical, social and economic information. Such reviews shall be coordinated with pertinent reviews

1. 이 의정서의 당사자회의의 역할을 수행하는 당사국총회는 기후변화와 그 영향에 대하여 이용 가능한 최선의 과학적 정보·평가와 기술적·사회적·경제적 관련 정보에 비추어 이 의정서를 정기적으로 검토한다. 이러한 검토는 협약상의 관련 검토, 특히 협약 제4조 제2항 라목 및 제7조 제2항 가목에서 요구되는 관련 검토와 조정된다.

under the Convention, in particular those required by Article 4, paragraph 2(d), and Article 7, paragraph 2(a), of the Convention. Based on these reviews, the Conference of the Parties serving as the meeting of the Parties to this Protocol shall take appropriate action.

2. The first review shall take place at the second session of the Conference of the Parties serving as the meeting of the Parties to this Protocol. Further reviews shall take place at regular intervals and in a timely manner.

Article 10

All Parties, taking into account their common but differentiated responsibilities and their specific national and regional development priorities, objectives and circumstances, without introducing any new commitments for Parties not included in Annex I, but reaffirming existing commitments under Article 4, paragraph 1, of the Convention, and continuing to advance the implementation of these commitments in order to achieve sustainable development, taking into account Article 4, paragraphs 3, 5 and 7, of the Convention, shall:

(a) Formulate, where relevant and to the extent possible, cost-effective national and, where appropriate, regional programmes to improve the quality of local emission factors, activity data and/or models which reflect the socioeconomic conditions of each Party for the preparation and periodic updating of national inventories of anthropogenic

---

이 의정서의 당사자회의의 역할을 수행하는 당사국총회는 이러한 검토에 기초하여 적절한 조치를 취한다.

2. 제1차 검토는 이 의정서의 당사자회의의 역할을 수행하는 당사국총회의 제2차 회기에서 이루어진다. 추가적 검토는 적절한 방식에 의하여 정기적으로 이루어진다.

제 10 조

모든 당사자는, 공통적이지만 그 정도에는 차이가 있는 각자의 책임과 국가 및 지역에 고유한 개발우선순위·목적·상황을 고려하고, 부속서 1에 포함되지 아니한 당사자에 대하여는 어떠한 새로운 공약도 도입하지 아니하나 협약 제4조 제1항의 기존 공약에 대하여는 이를 재확인하며, 지속가능한 개발을 달성하기 위하여 이들 공약의 이행을 계속 진전시키고, 협약 제4조 제3항·제5항 및 제7항을 고려하여 다음 사항을 수행한다.

가. 당사국총회가 채택한 국가보고서의 작성을 위한 지침에 부합하고 당사국총회가 합의한 비교가능한 방법론을 사용하여, 모든 온실가스(몬트리올의정서에 의하여 규제되는 것을 제외한다)의 배출원에 의한 인위적 배출량과 흡수원에 의한 제거량에 관한 국가통계목록을 작성하고 이를 정기적으로 갱신하기 위하여, 각 당사자

emissions by sources and removals by sinks of all greenhouse gases not controlled by the Montreal Protocol, using comparable methodologies to be agreed upon by the Conference of the Parties, and consistent with the guidelines for the preparation of national communications adopted by the Conference of the Parties;

(b) Formulate, implement, publish and regularly update national and, where appropriate, regional programmes containing measures to mitigate climate change and measures to facilitate adequate adaptation to climate change:

(i) programmes would, inter alia, concern the energy, transport and industry sectors as well as agriculture, forestry and waste management. Furthermore, adaptation technologies and methods for improving spatial planning would improve adaptation to climate change; and

(ii) Parties included in Annex I shall submit information on action under this Protocol, including national programmes, in accordance with Article 7; and other Parties shall seek to include in their national communications, as appropriate, information on programmes which contain measures that the Party believes contribute to addressing climate change and its adverse impacts, including the abatement of increases in greenhouse gas emissions, and enhancement of and removals by sinks, capacity building and adaptation measures;

의 사회·경제적 여건을 반영하는 국내배출요소·활동자료 및/또는 모델의 질을 개선하기 위한 비용효율적인 국가적 계획, 적절한 경우에는 지역적 계획을 타당하고 가능한 범위 안에서 수립할 것

나. 기후변화를 완화하는 조치와 기후변화에 대한 충분한 적응을 용이하게 하는 조치를 그 내용으로 하는 국가적 계획, 적절한 경우에는 지역적 계획을 수립·실시·공표하고 정기적으로 이를 갱신할 것

(1) 이러한 계획은, 특히 에너지·수송·산업·농업·임업 및 폐기물관리에 관한 것이며, 적응기술 및 국토관리 계획을 개선하기 위한 방법은 기후변화에 대한 적응을 향상시킨다.

(2) 부속서 1의 당사자는 제7조에 따라 국가적 계획과 이 의정서에 따른 조치에 관한 정보를 제출한다. 그 밖의 당사자는 기후변화 및 그 부정적 영향에 대한 대응에 기여하리라고 생각되는 조치(온실가스 배출량의 증가 완화, 흡수원의 증진 및 흡수원에 의한 제거, 능력형성 및 적응조치를 포함한다)를 내용으로 하는 계획에 관한 정보를 자국의 국가보고서에 적절히 포함시키도록 노력한다.

(c) Cooperate in the promotion of effective modalities for the development, application and diffusion of, and take all practicable steps to promote, facilitate and finance, as appropriate, the transfer of, or access to, environmentally sound technologies, know-how, practices and processes pertinent to climate change, in particular to developing countries, including the formulation of policies and programmes for the effective transfer of environmentally sound technologies that are publicly owned or in the public domain and the creation of an enabling environment for the private sector, to promote and enhance the transfer and access to, environmentally sound technologies;

(d) Cooperate in scientific and technical research and promote the maintenance and development of systematic observation systems and development of data archives to reduce uncertainties related to the climate system, the adverse impacts of climate change and the economic and social consequences of various response strategies, and promote the development and strengthening of endogenous capacities and capabilities to participate in international and intergovernmental efforts, programmes and networks on research and systematic observation, taking into account Article 5 of the Convention;

(e) Cooperate in and promote at the international level, and, where appropriate, using existing bodies, the development and implementation of education and training programmes, including the

다. 기후변화와 관련된 환경적으로 건전한 기술·노하우·관행 및 공정의 개발·적용·확산을 위한 효과적인 방식을 증진하는 데 협력한다. 특히 개발도상국에 대하여, 기후변화와 관련된 환경적으로 건전한 기술·노하우·관행 및 공정의 이전이나 이에 대한 접근을 적절히 증진·촉진하며, 이에 필요한 재원을 제공하기 위하여 실행가능한 모든 조치를 행한다. 이러한 조치는 공공소유 또는 사적 권리가 소멸된 환경적으로 건전한 기술의 효과적인 이전을 위한 정책 및 계획의 수립과 민간부문으로 하여금 환경적으로 건전한 기술의 이전과 이에 대한 접근을 증진하고 향상시킬 수 있도록 하는 환경의 조성을 포함한다.

라. 협약 제5조를 고려하여, 기후체계 및 기후변화의 부정적 영향이나 다양한 대응전략의 경제적·사회적 영향에 관한 불확실성을 줄이기 위하여 과학적·기술적 연구에서 협력하고, 체계적 관측체제의 유지·발전 및 자료보관제도의 정비를 증진하며, 연구 및 체계적 관측에 관한 국가간 및 정부간 노력·계획 및 협력망에 참여하기 위한 고유한 역량과 능력의 개발·강화를 증진한다.

마. 국제적 차원에서, 적절한 경우에는 기존 기구를 활용하여, 교육·훈련계획(국가적 능력, 특히 인적·제도적 능력형성의 강화, 특히 개발도상국에 있어서 이 분야의 전문가를 양성할 요원의 교류나 파견에

strengthening of national capacity buil-ding, in particular human and institu-nal capacities and the exchange or se-condment of personnel to train experts in this field, in particular for developing countries, and facilitate at the national level public awareness of, and public access to information on, climate change. Suitable modalities should be developed to implement these activities through the relevant bodies of the Convention, taking into account Article 6 of the Convention;

(f) Include in their national communications information on programmes and activ-ities undertaken pursuant to this Article in accordance with relevant decisions of the Conference of the Parties; and

(g) Give full consideration, in implement-ing the commitments under this Article, to Article 4, paragraph 8 of the Con-vention.

Article 11

1. In the implementation of Article 10, Par-ties shall take into account the provisions of Article 4, paragraphs 4, 5, 7, 8 and 9, of the Convention.

2. In the context of the implementation of Article 4, paragraph 1, of the Convention, in accordance with the provisions of Article 4, paragraph 3, and Article 11 of the Convention, and through the entity or entities entrusted with the operation of the financial mechanism of the Conven-tion, the developed country Parties and other developed Parties included in An-nex II to the Convention shall:

관한 것을 포함한다)의 개발·실시에 협력하고 이를 증진한다. 국가적 차원에서 기후변화에 관한 공중의 인식을 제고하고 관련 정보에 대한 공중의 접근을 용이하게 한다. 이러한 활동을 수행하기 위한 적절한 방식은, 협약 제6조를 고려하여, 이 협약의 관련기구를 통하여 개발된다.

바. 당사국총회의 관련 결정들에 따라, 이 조에 의하여 수행한 계획 및 활동에 관한 정보를 자국의 국가보고서에 포함시킨다.

사. 이 조의 공약을 이행함에 있어서 협약 제4조 제8항을 충분히 고려한다.

제11조

1. 제10조의 이행에 있어, 당사자는 협약 제4조 제4항·제5항 및 제7항 내지 제9항의 규정을 고려한다.

2. 협약 제4조 제1항의 이행과 관련하여, 협약 부속서 2의 선진국인 당사자와 그 밖의 선진당사자는 협약 제4조 제3항 및 제11조와 협약의 재정지원체제의 운영을 위임받은 기구를 통하여 다음을 행한다.

(a) Provide new and additional financial resources to meet the agreed full costs incurred by developing country Parties in advancing the implementation of existing commitments under Article 4, paragraph 1(a), of the Convention that are covered in Article 10, subparagraph (a); and

(b) Also provide such financial resources, including for the transfer of technology, needed by the developing country Parties to meet the agreed full incremental costs of advancing the implementation of existing commitments under Article 4, paragraph 1, of the Convention that are covered by Article 10 and that are agreed between a developing country Party and the international entity or entities referred to in Article 11 of the Convention, in accordance with that Article.

The implementation of these existing commitments shall take into account the need for adequacy and predictability in the flow of funds and the importance of appropriate burden sharing among developed country Parties. The guidance to the entity or entities entrusted with the operation of the financial mechanism of the Convention in relevant decisions of the Conference of the Parties, including those agreed before the adoption of this Protocol, shall apply mutatis mutandis to the provisions of this paragraph.

3. The developed country Parties and other developed Parties in Annex II to the Convention may also provide, and deve-

가. 협약 제4조 제1항가목의 규정에 의한 기존 공약으로서 제10조가목에 규정된 사항의 이행을 진전시키기 위하여 개발도상국인 당사자가 부담하는 합의된 총비용을 충당하기 위하여 신규의 추가적 재원을 제공할 것

나. 협약 제4조 제1항의 규정에 의한 기존 공약으로서 제10조에 규정되어 있고 개발도상국인 당사자와 협약 제11조에 규정된 국제기구간에 합의된 사항의 이행을 진전시키는데 소요되는 합의된 총증가비용을 개발도상국인 당사자가 충당하는데 필요한 신규의 추가적 재원(기술이전을 위한 재원을 포함한다)을 제11조에 따라 제공할 것

이러한 기존 공약의 이행에는 자금 흐름의 적정성 및 예측가능성이 필요하다는 점과 선진국인 당사자 간에 적절한 부담배분이 중요하다는 점이 고려되어야 한다. 이 의정서의 채택 이전에 합의된 결정을 포함하여 당사국총회의 관련 결정에서 협약상의 재정지원체제를 운영하도록 위임받은 기구에 대한 지침은 이 항의 규정에 준용한다.

3. 협약 부속서 2의 선진국인 당사자와 그 밖의 선진당사자는 양자적·지역적 및 그 밖의 다자적 경로를 통하여 제10조의 이행

loping country Parties avail themselves of, financial resources for the implementation of Article 10, through bilateral, regional and other multilateral channels.

Article 12

1. A clean development mechanism is hereby defined.

2. The purpose of the clean development mechanism shall be to assist Parties not included in Annex I in achieving sustainable development and in contributing to the ultimate objective of the Convention, and to assist Parties included in Annex I in achieving compliance their quantified emission limitation and reduction commitments under Article

3. Under the clean development mechanism:

(a) Parties not included in Annex I will benefit from project activities resulting in certified emission reductions; and

(b) Parties included in Annex I may use the certified emission reductions accruing from such project activities to contribute to compliance with part of their quantified emission limitation and reduction commitments under Article 3, as determined by the Conference of the serving as the meeting of the Parties to this Protocol.

4. The clean development mechanism shall be subject to the authority and guidance of the Conference of the Parties serving as the meeting of the Parties to this Pro-

을 위한 재원을 제공할 수 있고, 개발도상국인 당사자는 이를 이용할 수 있다.

제12조

1. 청정개발체제를 이에 규정한다.

2. 청정개발체제는 부속서 1에 포함되지 아니한 당사자가 지속가능한 개발을 달성하고 협약의 궁극적 목적에 기여할 수 있도록 지원하며, 부속서 1의 당사자가 제3조의 규정에 의한 수량적 배출량의 제한·감축을 위한 공약을 준수할 수 있도록 지원하는 것을 목적으로 한다.

3. 청정개발체제하에서,

가. 부속서 1에 포함되지 아니한 당사자는 인증받은 배출감축량을 발생시키는 사업활동으로부터 이익을 얻는다.

나. 부속서 1의 당사자는 제3조의 규정에 의한 수량적 배출량의 제한·감축을 위한 공약의 일부 준수에 기여하기 위하여 이러한 사업 활동으로부터 발생하는 인증받은 배출감축량을 이 의정서의 당사자회의의 역할을 수행하는 당사국총회가 결정하는 바에 따라 사용할 수 있다.

4. 청정개발체제는 이 의정서의 당사자회의의 역할을 수행하는 당사국총회의 권한 및 지도에 따르며, 청정개발체제 집행이사회의 감독을 받는다.

tocol and be supervised by an executive board of the clean development mechanism.

5. Emission reductions resulting from each project activity shall be certified by operational entities to be designated by the Conference of the Parties serving as the meeting of Parties to this Protocol, on the basis of:

(a) Voluntary participation approved by each Party involved;

(b) Real, measurable, and long-term benefits related to the mitigation of climate change; and

(c) Reductions in emissions that are additional to any that would occur in the absence of the certified project activity.

6. The clean development mechanism shall assist in arranging funding of certified project activities as necessary.

7. The Conference of the Parties serving as the meeting of the Parties to this Protocol shall, at its first session, elaborate modalities and procedures with the objective of ensuring transparency, efficiency and accountability through independent auditing and verification of project activities.

8. The Conference of the Parties serving as the meeting of the Parties to this Protocol shall ensure that a share of the proceeds from certified project activities is used to cover administrative expenses as well as to assist developing country

---

5. 각 사업 활동으로부터 발생하는 배출감축량은 다음에 기초하여, 이 의정서의 당사자회의의 역할을 수행하는 당사국총회가 지정하는 운영기구에 의하여 인증받는다.

가. 관련 각 당사자가 승인한 자발적 참여

나. 기후변화의 완화와 관련되는 실질적이고 측정가능한 장기적 이익

다. 인증받은 사업 활동이 없는 경우에 발생하는 배출량의 감축에 추가적인 배출량의 감축

6. 청정개발체제는, 필요한 경우, 인증받은 사업 활동을 위한 재원조달을 지원한다.

7. 이 의정서의 당사자회의의 역할을 수행하는 당사국총회는 제1차 회기에서 사업 활동에 대한 독립적인 감사·검증을 통하여 투명성·효율성 및 책임성을 보장하기 위한 방식 및 절차를 발전시킨다.

8. 이 의정서의 당사자회의의 역할을 수행하는 당사국총회는 인증받은 사업 활동의 수익 중 일부가 행정경비로 지불되고, 기후변화의 부정적 효과에 특히 취약한 개발도상국인 당사자의 적응비용의 충당을 지원하는 데 사용되도록 보장한다.

Parties that are particularly vulnerable to the adverse effects of climate change to meet the costs of adaptation.

9. Participation under the clean development mechanism, including in activities mentioned paragraph 3(a) above and in the acquisition of certified emission reductions, may private and/or public entities, and is to be subject to whatever guidance may be provided by the executive board of the clean development mechanism.

9. 청정개발체제에의 참여(제3항 가목에 규정된 활동에의 참여 및 인증받은 배출감축량의 취득에의 참여를 포함한다)는 민간 및/또는 공공 기구를 관여시킬 수 있으며, 이러한 참여는 청정개발체제의 집행이사회가 제공하는 지침에 따라 이루어진다.

10. Certified emission reductions obtained during the period from the year 2000 up to the beginning of the first commitment period can be used to assist in achieving compliance in the first commitment period.

10. 2000년부터 제1차 공약기간 개시 전의 기간 동안 취득된 인증받은 배출감축량은 제1차 공약기간동안의 공약준수를 지원하기 위하여 사용될 수 있다.

Article 13

제 13 조

1. The Conference of the Parties, the supreme body of the Convention, shall serve as the meeting of the Parties to this Protocol.

1. 협약의 최고기관인 당사국총회는 이 의정서의 당사자회의의 역할을 수행한다.

2. Parties to the Convention that are not Parties to this Protocol may participate as observers in the proceedings of any session of the Conference of the Parties serving as the meeting of the Parties to this Protocol. When the Conference of the Parties serves as the meeting of the Parties to this Protocol, decisions under this Protocol shall be taken only by those that are Parties to this Protocol.

2. 이 의정서의 당사자가 아닌 협약의 당사자는 이 의정서의 당사자회의의 역할을 수행하는 당사국총회의 모든 회기의 심의에 참관인으로 참여할 수 있다. 당사국총회가 이 의정서의 당사자회의의 역할을 수행하는 경우, 이 의정서에 따른 결정은 이 의정서의 당사자만이 할 수 있다.

3. When the Conference of the Parties serves

3. 당사국총회가 이 의정서의 당사자회의의

as the meeting of the Parties to this Protocol, any member of the Bureau of the Conference of the Parties representing a Party to the Convention but, at that time, not a Party to this Protocol, shall be replaced by an additional to be elected by and from amongst the Parties to this Protocol.

4. The Conference of the Parties serving as the meeting of the Parties to this Protocol shall keep under regular review the implementation of this Protocol and shall make, within its mandate, the decisions necessary to promote its effective implementation. It shall perform the assigned to it by this Protocol and shall:

(a) Assess, on the basis of all information made available to it in accordance with the provisions of this Protocol, the implementation of this Protocol by the Parties, the overall effects of the measures taken pursuant to this Protocol, in particular environmental, economic and social effects as well as their cumulative impacts and the extent to which progress towards objective of the Convention is being achieved;

(b) Periodically examine the obligations of the Parties under this Protocol, giving due consideration to any reviews required by Article 4, paragraph 2(d), and Article 7, paragraph 2, of the Convention, in the light of the objective of the Convention, the experience gained in its implementation and the evolution of scientific and technological knowledge, and in this respect consider and adopt regular reports on the implementation

역할을 수행하는 경우, 그 당시 이 의정서의 당사자가 아닌 협약의 당사자를 대표하는 자가 당사국총회의 의장단의 구성원인 때에는, 동 구성원은 이 의정서의 당사자들이 그들 중에서 선출한 추가구성원으로 대체된다.

4. 이 의정서의 당사자회의의 역할을 수행하는 당사국총회는 이 의정서의 이행상황을 정기적으로 검토하고, 그 권한의 범위 안에서 이 의정서의 효과적 이행의 증진에 필요한 결정을 한다. 당사국총회는 이 의정서에 의하여 부여된 기능을 수행하며 다음을 행한다.

가. 이 의정서의 규정에 따라 제공되는 이용 가능한 모든 정보에 입각하여, 당사자의 의정서 이행상황, 이 의정서에 따라 행한 조치의 전반적 효과, 특히 환경적·경제적·사회적 효과 및 이의 누적적 효과와 협약의 목적 성취도를 평가할 것

나. 협약 제4조 제2항 라목 및 제7조 제2항에서 요구되는 모든 검토를 충분히 고려하고, 협약의 목적 및 협약의 이행과정에서 얻은 경험과 과학·기술 지식의 발전에 비추어, 이 의정서에 따른 당사자의 의무를 정기적으로 검토하고, 이러한 측면에서 이 의정서의 이행에 관한 정기보고서를 심의·채택할 것

of this Protocol;

(c) Promote and facilitate the exchange of information on measures adopted by the Parties to address climate change and its effects, taking into account the differing circumstances, responsibilities and capabilities of the Parties and their respective commitments this Protocol;

(d) Facilitate, at the request of two or more Parties, the coordination of measures adopted by them to address climate change and its effects, taking into account the differing circumstances, responsibilities and capabilities of the Parties and their respective commitments this Protocol;

(e) Promote and guide, in accordance with the objective of the Convention and the provisions of this Protocol, and taking fully into account the relevant decisions by the Conference of the Parties, the development and periodic refinement of comparable methodologies for the effective implementation of this Protocol, to be agreed on by the Conference of the Parties serving as the meeting of the Parties to this Protocol;

(f) Make recommendations on any matters necessary for the implementation of this Protocol;

(g) Seek to mobilize additional financial resources in accordance with Article 11, paragraph 2;

(h) Establish such subsidiary bodies as are deemed necessary for the implementation of this Protocol;

(i) Seek and utilize, where appropriate, the services and cooperation of, and information provided by, competent inter-

다. 당사자의 서로 다른 여건·책임 및 능력과 이 의정서상의 각자의 공약을 고려하여, 기후변화와 그 효과에 대응하기 위하여 당사자가 채택한 조치에 관한 정보의 교환을 촉진하고 용이하게 할 것

라. 2 이상의 당사자의 요청이 있는 경우, 각 당사자의 서로 다른 여건·책임 및 능력과 이 의정서상의 각자의 공약을 고려하여, 기후변화와 그 효과에 대응하기 위하여 당사자가 채택한 조치의 조정을 용이하게 할 것

마. 협약의 목적 및 이 의정서의 규정에 따라, 그리고 당사국총회의 관련 결정을 충분히 고려하여, 이 의정서의 당사자회의의 역할을 수행하는 당사국총회가 합의한 방법론으로서 이 의정서의 효과적인 이행을 위한 비교가능한 방법론의 발전과 정기적인 개선을 촉진·지도할 것

바. 이 의정서의 이행에 필요한 사항에 대하여 권고할 것

사. 제11조 제2항에 따라 추가적 재원의 동원을 위하여 노력할 것

아. 이 의정서의 이행에 필요하다고 판단되는 보조기관을 설치할 것

자. 적절한 경우, 권한 있는 국제기구·정부간기구 및 비정부간기구로부터의 지원·협력 및 정보제공을 구하고 이를 활용할 것

national organizations and intergovernmental and non-governmental bodies;
and

(j) Exercise such other functions as may
be required for the implementation of
this and consider any assignment resulting from a decision by the Conference
of the Parties.

5. The rules of procedure of the Conference of the Parties and financial procedures applied under the Convention shall
be applied mutatis mutandis under this
Protocol, except as may be otherwise decided by consensus by the Conference
of the Parties serving as the meeting of
the Parties to this Protocol.

6. The first session of the Conference of
the Parties serving as the meeting of the
Parties to this Protocol shall be convened
by the secretariat in conjunction with the
first session of the Conference of the
Parties that is scheduled after the date
of the entry into force of this Protocol.
Subsequent ordinary sessions of the Conference of the Parties serving as the
meeting of the Parties to this Protocol
shall be held every year and in conjunction with ordinary sessions of the Conference of the Parties, unless otherwise
decided by the Conference the Parties
serving as the meeting of the Parties to
this Protocol.

7. Extraordinary sessions of the Conference of the Parties serving as the meeting of the Parties to this Protocol shall
be held at such other times as may be
deemed necessary by the Conference of

차. 이 의정서의 이행을 위하여 필요한 그 밖
의 기능을 수행하고, 당사국총회의 결정
에 의하여 부여되는 모든 과제를 심의할
것

5. 이 의정서의 당사자회의의 역할을 수행하
는 당사국총회가 컨센서스로 달리 결정하
는 경우를 제외하고는, 당사국총회의 의사
규칙 및 협약상 적용되는 재정절차는 이
의정서에 준용한다.

6. 이 의정서의 당사자회의의 역할을 수행하
는 당사국총회의 제1차 회기는 사무국에
의하여 이 의정서의 발효일 이후에 예정되
어 있는 당사국총회의 첫째 회기와 함께
소집된다. 이 의정서의 당사자회의의 역할
을 수행하는 당사국총회의 후속 정기회기
는, 동 당사국총회가 달리 결정하지 아니
하는 한, 당사국총회의 정기회기와 함께
매년 개최된다.

7. 이 의정서의 당사자회의의 역할을 수행하
는 당사국총회의 특별회기는 동 당사국총
회가 필요하다고 인정하거나 당사자의 서
면요청이 있는 때에 개최된다. 다만, 이러
한 서면요청은 사무국이 이를 당사자들에

the Parties serving as the meeting of the Parties to this Protocol, or at the written request of any Party, provided that, within six months of the request being communicated to the Parties by the secretariat, it is supported by at least one third of the Parties.

8. The United Nations, its specialized agencies and the International Atomic Energy Agency, as well as any State member thereof or observers thereto not party to the Convention, may be represented at sessions of the Conference of the Parties serving as the meeting of the Parties to this Protocol as observers. Any body or agency, whether national or international, governmental or non-governmental, which is qualified in matters covered by this Protocol and which has informed the secretariat of its wish to be represented at a session of the Conference of the Parties serving as the meeting of the Parties to this Protocol as an observer, may be so admitted unless at least one third of the Parties present object. The admission and participation of observers shall be subject to the rules of procedure, as referred to in paragraph 5 above.

Article 14

1. The secretariat established by Article 8 of the Convention shall serve as the secretariat of this Protocol.

2. Article 8, paragraph 2, of the Convention on the functions of the secretariat, and Article 8, paragraph 3, of the Con-

게 통보한 후 6월 이내에 최소한 당사자 3분의 1이상의 지지를 받아야 한다.

8. 국제연합 · 국제연합전문기구 · 국제원자력기구 및 이들 기구의 회원국이나 참관인인 협약의 비당사자는 이 의정서의 당사자회의의 역할을 수행하는 당사국총회의 회기에 참관인으로 참석할 수 있다. 국내적 · 국제적 또는 정부간 · 비정부간 기구나 기관을 불문하고 이 의정서가 규율하는 사항에 대하여 전문성을 갖는 기구나 기관이 이 의정서의 당사자회의의 역할을 수행하는 당사국총회의 회기에 참관인으로 참석하고자 하는 의사를 사무국에 통보하는 경우, 출석당사자의 3분의 1 이상이 반대하지 아니하는 한 그 참석이 허용될 수 있다. 참관인의 참석 허용 및 회의 참가는 제5항에 규정된 의사규칙에 따라 이루어진다.

제 14 조

1. 협약 제8조에 의하여 설치되는 사무국은 이 의정서의 사무국의 역할을 수행한다.

2. 사무국의 기능에 관하여 규정하고 있는 협약 제8조 제2항 및 사무국의 기능수행에 필요한 준비에 관하여 규정하고 있는 협약

vention on arrangements made for the functioning of the secretariat, shall apply mutatis mutandis to this Protocol. The secretariat shall, in addition, exercise the functions assigned to it under this Protocol.

제8조 제3항은 이 의정서에 준용한다. 또한 사무국은 이 의정서에 의하여 부여된 기능을 수행한다.

Article 15

1. The Subsidiary Body for Scientific and Technological Advice and the Subsidiary Body for Implementation established by Articles 9 and 10 of the Convention shall serve as, respectively, the Subsidiary Body for Scientific and Technological Advice and the Subsidiary Body for Implementation of this Protocol. The provisions relating to the functioning of these two bodies under the Convention shall apply mutatis mutandis to this Protocol. Sessions of the meetings of the Subsidiary Body for Scientific and Technological Advice and the Subsidiary Body for Implementation of this Protocol shall be held in conjunction with the meetings of, respectively, the Subsidiary Body for Scientific and Technological Advice and the Body for Implementation of the Convention.

2. Parties to the Convention that are not Parties to this Protocol may participate as observers in the proceedings of any session of the subsidiary bodies. When the subsidiary bodies serve as the subsidiary bodies of this Protocol, decisions under this Protocol shall be taken only by those that are Parties to this Protocol.

제15조

1. 협약 제9조 및 제10조에 의하여 설치된 과학·기술자문 보조기관 및 이행을 위한 보조기관은 각각 이 의정서의 과학·기술자문 보조기관 및 이행을 위한 보조기관의 역할을 수행한다. 과학·기술자문 보조기관 및 이행을 위한 보조기관의 기능수행에 관한 협약의 규정은 이 의정서에 준용한다. 이 의정서의 과학·기술자문 보조기관 및 이행을 위한 보조기관 회의의 회기는 각각 협약의 과학·기술 보조기관 및 이행을 위한 보조기관의 회의와 함께 개최된다.

2. 이 의정서의 당사자가 아닌 협약의 당사자는 보조기관의 모든 회기의 심의에 참관인으로 참여할 수 있다. 보조기관이 이 의정서의 보조기관의 역할을 수행하는 경우, 이 의정서에 따른 결정은 이 의정서의 당사자만이 할 수 있다.

3. When the subsidiary bodies established by Articles 9 and 10 of the Convention exercise their functions with regard to matters concerning this Protocol, any member of the Bureaux of those subsidiary bodies representing a Party to the Convention but, at that time, not a party to this Protocol, shall be replaced by an additional member to be elected by and from amongst the Parties to this Protocol.

3. 협약 제9조 및 제10조에 의하여 설치된 보조기관이 이 의정서와 관련된 사항에 대하여 그 기능을 수행하는 경우, 그 당시 이 의정서의 당사자가 아닌 협약의 당사자를 대표하는 자가 보조기관의 의장단의 구성원인 때에는 동 구성원은 이 의정서의 당사자들이 그들 중에서 선출한 추가구성원으로 대체된다.

Article 16

The Conference of the Parties serving as the meeting of the Parties to this Protocol shall, as soon as practicable, consider the application to this Protocol of, and modify as appropriate, the multilateral consultative process referred to in Article 13 of the Convention, in the light of any relevant decisions that may be taken by the Conference of the Parties. Any multilateral consultative process that may be applied to this Protocol shall operate without prejudice to the procedures and mechanisms established in accordance with Article 18.

제16조

이 의정서의 당사자회의의 역할을 수행하는 당사국총회는, 당사국총회가 채택한 모든 관련 결정에 비추어 가능한 한 조속히, 협약 제13조에 규정된 다자간 협의절차를 이 의정서에 적용하는 문제를 심의하고, 적절한 경우에는 이를 수정한다. 이 의정서에 적용될 수 있는 모든 다자간 협의절차는 제18조에 따라 마련된 절차 및 체제에 영향을 미치지 아니하도록 운영된다.

Article 17

The Conference of the Parties shall define the relevant principles, modalities, rules and in particular for verification, reporting and accountability for emissions trading. The Parties included in Annex B may participate in emissions trading for the purposes of fulfilling their commitments under Article 3. Any such trading shall be supplemental to domestic actions for the purpose

제17조

당사국총회는, 특히 검증·보고·책임 등에 관한 것을 비롯하여, 배출량거래에 관한 원칙·방식·규칙·지침을 규정한다. 부속서 나의 당사자는 제3조의 규정에 의한 공약을 이행하기 위하여 배출량거래에 참여할 수 있다. 이러한 모든 거래는 제3조의 규정에 의한 수량적 배출량의 제한·감축을 위한 공약의 이행을 위한 국내조치의 보조수단으로 활용되

of meeting quantified emission limitation and commitments under that Article.

어야 한다.

Article 18

The Conference of the Parties serving as the meeting of the Parties to this Protocol shall, at its first session, approve appropriate and effective procedures and mechanisms to determine and to address cases of non-compliance with the provisions of this Protocol, including through the development of an indicative list of consequences, taking into account the cause, type, degree and frequency of noncompliance. Any procedures and mechanisms under this Article entailing binding consequences shall be adopted by means of an amendment to this Protocol.

제 18 조

이 의정서의 당사자회의의 역할을 수행하는 당사국총회는 제1차 회기에서, 이 의정서가 준수되지 아니하는 원인·형태·정도 및 빈도를 고려하여, 그 결과에 관한 예시목록의 개발 등 그 사례를 결정하고 이에 대응하기 위한 적절하고 효과적인 절차 및 체제를 승인한다. 이 조의 규정에 의한 절차 및 체제로서 기속력 있는 결과를 수반하는 것은 이 의정서의 개정에 의하여 채택된다.

Article 19

The provisions of Article 14 of the Convention on settlement of disputes shall apply mutatis mutandis to this Protocol.

제 19 조

분쟁해결에 관한 협약 제14조의 규정은 이 의정서에 준용한다.

Article 20

1. Any Party may propose amendments to this Protocol.

2. Amendments to this Protocol shall be adopted at an ordinary session of the Conference of the Parties serving as the meeting of the Parties to this Protocol. The text of any proposed amendment to this Protocol shall be communicated to the Parties by the secretariat at least six months before the meeting at which it is proposed for adoption.

제 20 조

1. 모든 당사자는 이 의정서의 개정안을 제안할 수 있다.

2. 이 의정서의 개정안은 이 의정서의 당사자회의의 역할을 수행하는 당사국총회의 정기회기에서 채택된다. 사무국은 개정안의 채택여부가 상정되는 정기회기가 개최되기 최소 6월 전에 동 개정안을 당사자들에게 통보하고, 협약의 당사자와 그 서명자에게도 통보하며, 참고용으로 수탁자에게도 통보한다.

The secretariat shall also communicate the text of any proposed amendments to the Parties and signatories to the Convention and, for information, to the Depositary.

3. The Parties shall make every effort to reach agreement on any proposed amendment to this Protocol by consensus. If all efforts at consensus have been exhausted, and no agreement reached, the amendment shall as a last resort be adopted by a three-fourths majority vote of the Parties present and voting at the meeting. The adopted amendment shall be communicated the secretariat to the Depository, who shall circulate it to all Parties for their acceptance.

4. Instruments of acceptance in respect of an amendment shall be deposited with the Depositary. An amendment adopted in accordance with paragraph 3 above shall enter into force for those Parties having accepted it on the ninetieth day after the date of receipt by the Depositary of an instrument of acceptance by at least three fourths of the Parties to this Protocol.

5. The amendment shall enter into force for any other Party on the ninetieth day after the date on which that Party deposits with the Depositary its instrument of acceptance of the said amendment.

Article 21

1. Annexes to this Protocol shall form an

3. 당사자는 이 의정서의 개정안에 대하여 컨센서스에 의한 합의에 도달하도록 모든 노력을 다한다. 컨센서스를 위한 모든 노력을 다하였으나 합의에 도달하지 못한 경우, 동 개정안은 최종적으로 회의에 출석하여 투표하는 당사자의 4분의 3 이상의 다수결로 채택된다. 사무국은 채택된 개정안을 수탁자에게 통보하며, 수탁자는 동 개정안의 수락을 위하여 이를 모든 당사자에게 배포한다.

4. 개정안에 대한 수락서는 수탁자에게 기탁된다. 제3항에 따라 채택된 개정안은 이 의정서의 당사자중 최소 4분의 3 이상의 수락서가 수탁자에게 접수된 날부터 90일째 되는 날에 수락한 당사자에 대하여 발효한다.

5. 그 밖의 당사자가 그 후에 수탁자에게 수락서를 기탁한 경우에는, 그 개정안은 수락서를 기탁한 날부터 90일째 되는 날에 동 당사자에 대하여 발효한다.

제21조

1. 이 의정서의 부속서는 의정서의 불가분의

integral part thereof and, unless otherwise expressly provided, a reference to this Protocol constitutes at the same time a reference to any annexes thereto. Any annexes adopted after the entry into force of this Protocol shall be restricted to lists, forms and any other material of a descriptive nature that is of a scientific, technical, procedural or administrative character.

2. Any Party may make proposals for an annex to this Protocol and may propose amendments to annexes to this Protocol.

3. Annexes to this Protocol and amendments to annexes to this Protocol shall be adopted at an ordinary session of the Conference of the Parties serving as the meeting of the Parties to this Protocol. The text of any proposed annex or amendment to an annex shall be communicated to the Parties by the secretariat at least six months before the meeting at which it is proposed for adoption. The secretariat shall also communicate the text of any proposed annex or amendment to an annex to the Parties and signatories to the Convention and, for information, to the Depositary.

4. The Parties shall make every effort to reach agreement on any proposed annex or amendment to an annex by consensus. If all efforts at consensus have been exhausted, and no agreement reached, the annex or amendment to an annex shall as a last resort be adopted by a three—

일부를 구성하며, 명시적으로 달리 규정하지 아니하는 한, 이 의정서에 관한 언급은 동시에 그 부속서도 언급하는 것으로 본다. 이 의정서의 발효 이후에 채택되는 모든 부속서는 목록·양식이나 과학적·기술적·절차적·행정적 특성을 갖는 서술적 성격의 자료에 국한된다.

2. 모든 당사자는 이 의정서의 부속서안이나 이 의정서의 부속서의 개정안을 제안할 수 있다.

3. 이 의정서의 부속서안 및 이 의정서의 부속서의 개정안은 이 의정서의 당사자회의의 역할을 수행하는 당사국총회의 정기회기에서 채택된다. 사무국은 제안된 부속서안 또는 부속서의 개정안의 채택여부가 상정되는 정기회기가 개최되기 최소 6월 전에 동 부속서안 또는 부속서의 개정안을 당사자들에게 통보하고, 협약의 당사자와 그 서명자에게도 통보하며, 참고용으로 수탁자에게도 통보한다.

4. 당사자는 부속서안 또는 부속서의 개정안에 대하여 컨센서스에 의한 합의에 도달하도록 모든 노력을 다한다. 컨센서스를 위한 모든 노력을 다하였으나 합의에 도달하지 못한 경우, 부속서안 또는 부속서의 개정안은 최종적으로 회의에 출석하여 투표

fourths majority vote of the Parties present and voting at the meeting. The adopted annex or amendment to an annex shall be communicated by the secretariat to the Depositary, who shall circulate it to all Parties for their acceptance.

5. An annex, or amendment to an annex other than Annex A or B, that has been adopted in accordance with paragraphs 3 and 4 above shall enter into force for all Parties to this Protocol six months after the date of the communication by the Depositary to such Parties of the adoption of the annex or adoption of the amendment to the annex, except for those Parties that have notified the Depositary, in writing, within that period of their non-acceptance of the annex or amendment to the annex. The annex or amendment to an annex shall enter into force for Parties which withdraw their notification of nonacceptance on the ninetieth day after the date on which withdrawal of such notification has been received by the Depositary.

6. If the adoption of an annex or an amendment to an annex involves an amendment to this Protocol, that annex or amendment to an annex shall not enter into force until such time as amendment to this Protocol enters into force.

7. Amendments to Annexes A and B to this Protocol shall be adopted and enter into force in accordance with the procedure set out in Article 20, provided that any amendment to Annex B shall

하는 당사자의 4분의 3 이상의 다수결로 채택된다. 사무국은 채택된 부속서안 또는 부속서의 개정안을 수탁자에게 통보하며, 수탁자는 수락을 위하여 이를 모든 당사자에게 배포한다.

5. 제3항과 제4항에 따라 채택된 부속서안 또는 부속서(부속서 가 또는 나를 제외한다)의 개정안은 수탁자가 동 부속서안 또는 는 부속서의 개정안의 채택을 당사자에게 통보한 날부터 6월 후에 이 의정서의 모든 당사자(동 기간 내에 이를 수락하지 아니함을 수탁자에게 서면으로 통고한 당사자를 제외한다)에 대하여 발효한다. 부속서안 또는 부속서의 개정안을 수락하지 아니한다는 서면통고를 한 당사자가 이를 철회한 경우에는, 동 당사자에 대하여는 그 철회통고가 수탁자에게 접수된 날부터 90일째 되는 날에 발효한다.

6. 부속서안 또는 부속서의 개정안의 채택이 이 의정서의 개정을 수반하는 경우에는, 그 부속서안 또는 부속서의 개정안은 이 의정서의 개정안이 발효할 때까지 발효하지 아니한다.

7. 이 의정서의 부속서 가 및 나의 개정안은 제20조에 규정된 절차에 따라 채택되고 발효한다. 다만, 부속서 나의 개정안은 관련 당사자의 서면동의가 있는 경우에만 채택된다.

be adopted only with the written con-
sent of the Party concerned.

Article 22

1. Each Party shall have one vote, except
as provided for in paragraph 2 below.

2. Regional economic integration organizations, in matters within their competence, shall exercise their right to vote
with a number of votes equal to the
number of their member States that are
Parties to this Protocol. Such an organization shall not exercise its right to vote
if any of its member States exercises its
right, and vice versa.

Article 23

The Secretary-General of the United Nations shall be the Depositary of this Protocol.

Article 24

1. This Protocol shall be open for signature
and subject to ratification, acceptance
or approval by States and regional economic integration organizations which
are Parties to the Convention. It shall
be open for signature at United Nations
Headquarters in New York from 16
March 1998 to 15 March 1999. This
Protocol shall be open for accession
from the day after the date on which it
is closed for signature. Instruments of
ratification, acceptance, approval or accession shall be deposited with the Depositary.

제22조

1. 각 당사자는 제2항에 규정된 경우를 제외
하고는 하나의 투표권을 가진다.

2. 지역경제통합기구는 그 기구의 권한사항
에 대하여 이 의정서의 당사자인 기구 회원
국의 수와 동수의 투표권을 행사한다. 기
구 회원국 중 어느 한 국가라도 투표권을
행사하는 경우, 기구는 투표권을 행사하지
아니하며, 그 반대의 경우도 또한 같다.

제23조

국제연합사무총장은 이 의정서의 수탁자가
된다.

제24조

1. 이 의정서는 협약의 당사자인 국가와 지역
경제통합기구의 서명을 위하여 개방되며,
이들에 의하여 비준·수락·승인된다. 이
의정서는 1998년 3월 16일부터 1999년 3
월 15일까지 뉴욕의 국제연합본부에서 서
명을 위하여 개방되며, 그 서명기간이 종
료한 다음 날부터 가입을 위하여 개방된
다. 비준서·수락서·승인서·가입서는 수
탁자에게 기탁된다.

2. Any regional economic integration organization which becomes a Party to this Protocol without any of its member States being a Party shall be bound by all the obligations under this Protocol. In the case of such organizations, one or more of whose member States is a Party to this Protocol, the organization and its member States shall decide on their respective responsibilities for the performance of their obligations under this Protocol. In such the organization and the member States shall not be entitled to exercise rights under this Protocol concurrently.

3. In their instruments of ratification, acceptance, approval or accession, regional economic integration organizations shall declare the extent of their competence with respect to the matters governed by this Protocol. These organizations shall also inform the Depositary, who shall in turn inform the Parties, of any substantial modification in the extent of their competence.

Article 25

1. This Protocol shall enter into force on the ninetieth day after the date on which not less than 55 Parties to the Convention, incorporating Parties included in Annex I which accounted in total for at least 55 per cent of the total carbon dioxide emissions for 1990 of the Parties included in Annex I, have deposited their instruments of ratification, acceptance, approval or accession.

2. 이 의정서의 당사자가 되는 지역경제통합기구는, 기구 회원국 중 어느 한 국가도 이 의정서의 당사자가 아닌 경우에도 이 의정서상의 모든 의무에 구속된다. 기구의 1 이상의 회원국이 이 의정서의 당사자인 경우, 기구와 그 회원국은 이 의정서상의 의무를 수행하기 위한 각각의 책임을 결정한다. 이 경우, 기구와 그 회원국은 이 의정서상의 권리를 동시에 행사할 수 없다.

3. 지역경제통합기구는 그 비준서·수락서·승인서·가입서에서 이 의정서가 규율하는 사항에 관한 기구의 권한범위를 선언한다. 또한, 기구는 그 권한범위의 실질적 변동에 관하여 수탁자에게 통보하며, 수탁자는 이를 당사자에게 통보한다.

제25조

1. 이 의정서는 부속서 1의 당사자들의 1990년도 이산화탄소 총 배출량 중 55퍼센트 이상을 차지하는 부속서 1의 당사자를 포함하여, 55 이상의 협약의 당사자가 비준서·수락서·승인서·가입서를 기탁한 날부터 90일째 되는 날에 발효한다.

2. For the purposes of this Article, "the total carbon dioxide emissions for 1990 of the Parties included in Annex I" means the amount communicated on or before the date of adoption of this Protocol by the Parties included in Annex I in their first national communications submitted in accordance with Article 12 of the Convention.

3. For each State or regional economic integration organization that ratifies, accepts or approves this Protocol or accedes thereto after the conditions set out in paragraph 1 above for entry into force have been fulfilled, this Protocol shall enter into force on the ninetieth day following the date of deposit of its instrument of ratification, acceptance, approval or accession.

4. For the purposes of this Article, any instrument deposited by a regional economic integration organization shall not be counted as additional to those deposited by States members of the organization.

Article 26

No reservations may be made to this Protocol.

Article 27

1. At any time after three years from the date on which this Protocol has entered into force for a Party, that Party may withdraw from this Protocol by giving written notification to the Depositary.

2. 이 조의 목적상, "부속서 1의 당사자들의 1990년도 이산화탄소 총 배출량"이라 함은 부속서 1의 당사자들이 이 의정서의 채택일 또는 그 이전에 협약 제12조에 따라 제출한 제1차 국가보고서에서 통보한 양을 말한다.

3. 발효에 관한 제1항의 조건이 충족된 후 이 의정서를 비준·수락·승인·가입하는 국가 또는 지역경제통합기구의 경우에는, 그 비준서·수락서·승인서·가입서가 기탁된 날부터 90일째 되는 날에 동 국가 또는 기구에 대하여 발효한다.

4. 이 조의 목적상, 지역경제통합기구가 기탁하는 문서는 기구의 회원국이 기탁하는 문서에 추가되는 것으로 계산되지 아니한다.

제 26 조

이 의정서에 대하여는 어떠한 유보도 행할 수 없다.

제 27 조

1. 당사자는 의정서가 자신에 대하여 발효한 날부터 3년이 경과한 후에는 언제나 수탁자에게 서면통고를 함으로써 이 의정서로부터 탈퇴할 수 있다.

2. Any such withdrawal shall take effect upon expiry of one year from the date of receipt by the Depositary of the notification of withdrawal, or on such later date as may be specified in the notification of withdrawal.

3. Any Party that withdraws from the Convention shall be considered as also having withdrawn from this Protocol.

Article 28

The original of this Protocol, of which the Arabic, Chinese, English, French, Russian and Spanish texts are equally authentic, shall be deposited with the Secretary—General of the United Nations.

DONE AT Kyoto this eleventh day of December one thousand nine hundred and ninety—seven.

IN WITNESS WHEREOF the undersigned, being duly authorized to that effect, have affixed their signatures to this Protocol on the dates indicated.

2. 탈퇴는 수탁자가 탈퇴 통고를 접수한 날부터 1년이 경과한 날이나 탈퇴통고서에 이보다 더 늦은 날짜가 명시된 경우에는 그 늦은 날에 발효한다.

3. 협약으로부터 탈퇴한 당사자는 이 의정서로부터도 탈퇴한 것으로 본다.

제28조

아랍어·중국어·영어·불어·러시아어 및 서반아어본이 동등하게 정본인 이 의정서의 원본은 국제연합 사무총장에게 기탁된다.

1997년 12월 11일에 교토에서 작성하였다.

이상의 증거로, 정당하게 권한을 위임받은 아래 서명자가 명시된 일자에 이 의정서에 서명하였다.

Annex A

Greenhouse gases
Carbon dioxide(CO_2)
Methane(CH_4)
Nitrous oxide(N_2O)
Hydrofluorocarbons(HFCs)
Perfluorocarbons(PFCs)
Sulphur hexafluoride(SF_6)

Sectors/source categories
Energy
Fuel combustion
Energy industries
Manufacturing industries and construction
Transport
Other sectors
Other
Fugitive emissions from fuels
Solid fuels
Oil and natural gas
Other

Industrial processes
Mineral products
Chemical industry
Metal production
Other production
Production of halocarbons and sulphur hexafluoride
Consumption of halocarbons and sulphur hexafluoride
Other

Solvent and other product use

Agriculture
Enteric fermentation
Manure management
Rice cultivation
Agricultural soils
Prescribed burning of savannas
Field burning of agricultural residues
Other

Waste

    Solid waste disposal on land

    Wastewater handling

    Waste incineration

    Other

Annex B

Quantified Emission Limitation or Reduction Commitment
[percentage of base year(1990) or period]

Party	%	Party	%
Australia	108	Liechtenstein	92
Austria	92	Lithuania*	92
Belgium	92	Luxembourg	92
Bulgaria*	92	Monaco	92
Canada	94	Netherlands	92
Croatia*	95	New Zealand	100
Czech Republic*	92	Norway	101
Denmark	92	Poland*	94
Estonia*	92	Portugal	92
European Community	92	Romania*	92
Finland	92	Russian Federation*	100
France	92	Slovakia*	92
Germany	92	Slovenia*	92
Greece	92	Spain	92
Hungary*	94	Sweden	92
Iceland	110	Switzerland	92
Ireland	92	Ukraine*	100
Italy	92	United Kingdom	92
Japan	94	United States	93
Latvia*	92		

* Countries that are undergoing the process of transition to a market economy.

5. Paris Agreement (2015)

5. 파리협정

Date : 12 December 2015
In force : 4 November 2016
States Party : 153
Korea : 3 November 2016 (조약 제2315호)
Link : www.unfccc.int

The Parties to this Agreement,

Being Parties to the United Nations Framework Convention on Climate Change, hereinafter referred to as "the Convention",

Pursuant to the Durban Platform for Enhanced Action established by decision 1/CP.17 of the Conference of the Parties to the Convention at its seventeenth session,

In pursuit of the objective of the Convention, and being guided by its principles, including the principle of equity and common but differentiated responsibilities and respective capabilities, in the light of different national circumstances,

Recognizing the need for an effective and progressive response to the urgent threat of climate change on the basis of the best available scientific knowledge,

Also recognizing the specific needs and special circumstances of developing country Parties, especially those that are particularly vulnerable to the adverse effects of climate change, as provided for in the Convention,

이 협정의 당사자는,

「기후변화에 관한 국제연합 기본협약(이하 "협약"이라 한다)」의 당사자로서,

제17차 협약 당사자총회에서 결정(1/CP.17)으로 수립된 「행동 강화를 위한 더반플랫폼」에 따라,

협약의 목적을 추구하고, 상이한 국내 여건에 비추어 형평의 원칙 및 공통적이지만 그 정도에 차이가 나는 책임과 각자의 능력의 원칙을 포함하는 협약의 원칙에 따라,

이용 가능한 최선의 과학적 지식에 기초하여 기후변화라는 급박한 위협에 대하여 효과적이고 점진적으로 대응할 필요성을 인식하며,

또한, 협약에서 규정된 대로 개발도상국인 당사자, 특히 기후변화의 부정적 영향에 특별히 취약한 개발도상국 당사자의 특수한 필요와 특별한 사정을 인식하고,

Taking full account of the specific needs and special situations of the least developed countries with regard to fund ing and transfer of technology,

Recognizing that Parties may be affected not only by climate change, but also by the impacts of the measures taken in response to it,

Emphasizing the intrinsic relatiohip that climate change actions, responses and impacts have with equitable access to sustainable development and eradication of poverty,

Recognizing the fundamental priority of safeguarding food security and ending hunger, and the particular vulnerabilities of food production systems to the adverse impacts of climate change,

Taking into account the imperatives of a just transition of the workforce and the creation of decent work and quality jobs in accordance with nationally defined development priorities,

Acknowledging that climate change is a common concern of humankind, Parties should, when taking action to address climate change, respect, promote and consider their respective obligations on human rights, the right to health, the rights of indigenous peoples, local communities, migrants, children, persons with disabilities and people in vulnerable situations and the right to development, as well as gender equality, empowerment of

자금 제공 및 기술 이전과 관련하여 최빈개도국의 특수한 필요와 특별한 상황을 충분히 고려하며,

당사자들이 기후변화뿐만 아니라 그에 대한 대응 조치에서 비롯된 여파에 의해서도 영향을 받을 수 있음을 인식하고,

기후변화 행동, 대응 및 영향이 지속가능한 발전 및 빈곤 퇴치에 대한 형평한 접근과 본질적으로 관계가 있음을 강조하며,

식량안보 수호 및 기아 종식이 근본적인 우선 과제이며, 기후변화의 부정적 영향에 식량생산체계가 특별히 취약하다는 점을 인식하고,

국내적으로 규정된 개발우선순위에 따라 노동력의 정당한 전환과 좋은 일자리 및 양질의 직업 창출이 매우 필요함을 고려하며,

기후변화가 인류의 공통 관심사임을 인정하고, 당사자는 기후변화에 대응하는 행동을 할 때 양성평등, 여성의 역량 강화 및 세대 간 형평뿐만 아니라, 인권, 보건에 대한 권리, 원주민·지역공동체·이주민·아동·장애인·취약계층의 권리 및 발전권에 관한 각자의 의무를 존중하고 촉진하며 고려하여야 함을 인정하며,

women and intergenerational equity,

Recognizing the importance of the conservation and enhancement, as appropriate, of sinks and reservoirs of the greenhouse gases referred to in the Convention,

협약에 언급된 온실가스의 흡수원과 저장고의 적절한 보전 및 증진의 중요성을 인식하고,

Noting the importance of ensuring the integrity of all ecosystems, including oceans, and the protection of biodiversity, recognized by some cultures as Mother Earth, and noting the importance for some of the concept of "climate justice", when taking action to address climate change,

기후변화에 대응하는 행동을 할 때, 해양을 포함한 모든 생태계의 건전성을 보장하는 것과 일부 문화에서 어머니 대지로 인식되는 생물다양성의 보존을 보장하는 것의 중요성에 주목하고, 일각에게 "기후 정의"라는 개념이 갖는 중요성에 주목하며,

Affirming the importance of education, training, public awareness, public participation, public access to information and cooperation at all levels on the matters addressed in this Agreement,

이 협정에서 다루어지는 문제에 대한 교육, 훈련, 공중의 인식, 공중의 참여, 공중의 정보 접근, 그리고 모든 차원에서의 협력이 중요함을 확인하고,

Recognizing the importance of the engagements of all levels of government and various actors, in accordance with respective national legislations of Parties, in addressing climate change,

기후변화에 대한 대응에 당사자 각자의 국내 법령에 따라 모든 차원의 정부조직과 다양한 행위자의 참여가 중요함을 인식하며,

Also recognizing that sustainable lifestyles and sustainable patterns of consumption and production, with developed country Parties taking the lead, play an important role in addressing climate change,

또한, 선진국인 당사자가 주도하고 있는 지속가능한 생활양식과 지속가능한 소비 및 생산 방식이 기후변화에 대한 대응에 중요한 역할을 함을 인식하면서,

Have agreed as follows:

다음과 같이 합의하였다.

Article 1

For the purpose of this Agreement, the definitions contained in Article 1 of the Convention shall apply. In addition:

(a) "Convention" means the United Nations Framework Convention on Climate Change, adopted in New York on 9 May 1992;

(b) "Conference of the Parties" means the Conference of the Parties to the Convention;

(c) "Party" means a Party to this Agreement.

Article 2

1. This Agreement, in enhancing the implementation of the Convention, including its objective, aims to strengthen the global response to the threat of climate change, in the context of sustainable development and efforts to eradicate poverty, including by:

(a) Holding the increase in the global average temperature to well below 2°C above pre-industrial levels and pursuing efforts to limit the temperature increase to 1.5°C above pre-industrial levels, recognizing that this would significantly reduce the risks and impacts of climate change;

(b) Increasing the ability to adapt to the adverse impacts of climate change and foster climate resilience and low greenhouse gas emissions development, in a manner that does not threaten

제1조

이 협정의 목적상, 협약 제1조에 포함된 정의가 적용된다. 추가로,

가. "협약"이란 1992년 5월 9일 뉴욕에서 채택된 「기후변화에 관한 국제연합 기본협약」을 말한다.

나. "당사자총회"란 협약의 당사자총회를 말한다.

다. "당사자"란 이 협정의 당사자를 말한다.

제2조

1. 이 협정은, 협약의 목적을 포함하여 협약의 이행을 강화하는 데에, 지속가능한 발전과 빈곤 퇴치를 위한 노력의 맥락에서, 다음의 방법을 포함하여 기후변화의 위협에 대한 전지구적 대응을 강화하는 것을 목표로 한다.

가. 기후변화의 위험 및 영향을 상당히 감소시킬 것이라는 인식하에, 산업화 전 수준 대비 지구 평균 기온 상승을 섭씨 2도 보다 현저히 낮은 수준으로 유지하는 것 및 산업화 전 수준 대비 지구 평균 기온 상승을 섭씨 1.5도로 제한하기 위한 노력의 추구

나. 식량 생산을 위협하지 아니하는 방식으로, 기후변화의 부정적 영향에 적응하는 능력과 기후 회복력 및 온실가스 저배출 발전을 증진하는 능력의 증대, 그리고

food production; and

(c) Making finance flows consistent with a pathway towards low greenhouse gas emissions and climate-resilient development.

2. This Agreement will be implemented to reflect equity and the principle of common but differentiated responsibilities and respective capabilities, in the light of different national circumstances.

Article 3

As nationally determined contributions to the global response to climate change, all Parties are to undertake and communicate ambitious efforts as defined in Articles 4, 7, 9, 10, 11 and 13 with the view to achieving the purpose of this Agreement as set out in Article 2. The efforts of all Parties will represent a progression over time, while recognizing the need to support developing country Parties for the effective implementation of this Agreement.

Article 4

1. In order to achieve the long-term temperature goal set out in Article 2, Parties aim to reach global peaking of greenhouse gas emissions as soon as possible, recognizing that peaking will take longer for developing country Parties, and to undertake rapid reductions thereafter in accordance with best available science, so as to achieve a balance between anthropogenic emissions by sources and removals by

다. 온실가스 저배출 및 기후 회복적 발전이라는 방향에 부합하도록 하는 재정 흐름의 조성

2. 이 협정은 상이한 국내 여건에 비추어 형평 그리고 공통적이지만 그 정도에 차이가 나는 책임과 각자의 능력의 원칙을 반영하여 이행될 것이다.

제3조

기후변화에 전지구적으로 대응하기 위한 국가결정기여로서, 모든 당사자는 제2조에 규정된 이 협정의 목적을 달성하기 위하여 제4조, 제7조, 제9조, 제10조, 제11조 및 제13조에 규정된 바와 같이 의욕적인 노력을 수행하고 통보하여야 한다. 이 협정의 효과적인 이행을 위해서는 개발도상국 당사자에 대한 지원이 필요함을 인식하면서, 모든 당사자는 시간의 경과에 따라 진전되는 노력을 보여줄 것이다.

제4조

1. 형평에 기초하고 지속가능한 발전과 빈곤퇴치를 위한 노력의 맥락에서, 제2조에 규정된 장기 기온 목표를 달성하기 위하여, 개발도상국 당사자에게는 온실가스 배출최대치 달성에 더욱 긴 시간이 걸릴 것임을 인식하면서, 당사자는 전지구적 온실가스 배출최대치를 가능한 한 조속히 달성할 것을 목표로 하고, 그 후에는 이용 가능한 최선의 과학에 따라 급속한 감축을 실시하는 것을 목표로 하여 금세기의

sinks of greenhouse gases in the second half of this century, on the basis of equity, and in the context of sustainable development and efforts to eradicate poverty.

2. Each Party shall prepare, communicate and maintain successive nationally determined contributions that it intends to achieve. Parties shall pursue domestic mitigation measures, with the aim of achieving the objectives of such contributions.

3. Each Party's successive nationally determined contribution will represent a progression beyond the Party's then current nationally determined contribution and reflect its highest possible ambition, reflecting its common but differentiated responsibilities and respective capabilities, in the light of different national circumstances.

4. Developed country Parties should continue taking the lead by undertaking economy-wide absolute emission reduction targets. Developing country Parties should continue enhancing their mitigation efforts, and are encouraged to move over time towards economy-wide emission reduction or limitation targets in the light of different national circumstances.

5. Support shall be provided to developing country Parties for the implementation of this Article, in accordance with Articles 9, 10 and 11, recognizing that

하반기에 온실가스의 배출원에 의한 인위적 배출과 흡수원에 의한 제거 간에 균형을 달성할 수 있도록 한다.

2. 각 당사자는 달성하고자 하는 차기 국가결정기여를 준비하고, 통보하며, 유지한다. 당사자는 그러한 국가결정기여의 목적을 달성하기 위하여 국내적 완화 조치를 추구한다.

3. 각 당사자의 차기 국가결정기여는 상이한 국내 여건에 비추어 공통적이지만 그 정도에 차이가 나는 책임과 각자의 능력을 반영하고, 당사자의 현재 국가결정기여보다 진전되는 노력을 시현할 것이며 가능한 한 가장 높은 의욕 수준을 반영할 것이다.

4. 선진국 당사자는 경제 전반에 걸친 절대량 배출 감축목표를 약속함으로써 주도적 역할을 지속하여야 한다. 개발도상국 당사자는 완화 노력을 계속 강화하여야 하며, 상이한 국내 여건에 비추어 시간의 경과에 따라 경제 전반의 배출 감축 또는 제한 목표로 나아갈 것이 장려된다.

5. 개발도상국 당사자에 대한 지원 강화를 통하여 그들이 보다 의욕적으로 행동할 수 있을 것임을 인식하면서, 개발도상국 당사자에게 이 조의 이행을 위하여 제9

enhanced support for developing country Parties will allow for higher ambition in their actions.

조, 제10조 및 제11조에 따라 지원이 제공된다.

6. The least developed countries and small island developing States may prepare and communicate strategies, plans and actions for low greenhouse gas emissions development reflecting their special circumstances.

6. 최빈개도국과 소도서 개발도상국은 그들의 특별한 사정을 반영하여 온실가스 저배출 발전을 위한 전략, 계획 및 행동을 준비하고 통보할 수 있다.

7. Mitigation co-benefits resulting from Parties' adaptation actions and/or economic diversification plans can contribute to mitigation outcomes under this Article.

7. 당사자의 적응 행동 그리고/또는 경제 다변화 계획으로부터 발생하는 완화의 공통이익은 이 조에 따른 완화 성과에 기여할 수 있다.

8. In communicating their nationally determined contributions, all Parties shall provide the information necessary for clarity, transparency and understanding in accordance with decision 1/CP.21 and any relevant decisions of the Conference of the Parties serving as the meeting of the Parties to this Agreement.

8. 국가결정기여를 통보할 때, 모든 당사자는 결정 1/CP.21과 이 협정의 당사자회의 역할을 하는 당사자총회의 모든 관련 결정에 따라 명확성, 투명성 및 이해를 위하여 필요한 정보를 제공한다.

9. Each Party shall communicate a nationally determined contribution every five years in accordance with decision 1/CP.21 and any relevant decisions of the Conference of the Parties serving as the meeting of the Parties to this Agreement and be informed by the outcomes of the global stocktake referred to in Article 14.

9. 각 당사자는 결정 1/CP.21과 이 협정의 당사자회의 역할을 하는 당사자총회의 모든 관련 결정에 따라 5년마다 국가결정기여를 통보하며, 각 당사자는 제14조에 언급된 전지구적 이행점검의 결과를 통지받는다.

10. The Conference of the Parties serving as the meeting of the Parties to this

10. 이 협정의 당사자회의 역할을 하는 당사자총회는 제1차 회기에서 국가결정기여

Agreement shall consider common time frames for nationally determined contributions at its first session.

11. A Party may at any time adjust its existing nationally determined contribution with a view to enhancing its level of ambition, in accordance with guidance adopted by the Conference of the Parties serving as the meeting of the Parties to this Agreement.

12. Nationally determined contributions communicated by Parties shall be recorded in a public registry maintained by the secretariat.

13. Parties shall account for their nationally determined contributions. In accounting for anthropogenic emissions and removals corresponding to their nationally determined contributions, Parties shall promote environmental integrity, transparency, accuracy, completeness, comparability and consistency, and ensure the avoidance of double counting, in accordance with guidance adopted by the Conference of the Parties serving as the meeting of the Parties to this Agreement.

14. In the context of their nationally determined contributions, when recognizing and implementing mitigation actions with respect to anthropogenic emissions and removals, Parties should take into account, as appropriate, existing methods and guidance under the Convention, in the light of the provi-

를 위한 공통의 시간 계획에 대하여 고려한다.

11. 이 협정의 당사자회의 역할을 하는 당사자총회가 채택하는 지침에 따라, 당사자는 자신의 의욕 수준을 증진하기 위하여 기존의 국가결정기여를 언제든지 조정할 수 있다.

12. 당사자가 통보한 국가결정기여는 사무국이 유지하는 공공 등록부에 기록된다.

13. 당사자는 자신의 국가결정기여를 산정한다. 자신의 국가결정기여에 따른 인위적 배출과 제거를 산정할 때는, 당사자는 이 협정의 당사자회의 역할을 하는 당사자총회가 채택하는 지침에 따라, 환경적 건전성, 투명성, 정확성, 완전성, 비교가능성, 일관성을 촉진하며, 이중계산의 방지를 보장한다.

14. 국가결정기여의 맥락에서, 인위적 배출과 제거에 관한 완화 행동을 인식하고 이행할 때 당사자는, 이 조 제13항에 비추어, 협약상의 기존 방법론과 지침을 적절히 고려하여야 한다.

sions of paragraph 13 of this Article.

15. Parties shall take into consideration in the implementation of this Agreement the concerns of Parties with economies most affected by the impacts of response measures, particularly developing country Parties.

16. Parties, including regional economic integration organizations and their member States, that have reached an agreement to act jointly under paragraph 2 of this Article shall notify the secretariat of the terms of that agreement, including the emission level allocated to each Party within the relevant time period, when they communicate their nationally determined contributions. The secretariat shall in turn inform the Parties and signatories to the Convention of the terms of that agreement.

17. Each party to such an agreement shall be responsible for its emission level as set out in the agreement referred to in paragraph 16 of this Article in accordance with paragraphs 13 and 14 of this Article and Articles 13 and 15.

18. If Parties acting jointly do so in the framework of, and together with, a regional economic integration organization which is itself a Party to this Agreement, each member State of that regional economic integration organization individually, and together with the regional economic integra-

15. 당사자는 이 협정을 이행할 때, 대응조치의 영향으로 인하여 자국 경제가 가장 크게 영향을 받는 당사자, 특히 개발도상국 당사자의 우려사항을 고려한다.

16. 공동으로 이 조 제2항에 따라 행동할 것에 합의한 지역경제통합기구와 그 회원국을 포함하는 당사자는 자신의 국가결정기여를 통보할 때, 관련 기간 내에 각 당사자에 할당된 배출 수준을 포함하는 합의 내용을 사무국에 통고한다. 그 다음 순서로 사무국은 협약의 당사자 및 서명자에게 그 합의 내용을 통지한다.

17. 그러한 합의의 각 당사자는 이 조 제13항 및 제14항 그리고 제13조 및 제15조에 따라 이 조 제16항에서 언급된 합의에 규정된 배출 수준에 대하여 책임을 진다.

18. 공동으로 행동하는 당사자들이 이 협정의 당사자인 지역경제통합기구의 프레임워크 안에서 그리고 지역경제통합기구와 함께 공동으로 행동하는 경우, 그 지역경제통합기구의 각 회원국은 개별적으로 그리고 지역경제통합기구와 함께, 이 조 제13항 및 제14항 그리고 제

tion organization, shall be responsible for its emission level as set out in the agreement communicated under paragraph 16 of this Article in accordance with paragraphs 13 and 14 of this Article and Articles 13 and 15.

19. All Parties should strive to formulate and communicate long—term low greenhouse gas emission development strategies, mindful of Article 2 taking into account their common but differentiated responsibilities and respective capabilities, in the light of different national circumstances.

Article 5

1. Parties should take action to conserve and enhance, as appropriate, sinks and reservoirs of greenhouse gases as referred to in Article 4, paragraph 1(d), of the Convention, including forests.

2. Parties are encouraged to take action to implement and support, including through results—based payments, the existing framework as set out in related guidance and decisions already agreed under the Convention for: policy approaches and positive incentives for activities relating to reducing emissions from deforestation and forest degradation, and the role of conservation, sustainable management of forests and enhancement of forest carbon stocks in developing countries; and alternative policy approaches, such

13조 및 제15조에 따라 이 조 제16항에 따라 통보된 합의에서 명시된 배출 수준에 대하여 책임을 진다.

19. 모든 당사자는 상이한 국내 여건에 비추어, 공통적이지만 그 정도에 차이가 나는 책임과 각자의 능력을 고려하는 제2조를 유념하며 장기적인 온실가스 저배출 발전 전략을 수립하고 통보하기 위하여 노력하여야 한다.

제5조

1. 당사자는 협약 제4조제1항라목에 언급된 바와 같이, 산림을 포함한 온실가스 흡수원 및 저장고를 적절히 보전하고 증진하는 조치를 하여야 한다.

2. 당사자는, 협약하 이미 합의된 관련 지침과 결정에서 규정하고 있는 기존의 프레임워크인: 개발도상국에서의 산림 전용과 산림 황폐화로 인한 배출의 감축 관련 활동, 그리고 산림의 보전, 지속가능한 관리 및 산림 탄소 축적 증진 역할에 관한 정책적 접근 및 긍정적 유인과; 산림의 통합적이고 지속가능한 관리를 위한 완화 및 적응 공동 접근과 같은 대안적 정책 접근을, 이러한 접근과 연계된 비탄소 편익에 대하여 적절히 긍정적인 유인을 제공하는 것의 중요성을 재확인하면서, 결과기반지불 등의 방식을 통하여, 이행하고 지원하

as joint mitigation and adaptation approaches for the integral and sustainable management of forests, while reaffirming the importance of incentivizing, as appropriate, non—carbon benefits associated with such approaches.

는 조치를 하도록 장려된다.

Article 6

제6조

1. Parties recognize that some Parties choose to pursue voluntary cooperation in the implementation of their nationally determined contributions to allow for higher ambition in their mitigation and adaptation actions and to promote sustainable development and environmental integrity.

1. 당사자는 일부 당사자가 완화 및 적응 행동을 하는 데에 보다 높은 수준의 의욕을 가능하게 하고 지속가능한 발전과 환경적 건전성을 촉진하도록 하기 위하여, 국가결정기여 이행에서 자발적 협력 추구를 선택하는 것을 인정한다.

2. Parties shall, where engaging on a voluntary basis in cooperative approaches that involve the use of internationally transferred mitigation outcomes towards nationally determined contributions, promote sustainable development and ensure environmental integrity and transparency, including in governance, and shall apply robust accounting to ensure, inter alia, the avoidance of double counting, consistent with guidance adopted by the Conference of the Parties serving as the meeting of the Parties to this Agreement.

2. 국가결정기여를 위하여 당사자가 국제적으로 이전된 완화 성과의 사용을 수반하는 협력적 접근에 자발적으로 참여하는 경우, 당사자는 지속가능한 발전을 촉진하고 거버넌스 등에서 환경적 건전성과 투명성을 보장하며, 이 협정의 당사자회의 역할을 하는 당사자총회가 채택하는 지침에 따라, 특히 이중계산의 방지 등을 보장하기 위한 엄격한 계산을 적용한다.

3. The use of internationally transferred mitigation outcomes to achieve nationally determined contributions under this Agreement shall be voluntary and authorized by participating Parties.

3. 이 협정에 따라 국가결정기여를 달성하기 위하여 국제적으로 이전된 완화 성과는 자발적으로 사용되며, 참여하는 당사자에 의하여 승인된다.

4. A mechanism to contribute to the mitigation of greenhouse gas emissions and support sustainable development is hereby established under the authority and guidance of the Conference of the Parties serving as the meeting of the Parties to this Agreement for use by Parties on a voluntary basis. It shall be supervised by a body designated by the Conference of the Parties serving as the meeting of the Parties to this Agreement, and shall aim:

(a) To promote the mitigation of greenhouse gas emissions while fostering sustainable development;

(b) To incentivize and facilitate participation in the mitigation of greenhouse gas emissions by public and private entities authorized by a Party;

(c) To contribute to the reduction of emission levels in the host Party, which will benefit from mitigation activities resulting in emission reductions that can also be used by another Party to fulfil its nationally determined contribution; and

(d) To deliver an overall mitigation in global emissions.

5. Emission reductions resulting from the mechanism referred to in paragraph 4 of this Article shall not be used to demonstrate achievement of the host Party's nationally determined contribution if used by another Party to demonstrate achievement of its nationally determined contribution.

4. 당사자가 자발적으로 사용할 수 있도록 온실가스 배출 완화에 기여하고 지속가능한 발전을 지원하는 메커니즘을 이 협정의 당사자회의 역할을 하는 당사자총회의 권한과 지침에 따라 설립한다. 이 메커니즘은 이 협정의 당사자회의 역할을 하는 당사자총회가 지정한 기구의 감독을 받으며, 다음을 목표로 한다.

가. 지속가능한 발전 증진 및 온실가스 배출의 완화 촉진

나. 당사자가 허가한 공공 및 민간 실체가 온실가스 배출 완화에 참여하도록 유인 제공 및 촉진

다. 유치당사자 국내에서의 배출 수준 하락에 기여. 유치당사자는 배출 감축으로 이어질 완화 활동으로부터 이익을 얻을 것이며 그러한 배출 감축은 다른 당사자가 자신의 국가결정기여를 이행하는 데에도 사용될 수 있다. 그리고

라. 전지구적 배출의 전반적 완화 달성

5. 이 조 제4항에 언급된 메커니즘으로부터 발생하는 배출 감축을 다른 당사자가 자신의 국가결정기여 달성을 증명하는 데 사용하는 경우, 그러한 배출 감축은 유치당사자의 국가결정기여 달성을 증명하는 데 사용되지 아니한다.

6. The Conference of the Parties serving as the meeting of the Parties to this Agreement shall ensure that a share of the proceeds from activities under the mechanism referred to in paragraph 4 of this Article is used to cover administrative expenses as well as to assist developing country Parties that are particularly vulnerable to the adverse effects of climate change to meet the costs of adaptation.

7. The Conference of the Parties serving as the meeting of the Parties to this Agreement shall adopt rules, modalities and procedures for the mechanism referred to in paragraph 4 of this Article at its first session.

8. Parties recognize the importance of integrated, holistic and balanced non-market approaches being available to Parties to assist in the implementation of their nationally determined contributions, in the context of sustainable development and poverty eradication, in a coordinated and effective manner, including through, inter alia, mitigation, adaptation, finance, technology transfer and capacity-building, as appropriate. These approaches shall aim to:

  (a) Promote mitigation and adaptation ambition;
  (b) Enhance public and private sector participation in the implementation of nationally determined contributions; and
  (c) Enable opportunities for coordination

6. 이 협정의 당사자회의 역할을 하는 당사자총회는 이 조 제4항에 언급된 메커니즘 하에서의 활동 수익 중 일부가 행정 경비로 지불되고, 기후변화의 부정적 영향에 특별히 취약한 개발도상국 당사자의 적응 비용의 충당을 지원하는 데 사용되도록 보장한다.

7. 이 협정의 당사자회의 역할을 하는 당사자총회는 제1차 회기에서 이 조 제4항에 언급된 메커니즘을 위한 규칙, 방식 및 절차를 채택한다.

8. 당사자는 지속가능한 발전과 빈곤퇴치의 맥락에서, 특히 완화, 적응, 금융, 기술 이전 및 역량배양 등을 통하여 적절히 조율되고 효과적인 방식으로 국가결정기여의 이행을 지원하기 위하여 당사자가 이용 가능한 통합적이고, 전체적이며, 균형적인 비시장 접근의 중요성을 인식한다. 이러한 접근은 다음을 목표로 한다.

가. 완화 및 적응 의욕 촉진

나. 국가결정기여 이행에 공공 및 민간 부문의 참여 강화, 그리고

다. 여러 기제 및 관련 제도적 장치 전반에

across instruments and relevant institutional arrangements.

9. A framework for non-market approaches to sustainable development is hereby defined to promote the non-market approaches referred to in paragraph 8 of this Article.

Article 7

1. Parties hereby establish the global goal on adaptation of enhancing adaptive capacity, strengthening resilience and reducing vulnerability to climate change, with a view to contributing to sustainable development and ensuring an adequate adaptation response in the context of the temperature goal referred to in Article 2.

2. Parties recognize that adaptation is a global challenge faced by all with local, subnational, national, regional and international dimensions, and that it is a key component of and makes a contribution to the long-term global response to climate change to protect people, livelihoods and ecosystems, taking into account the urgent and immediate needs of those developing country Parties that are particularly vulnerable to the adverse effects of climate change.

3. The adaptation efforts of developing country Parties shall be recognized, in accordance with the modalities to be adopted by the Conference of the

서 조정의 기회를 마련

9. 지속가능한 발전에 대한 비시장 접근 프레임워크를 이 조 제8항에 언급된 비시장 접근을 촉진하기 위하여 정의한다.

제7조

1. 당사자는 지속가능한 발전에 기여하고 제2조에서 언급된 기온 목표의 맥락에서 적절한 적응 대응을 보장하기 위하여, 적응 역량 강화, 회복력 강화 그리고 기후변화에 대한 취약성 경감이라는 전지구적 적응목표를 수립한다.

2. 당사자는 기후변화의 부정적 영향에 특별히 취약한 개발도상국 당사자의 급박하고 즉각적인 요구를 고려하면서, 적응이 현지적, 지방적, 국가적, 지역적 및 국제적 차원에서 모두가 직면한 전지구적 과제라는 점과, 적응이 인간, 생계 및 생태계를 보호하기 위한 장기적이며 전지구적인 기후변화 대응의 핵심 요소이며 이에 기여한다는 점을 인식한다.

3. 개발도상국 당사자의 적응 노력은 이 협정의 당사자회의 역할을 하는 당사자총회 제1차 회기에서 채택되는 방식에 따라 인정된다.

Parties serving as the meeting of the Parties to this Agreement at its first session.

4. Parties recognize that the current need for adaptation is significant and that greater levels of mitigation can reduce the need for additional adaptation efforts, and that greater adaptation needs can involve greater adaptation costs.

5. Parties acknowledge that adaptation action should follow a country-driven, gender-responsive, participatory and fully transparent approach, taking into consideration vulnerable groups, communities and ecosystems, and should be based on and guided by the best available science and, as appropriate, traditional knowledge, knowledge of indigenous peoples and local knowledge systems, with a view to integrating adaptation into relevant socio-economic and environmental policies and actions, where appropriate.

6. Parties recognize the importance of support for and international cooperation on adaptation efforts and the importance of taking into account the needs of developing country Parties, especially those that are particularly vulnerable to the adverse effects of climate change.

7. Parties should strengthen their cooperation on enhancing action on adaptation, taking into account the Cancun Adaptation Framework, including with

4. 당사자는 현재 적응에 대한 필요성이 상당하고, 더 높은 수준의 완화가 추가적인 적응 노력의 필요성을 줄일 수 있으며, 적응 필요성이 더 클수록 더 많은 적응 비용이 수반될 수 있다는 점을 인식한다.

5. 당사자는, 적절한 경우 적응을 관련 사회경제적 및 환경적 정책과 행동에 통합하기 위하여, 취약계층, 지역공동체 및 생태계를 고려하면서 적응 행동이 국가 주도적이고 성 인지적이며 참여적이고 전적으로 투명한 접근을 따라야 한다는 점과, 이용 가능한 최선의 과학, 그리고 적절히 전통 지식, 원주민 지식 및 지역 지식체계에 기반을 두고 따라야 한다는 점을 확인한다.

6. 당사자는 적응 노력에 대한 지원과 국제협력의 중요성을 인식하고, 개발도상국 당사자, 특히 기후변화의 부정적 영향에 특별히 취약한 국가의 요구를 고려하는 것의 중요성을 인식한다.

7. 당사자는 다음에 관한 것을 포함하여 「칸쿤 적응 프레임워크」를 고려하면서 적응 행동 강화를 위한 협력을 증진하여야 한다.

regard to:

(a) Sharing information, good practices, experiences and lessons learned, including, as appropriate, as these relate to science, planning, policies and implementation in relation to adaptation actions;

(b) Strengthening institutional arrangements, including those under the Convention that serve this Agreement, to support the synthesis of relevant information and knowledge, and the provision of technical support and guidance to Parties;

(c) Strengthening scientific knowledge on climate, including research, systematic observation of the climate system and early warning systems, in a manner that informs climate services and supports decision—making;

(d) Assisting developing country Parties in identifying effective adaptation practices, adaptation needs, priorities, support provided and received for adaptation actions and efforts, and challenges and gaps, in a manner consistent with encouraging good practices; and

(e) Improving the effectiveness and durability of adaptation actions.

8. United Nations specialized organizations and agencies are encouraged to support the efforts of Parties to implement the actions referred to in paragraph 7 of this Article, taking into account the provisions of paragraph 5 of this Article.

가. 적응 행동과 관련 있는 과학, 계획, 정책 및 이행에 관한 것을 적절히 포함하여, 정보, 모범관행, 경험 및 교훈의 공유

나. 관련 정보와 지식의 취합 및 당사자에 대한 기술적 지원 및 지침의 제공을 지원하기 위하여, 이 협정을 지원하는 협약상의 것을 포함한 제도적 장치의 강화

다. 기후 서비스에 정보를 제공하고 의사결정을 지원하는 방식으로, 연구, 기후체계에 관한 체계적 관측, 조기경보시스템 등을 포함하여 기후에 관한 과학적 지식의 강화

라. 개발도상국 당사자가 효과적인 적응 관행, 적응 요구, 우선순위, 적응 행동과 노력을 위하여 제공하고 제공받은 지원, 문제점과 격차를 파악할 수 있도록, 모범관행 장려에 부합하는 방식으로의 지원, 그리고

마. 적응 행동의 효과성 및 지속성 향상

8. 국제연합 전문기구 및 기관들은 이 조 제5항을 고려하면서 이 조 제7항에서 언급된 행동을 이행하기 위한 당사자의 노력을 지원하도록 장려된다.

9. Each Party shall, as appropriate, engage in adaptation planning processes and the implementation of actions, including the development or enhancement of relevant plans, policies and/or contributions, which may include:

(a) The implementation of adaptation actions, undertakings and/or efforts;

(b) The process to formulate and implement national adaptation plans;

(c) The assessment of climate change impacts and vulnerability, with a view to formulating nationally determined prioritized actions, taking into account vulnerable people, places and ecosystems;

(d) Monitoring and evaluating and learning from adaptation plans, policies, programmes and actions; and

(e) Building the resilience of socioeconomic and ecological systems, including through economic diversification and sustainable management of natural resources.

10. Each Party should, as appropriate, submit and update periodically an adaptation communication, which may include its priorities, implementation and support needs, plans and actions, without creating any additional burden for developing country Parties.

11. The adaptation communication referred to in paragraph 10 of this Article shall be, as appropriate, submitted and updated periodically, as a component of or in conjunction with other

9. 각 당사자는, 관련 계획, 정책 그리고/또는 기여의 개발 또는 강화를 포함하는 적응계획 과정과 행동의 이행에 적절히 참여하며, 이는 다음을 포함할 수 있다.

가. 적응 행동, 조치, 그리고/또는 노력의 이행

나. 국가별 적응계획을 수립하고 이행하는 절차

다. 취약인구, 지역 및 생태계를 고려하면서, 국가별로 결정된 우선 행동을 정하기 위하여 기후변화 영향과 취약성 평가

라. 적응 계획, 정책, 프로그램 및 행동에 대한 모니터링, 평가 및 그로부터의 학습, 그리고

마. 경제 다변화와 천연자원의 지속가능한 관리 등의 방식을 통하여 사회경제적 그리고 생태계의 회복력 구축

10. 각 당사자는 개발도상국 당사자에게 어떤 추가적 부담도 발생시키지 아니하면서 적절히 적응 보고서를 정기적으로 제출하고 갱신하여야 하며, 이 보고서는 당사자의 우선순위, 이행 및 지원 필요성, 계획 및 행동을 포함할 수 있다.

11. 이 조 제10항에 언급된 적응 보고서는 국가별 적응계획, 제4조제2항에 언급된 국가결정기여, 그리고/또는 국가별보고서를 포함하여 그 밖의 보고서나 문서의 일부로서 또는 이와 함께 정기적으로 적

communications or documents, including a national adaptation plan, a nationally determined contribution as referred to in Article 4, paragraph 2, and/or a national communication.

12. The adaptation communications referred to in paragraph 10 of this Article shall be recorded in a public registry maintained by the secretariat.

13. Continuous and enhanced international support shall be provided to developing country Parties for the implementation of paragraphs 7, 9, 10 and 11 of this Article, in accordance with the provisions of Articles 9, 10 and 11.

14. The global stocktake referred to in Article 14 shall, inter alia:

(a) Recognize adaptation efforts of developing country Parties;
(b) Enhance the implementation of adaptation action taking into account the adaptation communication referred to in paragraph 10 of this Article;
(c) Review the adequacy and effectiveness of adaptation and support provided for adaptation; and
(d) Review the overall progress made in achieving the global goal on adaptation referred to in paragraph 1 of this Article.

Article 8

1. Parties recognize the importance of averting, minimizing and addressing

절히 제출되고 갱신된다.

12. 이 조 제10항에 언급된 적응 보고서는 사무국이 유지하는 공공 등록부에 기록된다.

13. 제9조, 제10조 및 제11조의 규정에 따라 이 조 제7항, 제9항, 제10항 및 제11항을 이행하기 위하여 지속적이고 강화된 국제적 지원이 개발도상국 당사자에게 제공된다.

14. 제14조에 언급된 전지구적 이행점검은 특히 다음의 역할을 한다.

가. 개발도상국 당사자의 적응 노력 인정

나. 이 조 제10항에 언급된 적응보고서를 고려하며 적응 행동의 이행 강화

다. 적응과 적응을 위하여 제공되는 지원의 적절성과 효과성 검토, 그리고

라. 이 조 제1항에 언급된 전지구적 적응목표를 달성하면서 나타난 전반적인 진전 검토

제8조

1. 당사자는 기상이변과 서서히 발생하는 현상을 포함한 기후변화의 부정적 영향과

loss and damage associated with the adverse effects of climate change, including extreme weather events and slow onset events, and the role of sustainable development in reducing the risk of loss and damage.

2. The Warsaw International Mechanism for Loss and Damage associated with Climate Change Impacts shall be subject to the authority and guidance of the Conference of the Parties serving as the meeting of the Parties to this Agreement and may be enhanced and strengthened, as determined by the Conference of the Parties serving as the meeting of the Parties to this Agreement.

3. Parties should enhance understanding, action and support, including through the Warsaw International Mechanism, as appropriate, on a cooperative and facilitative basis with respect to loss and damage associated with the adverse effects of climate change.

4. Accordingly, areas of cooperation and facilitation to enhance understanding, action and support may include:

(a) Early warning systems;
(b) Emergency preparedness;
(c) Slow onset events;
(d) Events that may involve irreversible and permanent loss and damage;
(e) Comprehensive risk assessment and management;
(f) Risk insurance facilities, climate risk

관련된 손실 및 피해를 방지하고, 최소화하며, 해결해 나가는 것의 중요성과, 그 손실과 피해의 위험을 줄이기 위한 지속가능한 발전의 역할을 인식한다.

2. 기후변화의 영향과 관련된 손실 및 피해에 관한 바르샤바 국제 메커니즘은 이 협정의 당사자회의 역할을 하는 당사자총회의 권한 및 지침을 따르며, 이 협정의 당사자회의 역할을 하는 당사자총회가 결정하는 바에 따라 증진되고 강화될 수 있다.

3. 당사자는 협력과 촉진을 기반으로, 적절한 경우 바르샤바 국제 메커니즘 등을 통하여 기후변화의 부정적 영향과 관련된 손실 및 피해에 관한 이해, 행동 및 지원을 강화하여야 한다.

4. 이에 따라, 이해, 행동 및 지원을 강화하기 위한 협력과 촉진 분야는 다음을 포함할 수 있다.

가. 조기경보시스템
나. 비상준비태세
다. 서서히 발생하는 현상
라. 돌이킬 수 없고 영구적인 손실과 피해를 수반할 수 있는 현상
마. 종합적 위험 평가 및 관리

바. 위험 보험 제도, 기후 위험 분산 그리고

pooling and other insurance solutions;

(g) Non-economic losses; and

(h) Resilience of communities, livelihoods and ecosystems.

5. The Warsaw International Mechanism shall collaborate with existing bodies and expert groups under the Agreement, as well as relevant organizations and expert bodies outside the Agreement.

Article 9

1. Developed country Parties shall provide financial resources to assist developing country Parties with respect to both mitigation and adaptation in continuation of their existing obligations under the Convention.

2. Other Parties are encouraged to provide or continue to provide such support voluntarily.

3. As part of a global effort, developed country Parties should continue to take the lead in mobilizing climate finance from a wide variety of sources, instruments and channels, noting the significant role of public funds, through a variety of actions, including supporting country-driven strategies, and taking into account the needs and priorities of developing country Parties. Such mobilization of climate finance should represent a progression beyond previous efforts.

4. The provision of scaled-up financial

그 밖의 보험 해결책

사. 비경제적 손실, 그리고

아. 공동체, 생계 및 생태계의 회복력

5. 바르샤바 국제 메커니즘은 이 협정상의 기존 기구 및 전문가그룹, 그리고 이 협정 밖에 있는 관련 기구 및 전문가 단체와 협력한다.

제9조

1. 선진국 당사자는 협약상의 자신의 기존 의무의 연속선상에서 완화 및 적응 모두와 관련하여 개발도상국 당사자를 지원하기 위하여 재원을 제공한다.

2. 그 밖의 당사자는 자발적으로 그러한 지원을 제공하거나 제공을 지속하도록 장려된다.

3. 전지구적 노력의 일환으로, 선진국 당사자는 다양한 행동을 통하여 국가 주도적 전략 지원을 포함한 공적 재원의 중요한 역할에 주목하고 개발도상국 당사자의 요구와 우선순위를 고려하면서, 다양한 재원, 기제 및 경로를 통하여 기후재원을 조성하는 데 주도적 역할을 지속하여야 한다. 그러한 기후재원 조성은 이전보다 진전되는 노력을 보여주어야 한다.

4. 확대된 재원의 제공은 적응을 위한 공적

resources should aim to achieve a balance between adaptation and mitigation, taking into account country-driven strategies, and the priorities and needs of developing country Parties, especially those that are particularly vulnerable to the adverse effects of climate change and have significant capacity constraints, such as the least developed countries and small island developing States, considering the need for public and grant-based resources for adaptation.

5. Developed country Parties shall biennially communicate indicative quantitative and qualitative information related to paragraphs 1 and 3 of this Article, as applicable, including, as available, projected levels of public financial resources to be provided to developing country Parties. Other Parties providing resources are encouraged to communicate biennially such information on a voluntary basis.

6. The global stocktake referred to in Article 14 shall take into account the relevant information provided by developed country Parties and/or Agreement bodies on efforts related to climate finance.

7. Developed country Parties shall provide transparent and consistent information on support for developing country Parties provided and mobilized through public interventions biennially in accordance with the modalities, procedu-

증여기반 재원의 필요성을 고려하고, 국가 주도적 전략과 개발도상국, 특히, 최빈개도국, 소도서 개발도상국과 같이 기후변화의 부정적 영향에 특별히 취약하고 그 역량상 상당한 제약이 있는 개발도상국 당사자의 우선순위와 요구를 감안하면서 완화와 적응 간 균형 달성을 목표로 하여야 한다.

5. 선진국 당사자는 가능하다면 개발도상국 당사자에게 제공될 공적 재원의 예상 수준을 포함하여, 이 조 제1항 및 제3항과 관련된 예시적인 성격의 정성적·정량적 정보를 적용 가능한 범위에서 2년마다 통보한다. 재원을 제공하는 그 밖의 당사자는 그러한 정보를 자발적으로 2년마다 통보하도록 장려된다.

6. 제14조에 언급된 전지구적 이행점검은 기후재원 관련 노력에 관하여 선진국 당사자 그리고/또는 협정상의 기구가 제공하는 관련 정보를 고려한다.

7. 선진국 당사자는, 제13조제13항에 명시된 바와 같이 이 협정의 당사자회의 역할을 하는 당사자총회 제1차 회기에서 채택되는 방식, 절차 및 지침에 따라, 공적 개입을 통하여 제공 및 조성된 개발도상국 당

res and guidelines to be adopted by the Conference of the Parties serving as the meeting of the Parties to this Agreement, at its first session, as stipulated in Article 13, paragraph 13. Other Parties are encouraged to do so.

8. The Financial Mechanism of the Convention, including its operating entities, shall serve as the financial mechanism of this Agreement.

9. The institutions serving this Agreement, including the operating entities of the Financial Mechanism of the Convention, shall aim to ensure efficient access to financial resources through simplified approval procedures and enhanced readiness support for developing country Parties, in particular for the least developed countries and small island developing States, in the context of their national climate strategies and plans.

Article 10

1. Parties share a long-term vision on the importance of fully realizing technology development and transfer in order to improve resilience to climate change and to reduce greenhouse gas emissions.

2. Parties, noting the importance of technology for the implementation of mitigation and adaptation actions under this Agreement and recognizing existing technology deployment and dissemination efforts, shall strengthen coopera-

---

사자에 대한 지원에 관하여 투명하고 일관된 정보를 2년마다 제공한다. 그 밖의 당사자는 그와 같이 하도록 장려된다.

8. 운영 실체를 포함한 협약의 재정메커니즘은 이 협정의 재정메커니즘의 역할을 한다.

9. 협약의 재정메커니즘의 운영 실체를 포함하여 이 협정을 지원하는 기관은, 국가별 기후 전략과 계획의 맥락에서, 개발도상국 당사자, 특히 최빈개도국 및 소도서 개발도상국이 간소한 승인 절차 및 향상된 준비수준 지원을 통하여 재원에 효율적으로 접근하도록 보장하는 것을 목표로 한다.

제 10 조

1. 당사자는 기후변화에 대한 회복력을 개선하고 온실가스 배출을 감축하기 위하여 기술 개발 및 이전을 완전히 실현하는 것의 중요성에 대한 장기적 전망을 공유한다.

2. 당사자는, 이 협정상의 완화 및 적응 행동의 이행을 위한 기술의 중요성에 주목하고 기존의 효율적 기술 사용 및 확산 노력을 인식하면서, 기술의 개발 및 이전을 위한 협력적 행동을 강화한다.

tive action on technology development and transfer.

3. The Technology Mechanism established under the Convention shall serve this Agreement.

4. A technology framework is hereby established to provide overarching guidance to the work of the Technology Mechanism in promoting and facilitating enhanced action on technology development and transfer in order to support the implementation of this Agreement, in pursuit of the long-term vision referred to in paragraph 1 of this Article.

5. Accelerating, encouraging and enabling innovation is critical for an effective, long-term global response to climate change and promoting economic growth and sustainable development. Such effort shall be, as appropriate, supported, including by the Technology Mechanism and, through financial means, by the Financial Mechanism of the Convention, for collaborative approaches to research and development, and facilitating access to technology, in particular for early stages of the technology cycle, to developing country Parties.

6. Support, including financial support, shall be provided to developing country Parties for the implementation of this Article, including for strengthening cooperative action on technology development and transfer at different stages of the technology cycle, with a

3. 협약에 따라 설립된 기술메커니즘은 이 협정을 지원한다.

4. 이 조 제1항에 언급된 장기적 전망을 추구하면서, 이 협정의 이행을 지원하기 위하여 기술 개발 및 이전 행동 강화를 촉진하고 증진하는 데 기술메커니즘의 작업에 포괄적인 지침을 제공하도록 기술에 관한 프레임워크를 설립한다.

5. 혁신을 가속화하고 장려하고 가능하게 하는 것은 기후변화에 대한 효과적이고 장기적인 전지구적 대응과 경제 성장 및 지속가능한 발전을 촉진하는 데 매우 중요하다. 그러한 노력은, 연구개발에 대한 협업적 접근을 위하여 그리고 특히 기술 주기의 초기 단계에 개발도상국 당사자가 기술에 쉽게 접근할 수 있도록 하기 위하여, 기술메커니즘 등에 의하여, 그리고 재정적 수단을 통하여 협약의 재정메커니즘 등에 의하여 적절히 지원된다.

6. 이 조의 이행을 위하여 재정적 지원 등의 지원이 개발도상국 당사자에게 제공되며, 이에는 완화와 적응을 위한 지원 간의 균형을 이루기 위하여, 상이한 기술 주기 단계에서의 기술 개발 및 이전에 관한 협력 행동을 강화하기 위한 지원이 포함된다.

view to achieving a balance between support for mitigation and adaptation. The global stocktake referred to in Article 14 shall take into account available information on efforts related to support on technology development and transfer for developing country Parties.

제14조에 언급된 전지구적 이행점검은 개발도상국 당사자를 위한 기술 개발 및 이전 지원 관련 노력에 대한 이용 가능한 정보를 고려한다.

Article 11

1. Capacity-building under this Agreement should enhance the capacity and ability of developing country Parties, in particular countries with the least capacity, such as the least developed countries, and those that are particularly vulnerable to the adverse effects of climate change, such as small island developing States, to take effective climate change action, including, inter alia, to implement adaptation and mitigation actions, and should facilitate technology development, dissemination and deployment, access to climate finance, relevant aspects of education, training and public awareness, and the transparent, timely and accurate communication of information.

2. Capacity-building should be country-driven, based on and responsive to national needs, and foster country ownership of Parties, in particular, for developing country Parties, including at the national, subnational and local levels. Capacity-building should be guided by lessons learned, including those from capacity-building activ-

제11조

1. 이 협정에 따른 역량배양은, 특히 적응 및 완화 행동의 이행을 포함한 효과적인 기후변화 행동을 위하여 최빈개도국과 같은 역량이 가장 부족한 개발도상국 및 소도서 개발도상국과 같은 기후변화의 부정적 효과에 특별히 취약한 개발도상국 당사자의 역량과 능력을 강화하여야 하고, 기술의 개발·확산 및 효과적 사용, 기후재원에 대한 접근, 교육·훈련 및 공중의 인식과 관련된 측면, 그리고 투명하고 시의적절하며 정확한 정보의 소통을 원활하게 하여야 한다.

2. 역량배양은 국가별 필요를 기반으로 반응하는 국가 주도적인 것이어야 하고, 국가적, 지방적 그리고 현지적 차원을 포함하여 당사자, 특히 개발도상국 당사자의 국가 주인의식을 조성하여야 한다. 역량배양은 협약상의 역량배양 활동을 통한 교훈을 포함하여 습득한 교훈을 따라야 하고, 참여적이고 종합적이며 성 인지적인

ities under the Convention, and should be an effective, iterative process that is participatory, cross—cutting and gender—responsive.

3. All Parties should cooperate to enhance the capacity of developing country Parties to implement this Agreement. Developed country Parties should enhance support for capacity—building actions in developing country Parties.

4. All Parties enhancing the capacity of developing country Parties to implement this Agreement, including through regional, bilateral and multilateral approaches, shall regularly communicate on these actions or measures on capacity—building. Developing country Parties should regularly communicate progress made on implementing capacity—building plans, policies, actions or measures to implement this Agreement.

5. Capacity—building activities shall be enhanced through appropriate institutional arrangements to support the implementation of this Agreement, including the appropriate institutional arrangements established under the Convention that serve this Agreement. The Conference of the Parties serving as the meeting of the Parties to this Agreement shall, at its first session, consider and adopt a decision on the initial institutional arrangements for capacity—building.

효과적·반복적 과정이 되어야 한다.

3. 모든 당사자는 이 협정을 이행하는 개발도상국 당사자의 역량을 강화하기 위하여 협력하여야 한다. 선진국 당사자는 개발도상국에서의 역량배양 행동에 대한 지원을 강화하여야 한다.

4. 지역적·양자적 및 다자적 접근 등의 수단을 통하여 이 협정의 이행을 위한 개발도상국 당사자의 역량을 강화하는 모든 당사자는, 역량배양을 위한 그러한 행동이나 조치에 대하여 정기적으로 통보한다. 개발도상국 당사자는 이 협정의 이행을 위한 역량배양 계획, 정책, 행동이나 조치를 이행하면서 얻은 진전을 정기적으로 통보하여야 한다.

5. 역량배양 활동은, 협약에 따라 설립되어 이 협정을 지원하는 적절한 제도적 장치 등 이 협정의 이행을 지원하기 위한 적절한 제도적 장치를 통하여 강화된다. 이 협정의 당사자회의 역할을 하는 당사자총회는 제1차 회기에서 역량배양을 위한 최초의 제도적 장치에 관한 결정을 고려하고 채택한다.

Article 12

Parties shall cooperate in taking measures, as appropriate, to enhance climate change education, training, public awareness, public participation and public access to information, recognizing the importance of these steps with respect to enhancing actions under this Agreement.

Article 13

1. In order to build mutual trust and confidence and to promote effective implementation, an enhanced transparency framework for action and support, with built-in flexibility which takes into account Parties' different capacities and builds upon collective experience is hereby established.

2. The transparency framework shall provide flexibility in the implementation of the provisions of this Article to those developing country Parties that need it in the light of their capacities. The modalities, procedures and guidelines referred to in paragraph 13 of this Article shall reflect such flexibility.

3. The transparency framework shall build on and enhance the transparency arrangements under the Convention, recognizing the special circumstances of the least developed countries and small island developing States, and be implemented in a facilitative, non-intrusive, non-punitive manner, respectful of national sovereignty, and avoid plac-

제12조

당사자는 이 협정상에서의 행동 강화와 관련하여 기후변화 교육, 훈련, 공중의 인식, 공중의 참여 그리고 정보에 대한 공중의 접근을 강화하기 위한 적절한 조치의 중요성을 인식하면서, 이러한 조치를 할 때 서로 협력한다.

제13조

1. 상호 신뢰와 확신을 구축하고 효과적 이행을 촉진하기 위하여, 당사자의 상이한 역량을 고려하고 공동의 경험에서 비롯된 유연성을 내재하고 있는, 행동 및 지원을 위하여 강화된 투명성 프레임워크를 설립한다.

2. 투명성 프레임워크는 각자의 역량에 비추어 유연성이 필요한 개발도상국 당사자가 이 조의 규정을 이행하는 데 유연성을 제공한다. 이 조 제13항에 언급된 방식, 절차 및 지침은 그러한 유연성을 반영한다.

3. 투명성 프레임워크는 최빈개도국과 소도서 개발도상국의 특수한 여건을 인식하면서 협약상의 투명성 장치를 기반으로 이를 강화하고, 국가주권을 존중하면서 촉진적·비침해적·비징벌적 방식으로 이행되며, 당사자에게 지나친 부담을 지우지 아니한다.

ing undue burden on Parties.

4. The transparency arrangements under the Convention, including national communications, biennial reports and biennial update reports, international assessment and review and international consultation and analysis, shall form part of the experience drawn upon for the development of the modalities, procedures and guidelines under paragraph 13 of this Article.

5. The purpose of the framework for transparency of action is to provide a clear understanding of climate change action in the light of the objective of the Convention as set out in its Article 2, including clarity and tracking of progress towards achieving Parties' individual nationally determined contributions under Article 4, and Parties' adaptation actions under Article 7, including good practices, priorities, needs and gaps, to inform the global stocktake under Article 14.

6. The purpose of the framework for transparency of support is to provide clarity on support provided and received by relevant individual Parties in the context of climate change actions under Articles 4, 7, 9, 10 and 11, and, to the extent possible, to provide a full overview of aggregate financial support provided, to inform the global stocktake under Article 14.

7. Each Party shall regularly provide the

4. 국가별보고서, 격년보고서, 격년갱신보고서, 국제 평가 및 검토, 그리고 국제 협의 및 분석을 포함하는 협약상의 투명성 장치는 이 조 제13항에 따른 방식, 절차 및 지침을 개발하기 위하여 얻은 경험의 일부를 구성한다.

5. 행동의 투명성을 위한 프레임워크의 목적은, 제14조에 따른 전지구적 이행점검에 알려주기 위하여, 제4조에 따른 당사자의 국가결정기여와 모범관행·우선순위·필요·격차 등 제7조에 따른 당사자들의 적응 행동을 완수하도록 명확성 및 그 진전을 추적하는 것을 포함하여, 협약 제2조에 설정된 목적에 비추어 기후변화 행동에 대한 명확한 이해를 제공하는 것이다.

6. 지원의 투명성을 위한 프레임워크의 목적은, 제14조에 따른 전지구적 이행점검에 알려주기 위하여, 제4조, 제7조, 제9조, 제10조 및 제11조에 따른 기후변화 행동의 맥락에서 관련 개별 당사자가 제공하고 제공받은 지원과 관련하여 명확성을 제공하고, 제공된 총 재정지원의 전체적인 개관을 가능한 수준까지 제공하는 것이다.

7. 각 당사자는 다음의 정보를 정기적으로

following information:

(a) A national inventory report of anthropogenic emissions by sources and removals by sinks of greenhouse gases, prepared using good practice methodologies accepted by the Intergovernmental Panel on Climate Change and agreed upon by the Conference of the Parties serving as the meeting of the Parties to this Agreement; and

(b) Information necessary to track progress made in implementing and achieving its nationally determined contribution under Article 4.

8. Each Party should also provide information related to climate change impacts and adaptation under Article 7, as appropriate.

9. Developed country Parties shall, and other Parties that provide support should, provide information on financial, technology transfer and capacity-building support provided to developing country Parties under Articles 9, 10 and 11.

10. Developing country Parties should provide information on financial, technology transfer and capacitybuilding support needed and received under Articles 9, 10 and 11.

11. Information submitted by each Party under paragraphs 7 and 9 of this Article shall undergo a technical ex-

---

제공한다.

가. 기후변화에 관한 정부 간 패널에서 수락되고 이 협정의 당사자회의 역할을 하는 당사자총회에서 합의된 모범관행 방법론을 사용하여 작성된 온실가스의 배출원에 의한 인위적 배출과 흡수원에 의한 제거에 관한 국가별 통계 보고서, 그리고

나. 제4조에 따른 국가결정기여를 이행하고 달성하는 데에서의 진전 추적에 필요한 정보

8. 각 당사자는 또한 제7조에 따라 기후변화의 영향과 적응에 관련된 정보를 적절히 제공하여야 한다.

9. 선진국 당사자는 제9조, 제10조 및 제11조에 따라 개발도상국 당사자에게 제공된 재정지원, 기술 이전 지원 및 역량배양 지원에 관한 정보를 제공하고, 지원을 제공하는 그 밖의 당사자는 이러한 정보를 제공하여야 한다.

10. 개발도상국 당사자는 제9조, 제10조 및 제11조에 따라 필요로 하고 제공받은 재정지원, 기술 이전 지원 및 역량배양 지원에 관한 정보를 제공하여야 한다.

11. 이 조 제7항과 제9항에 따라 각 당사자가 제출한 정보는 결정 1/CP.21에 따라 기술 전문가의 검토를 받는다. 개발도상

pert review, in accordance with deci-sion 1/CP.21. For those developing country Parties that need it in the light of their capacities, the review process shall include assistance in identifying capacity-building needs. In addition, each Party shall partic-ipate in a facilitative, multilateral con-sideration of progress with respect to efforts under Article 9, and its re-spective implementation and achieve-ment of its nationally determined con-tribution.

국 당사자의 역량에 비추어 필요한 경우 역량배양 필요를 파악하기 위한 지원을 검토 절차에 포함한다. 또한 각 당사자는 제9조에 따른 노력과 관련하여 그리고 국가결정기여에 대한 당사자 각자의 이행 및 달성과 관련하여 그 진전에 대한 촉진적·다자적 고려에 참여한다.

12. The technical expert review under this paragraph shall consist of a con-sideration of the Party's support provided, as relevant, and its imple-mentation and achievement of its na-tionally determined contribution. The review shall also identify areas of improvement for the Party, and in-clude a review of the consistency of the information with the modalities, procedures and guidelines referred to in paragraph 13 of this Article, taking into account the flexibility accorded to the Party under paragraph 2 of this Article. The review shall pay partic-ular attention to the respective natio-nal capabilities and circumstances of developing country Parties.

12. 이 항에 따른 기술 전문가의 검토는, 관련이 있을 경우 당사자가 제공한 지원에 대한 고려와, 국가결정기여의 이행 및 달성에 대한 고려로 구성된다. 또한 검토는 당사자를 위한 개선 분야를 파악하고, 이 조 제2항에 따라 당사자에 부여된 유연성을 고려하여 이 조 제13항에 언급된 방식·절차 및 지침과 제출된 정보 간 일관성에 대한 검토를 포함한다. 검토는 개발도상국 당사자 각자의 국가적 능력과 여건에 특별한 주의를 기울인다.

13. The Conference of the Parties serving as the meeting of the Parties to this Agreement shall, at its first session, building on experience from the ar-rangements related to transparency under the Convention, and elaborating

13. 이 협정의 당사자회의 역할을 하는 당사자총회는 제1차 회기에서 협약상의 투명성과 관련된 장치로부터 얻은 경험을 기반으로 이 조의 규정을 구체화하여, 행동과 지원의 투명성을 위한 공통의 방식, 절차 및 지침을 적절히 채택한다.

on the provisions in this Article, adopt common modalities, procedures and guidelines, as appropriate, for the transparency of action and support.

14. Support shall be provided to developing countries for the implementation of this Article.

15. Support shall also be provided for the building of transparency-related capacity of developing country Parties on a continuous basis.

Article 14

1. The Conference of the Parties serving as the meeting of the Parties to this Agreement shall periodically take stock of the implementation of this Agreement to assess the collective progress towards achieving the purpose of this Agreement and its long-term goals (referred to as the "global stocktake"). It shall do so in a comprehensive and facilitative manner, considering mitigation, adaptation and the means of implementation and support, and in the light of equity and the best available science.

2. The Conference of the Parties serving as the meeting of the Parties to this Agreement shall undertake its first global stocktake in 2023 and every five years thereafter unless otherwise decided by the Conference of the Parties serving as the meeting of the Parties to this Agreement.

14. 이 조의 이행을 위하여 개발도상국에 지원이 제공된다.

15. 또한 개발도상국 당사자의 투명성 관련 역량배양을 위하여 지속적인 지원이 제공된다.

제 14 조

1. 이 협정의 당사자회의 역할을 하는 당사자총회는 이 협정의 목적과 그 장기적 목표의 달성을 위한 공동의 진전을 평가하기 위하여 이 협정의 이행을 정기적으로 점검(이하 "전지구적 이행점검"이라 한다) 한다. 이는 완화, 적응 및 이행 수단과 지원 수단을 고려하면서, 형평과 이용 가능한 최선의 과학에 비추어 포괄적이고 촉진적인 방식으로 행하여진다.

2. 이 협정의 당사자회의 역할을 하는 당사자총회는 이 협정의 당사자회의 역할을 하는 당사자총회에서 달리 결정하는 경우가 아니면 2023년에 첫 번째 전지구적 이행점검을 실시하고 그 후 5년마다 이를 실시한다.

3. The outcome of the global stocktake shall inform Parties in updating and enhancing, in a nationally determined manner, their actions and support in accordance with the relevant provisions of this Agreement, as well as in enhancing international cooperation for climate action.

Article 15

1. A mechanism to facilitate implementation of and promote compliance with the provisions of this Agreement is hereby established.

2. The mechanism referred to in paragraph 1 of this Article shall consist of a committee that shall be expert-based and facilitative in nature and function in a manner that is transparent, non-adversarial and non-punitive. The committee shall pay particular attention to the respective national capabilities and circumstances of Parties.

3. The committee shall operate under the modalities and procedures adopted by the Conference of the Parties serving as the meeting of the Parties to this Agreement at its first session and report annually to the Conference of the Parties serving as the meeting of the Parties to this Agreement.

Article 16

1. The Conference of the Parties, the supreme body of the Convention, shall

---

3. 전지구적 이행점검의 결과는, 이 협정의 관련 규정에 따라 당사자가 국내적으로 결정한 방식으로 행동과 지원을 갱신하고 강화하도록 또한 기후 행동을 위한 국제 협력을 강화하도록 당사자에게 알려준다.

제 15 조

1. 이 협정 규정의 이행을 원활하게 하고 그 준수를 촉진하기 위한 메커니즘을 설립한다.

2. 이 조 제1항에 언급된 메커니즘은 전문가를 기반으로 한 촉진적 성격의 위원회로 구성되고, 이 위원회는 투명하고 비대립적이며 비징벌적인 방식으로 기능한다. 위원회는 당사자 각자의 국가적 능력과 여건에 특별한 주의를 기울인다.

3. 위원회는 이 협정의 당사자회의 역할을 하는 당사자총회 제1차 회기에서 채택되는 방식 및 절차에 따라 운영되며, 매년 이 협정의 당사자회의 역할을 하는 당사자총회에 보고한다.

제 16 조

1. 협약의 최고기구인 당사자총회는 이 협정의 당사자회의 역할을 한다.

serve as the meeting of the Parties to this Agreement.

2. Parties to the Convention that are not Parties to this Agreement may participate as observers in the proceedings of any session of the Conference of the Parties serving as the meeting of the Parties to this Agreement. When the Conference of the Parties serves as the meeting of the Parties to this Agreement, decisions under this Agreement shall be taken only by those that are Parties to this Agreement.

3. When the Conference of the Parties serves as the meeting of the Parties to this Agreement, any member of the Bureau of the Conference of the Parties representing a Party to the Convention but, at that time, not a Party to this Agreement, shall be replaced by an additional member to be elected by and from amongst the Parties to this Agreement.

4. The Conference of the Parties serving as the meeting of the Parties to this Agreement shall keep under regular review the implementation of this Agreement and shall make, within its mandate, the decisions necessary to promote its effective implementation. It shall perform the functions assigned to it by this Agreement and shall:

(a) Establish such subsidiary bodies as deemed necessary for the implementation of this Agreement; and

2. 이 협정의 당사자가 아닌 협약의 당사자는 이 협정의 당사자회의 역할을 하는 당사자총회의 모든 회기 절차에 옵서버로 참석할 수 있다. 당사자총회가 이 협정의 당사자회의 역할을 할 때, 이 협정에 따른 결정권은 이 협정의 당사자만이 갖는다.

3. 당사자총회가 이 협정의 당사자회의 역할을 할 때, 당사자총회 의장단의 구성원으로서 해당 시점에 이 협정의 당사자가 아닌 협약의 당사자를 대표하는 자는 이 협정의 당사자들이 그들 중에서 선출한 추가 구성원으로 대체된다.

4. 이 협정의 당사자회의 역할을 하는 당사자총회는 이 협정의 이행상황을 정기적으로 검토하고, 그 권한의 범위에서 이 협정의 효과적 이행의 증진에 필요한 결정을 한다. 이 협정의 당사자회의 역할을 하는 당사자총회는 이 협정에 의하여 부여된 기능을 수행하며 다음을 한다.

가. 이 협정의 이행에 필요하다고 간주되는 보조기구의 설립, 그리고

(b) Exercise such other functions as may be required for the implementation of this Agreement.

5. The rules of procedure of the Conference of the Parties and the financial procedures applied under the Convention shall be applied mutatis mutandis under this Agreement, except as may be otherwise decided by consensus by the Conference of the Parties serving as the meeting of the Parties to this Agreement.

6. The first session of the Conference of the Parties serving as the meeting of the Parties to this Agreement shall be convened by the secretariat in conjunction with the first session of the Conference of the Parties that is scheduled after the date of entry into force of this Agreement. Subsequent ordinary sessions of the Conference of the Parties serving as the meeting of the Parties to this Agreement shall be held in conjunction with ordinary sessions of the Conference of the Parties, unless otherwise decided by the Conference of the Parties serving as the meeting of the Parties to this Agreement.

7. Extraordinary sessions of the Conference of the Parties serving as the meeting of the Parties to this Agreement shall be held at such other times as may be deemed necessary by the Conference of the Parties serving as the meeting of the Parties to this Agreement or at the

나. 이 협정의 이행을 위하여 요구될 수 있는 그 밖의 기능의 수행

5. 이 협정의 당사자회의 역할을 하는 당사자총회가 만장일치로 달리 결정하는 경우를 제외하고는, 당사자총회의 절차규칙 및 협약에 따라 적용되는 재정 절차는 이 협정에 준용된다.

6. 이 협정의 당사자회의 역할을 하는 당사자총회의 제1차 회기는 이 협정의 발효일 후에 예정되어 있는 당사자총회의 제1차 회기와 함께 사무국에 의하여 소집된다. 이 협정의 당사자회의 역할을 하는 당사자총회의 후속 정기회기는, 이 협정의 당사자회의 역할을 하는 당사자총회가 달리 결정하는 경우가 아니면, 당사자총회의 정기회기와 함께 개최된다.

7. 이 협정의 당사자회의 역할을 하는 당사자총회의 특별회기는 이 협정의 당사자회의 역할을 하는 당사자총회에서 필요하다고 간주되는 다른 때에 또는 어느 당사자의 서면요청이 있는 때에 개최된다. 다만, 그러한 서면 요청은 사무국에 의하여 당사자들에게 통보된 후 6개월 이내에 최소

written request of any Party, provided that, within six months of the request being communicated to the Parties by the secretariat, it is supported by at least one third of the Parties.

8. The United Nations and its specialized agencies and the International Atomic Energy Agency, as well as any State member thereof or observers thereto not party to the Convention, may be represented at sessions of the Conference of the Parties serving as the meeting of the Parties to this Agreement as observers. Any body or agency, whether national or international, governmental or non-governmental, which is qualified in matters covered by this Agreement and which has informed the secretariat of its wish to be represented at a session of the Conference of the Parties serving as the meeting of the Parties to this Agreement as an observer, may be so admitted unless at least one third of the Parties present object. The admission and participation of observers shall be subject to the rules of procedure referred to in paragraph 5 of this Article.

Article 17

1. The secretariat established by Article 8 of the Convention shall serve as the secretariat of this Agreement.

2. Article 8, paragraph 2, of the Convention on the functions of the secretariat, and Article 8, paragraph 3, of the Con-

한 당사자 3분의 1의 지지를 받아야 한다.

8. 국제연합, 국제연합 전문기구, 국제원자력기구 및 이들 기구의 회원국이나 옵서버인 협약의 비당사자는 이 협정의 당사자회의 역할을 하는 당사자총회의 회기에 옵서버로 참석할 수 있다. 이 협정이 다루는 문제와 관련하여 자격을 갖추고 이 협정의 당사자회의 역할을 하는 당사자총회의 회기에 옵서버로 참석하고자 하는 의사를 사무국에 통지한 기구나 기관은, 국내적 또는 국제적, 정부 간 또는 비정부 간인지를 불문하고, 출석당사자의 3분의 1 이상이 반대하는 경우가 아니면 참석이 승인될 수 있다. 옵서버의 승인 및 참석은 이 조 제5항에 언급된 절차규칙에 따른다.

제 17 조

1. 협약 제8조에 의하여 설립되는 사무국은 이 협정의 사무국 역할을 한다.

2. 사무국의 기능에 관한 협약 제8조제2항 및 사무국의 기능 수행에 필요한 장치에 관한 협약 제8조제3항은 이 협정에 준용

vention, on the arrangements made for the functioning of the secretariat, shall apply mutatis mutandis to this Agreement. The secretariat shall, in addition, exercise the functions assigned to it under this Agreement and by the Conference of the Parties serving as the meeting of the Parties to this Agreement.

된다. 또한 사무국은 이 협정에 따라 부여된 기능과 이 협정의 당사자회의 역할을 하는 당사자총회에 의하여 부여된 기능을 수행한다.

Article 18

1. The Subsidiary Body for Scientific and Technological Advice and the Subsidiary Body for Implementation established by Articles 9 and 10 of the Convention shall serve, respectively, as the Subsidiary Body for Scientific and Technological Advice and the Subsidiary Body for Implementation of this Agreement. The provisions of the Convention relating to the functioning of these two bodies shall apply *mutatis mutandis* to this Agreement. Sessions of the meetings of the Subsidiary Body for Scientific and Technological Advice and the Subsidiary Body for Implementation of this Agreement shall be held in conjunction with the meetings of, respectively, the Subsidiary Body for Scientific and Technological Advice and the Subsidiary Body for Implementation of the Convention.

2. Parties to the Convention that are not Parties to this Agreement may participate as observers in the proceedings of any session of the subsidiary bodies. When the subsidiary bodies serve as

제 18 조

1. 협약 제9조 및 제10조에 의하여 설립된 과학기술자문 보조기구와 이행보조기구는 각각 이 협정의 과학기술자문 보조기구와 이행보조기구의 역할을 한다. 이들 두 기구의 기능 수행에 관한 협약 규정은 이 협정에 준용된다. 이 협정의 과학기술자문 보조기구와 이행보조기구 회의의 회기는 각각 협약의 과학기술 보조기구 및 이행보조기구의 회의와 함께 개최된다.

2. 이 협정의 당사자가 아닌 협약의 당사자는 그 보조기구의 모든 회기의 절차에 옵서버로 참석할 수 있다. 보조기구가 이 협정의 보조기구의 역할을 할 때, 이 협정에 따른 결정권은 이 협정의 당사자만 가진다.

the subsidiary bodies of this Agreement, decisions under this Agreement
shall be taken only by those that are
Parties to this Agreement.

3. When the subsidiary bodies established
by Articles 9 and 10 of the Convention
exercise their functions with regard to
matters concerning this Agreement, any
member of the bureaux of those subsidiary bodies representing a Party to the
Convention but, at that time, not a
Party to this Agreement, shall be replaced by an additional member to be
elected by and from amongst the
Parties to this Agreement.

3. 협약 제9조 및 제10조에 의하여 설립된
보조기구가 이 협정에 대한 문제와 관련
하여 그 기능을 수행할 때, 보조기구 의
장단의 구성원으로서 해당 시점에 이 협
정의 당사자가 아닌 협약의 당사자를 대
표하는 자는 이 협정의 당사자들이 그들
중에서 선출한 추가 구성원으로 대체된다.

Article 19

1. Subsidiary bodies or other institutional
arrangements established by or under
the Convention, other than those referred to in this Agreement, shall serve
this Agreement upon a decision of the
Conference of the Parties serving as
the meeting of the Parties to this
Agreement. The Conference of the
Parties serving as the meeting of the
Parties to this Agreement shall specify
the functions to be exercised by such
subsidiary bodies or arrangements.

2. The Conference of the Parties serving
as the meeting of the Parties to this
Agreement may provide further guidance to such subsidiary bodies and institutional arrangements.

제 19 조

1. 이 협정에서 언급되지 아니한, 협약에 의
하여 또는 협약에 따라 설립된 보조기구
나 그 밖의 제도적 장치는 이 협정의 당
사자회의 역할을 하는 당사자총회의 결정
에 따라 이 협정을 지원한다. 이 협정의
당사자회의 역할을 하는 당사자총회는 그
러한 보조기구나 장치가 수행할 기능을
명확히 한다.

2. 이 협정의 당사자회의 역할을 하는 당사
자총회는 그러한 보조기구와 제도적 장치
에 추가적인 지침을 제공할 수 있다.

Article 20

1. This Agreement shall be open for signature and subject to ratification, acceptance or approval by States and regional economic integration organizations that are Parties to the Convention. It shall be open for signature at the United Nations Headquarters in New York from 22 April 2016 to 21 April 2017. Thereafter, this Agreement shall be open for accession from the day following the date on which it is closed for signature. Instruments of ratification, acceptance, approval or accession shall be deposited with the Depositary.

2. Any regional economic integration organization that becomes a Party to this Agreement without any of its member States being a Party shall be bound by all the obligations under this Agreement. In the case of regional economic integration organizations with one or more member States that are Parties to this Agreement, the organization and its member States shall decide on their respective responsibilities for the performance of their obligations under this Agreement. In such cases, the organization and the member States shall not be entitled to exercise rights under this Agreement concurrently.

3. In their instruments of ratification, acceptance, approval or accession, regional economic integration organizations shall declare the extent of their competence with respect to the matters

제 20 조

1. 이 협정은 협약의 당사자인 국가와 지역경제통합기구의 서명을 위하여 개방되며, 이들에 의한 비준, 수락 또는 승인을 조건으로 한다. 이 협정은 뉴욕의 국제연합 본부에서 2016년 4월 22일부터 2017년 4월 21일까지 서명을 위하여 개방된다. 그 후 이 협정은 서명기간이 종료한 날의 다음 날부터 가입을 위하여 개방된다. 비준서, 수락서, 승인서 또는 가입서는 수탁자에게 기탁된다.

2. 그 회원국 중 어느 국가도 이 협정의 당사자가 아니면서 이 협정의 당사자가 되는 모든 지역경제통합기구는, 이 협정상의 모든 의무에 구속된다. 하나 또는 둘 이상의 회원국이 이 협정의 당사자인 지역경제통합기구의 경우, 그 기구와 그 회원국은 이 협정상의 의무를 이행하기 위한 각자의 책임에 관하여 결정한다. 그러한 경우, 그 기구와 그 회원국은 이 협정상의 권리를 동시에 행사하지 아니한다.

3. 지역경제통합기구는 그 비준서, 수락서, 승인서 또는 가입서에서 이 협정이 규율하는 문제에 관한 기구의 권한범위를 선언한다. 또한, 이러한 기구는 그 권한범위의 실질적 변동을 수탁자에게 통지하

governed by this Agreement. These organizations shall also inform the Depositary, who shall in turn inform the Parties, of any substantial modification in the extent of their competence.

며, 수탁자는 이를 당사자에게 통지한다.

Article 21

1. This Agreement shall enter into force on the thirtieth day after the date on which at least 55 Parties to the Convention accounting in total for at least an estimated 55 per cent of the total global greenhouse gas emissions have deposited their instruments of ratification, acceptance, approval or accession.

2. Solely for the limited purpose of paragraph 1 of this Article, "total global greenhouse gas emissions" means the most up-to-date amount communicated on or before the date of adoption of this Agreement by the Parties to the Convention.

3. For each State or regional economic integration organization that ratifies, accepts or approves this Agreement or accedes thereto after the conditions set out in paragraph 1 of this Article for entry into force have been fulfilled, this Agreement shall enter into force on the thirtieth day after the date of deposit by such State or regional economic integration organization of its instrument of ratification, acceptance, approval or accession.

제21조

1. 이 협정은 지구 온실가스 총 배출량 중 최소한 55퍼센트를 차지하는 것으로 추정되는 55개 이상의 협약 당사자가 비준서, 수락서, 승인서 또는 가입서를 기탁한 날부터 30일 후에 발효한다.

2. 오직 이 조 제1항의 제한적 목적상, "지구 온실가스 총 배출량"이란 협약의 당사자가 이 협정의 채택일에 또는 그 전에 통보한 가장 최신의 배출량을 말한다.

3. 발효에 관한 이 조 제1항의 조건이 충족된 후 이 협정을 비준, 수락 또는 승인하거나 이에 가입하는 국가 또는 지역경제통합기구의 경우, 이 협정은 그러한 국가 또는 지역경제통합기구의 비준서, 수락서, 승인서 또는 가입서가 기탁된 날부터 30일 후에 발효한다.

4. For the purposes of paragraph 1 of this Article, any instrument deposited by a regional economic integration organization shall not be counted as additional to those deposited by its member States.

Article 22

The provisions of Article 15 of the Convention on the adoption of amendments to the Convention shall apply mutatis mutandis to this Agreement.

Article 23

1. The provisions of Article 16 of the Convention on the adoption and amendment of annexes to the Convention shall apply mutatis mutandis to this Agreement.

2. Annexes to this Agreement shall form an integral part thereof and, unless otherwise expressly provided for, a reference to this Agreement constitutes at the same time a reference to any annexes thereto. Such annexes shall be restricted to lists, forms and any other material of a descriptive nature that is of a scientific, technical, procedural or administrative character.

Article 24

The provisions of Article 14 of the Convention on settlement of disputes shall apply mutatis mutandis to this Agreement.

4. 이 조 제1항의 목적상, 지역경제통합기구가 기탁하는 모든 문서는 그 기구의 회원국이 기탁하는 문서에 추가하여 계산되지 아니한다.

제 22 조

협약의 개정안 채택에 관한 협약 제15조는 이 협정에 준용된다.

제 23 조

1. 협약의 부속서 채택 및 개정에 관한 협약 제16조는 이 협정에 준용된다.

2. 이 협정의 부속서는 이 협정의 불가분의 일부를 구성하며, 명시적으로 달리 규정되는 경우가 아니면, 이 협정을 언급하는 것은 이 협정의 모든 부속서도 언급하는 것으로 본다. 그러한 부속서는 목록, 양식 및 과학적·기술적·절차적 또는 행정적 특성을 갖는 서술적 성격의 그 밖의 자료에 국한된다.

제 24 조

분쟁해결에 관한 협약 제14조는 이 협정에 준용된다.

Article 25

1. Each Party shall have one vote, except as provided for in paragraph 2 of this Article.

2. Regional economic integration organizations, in matters within their competence, shall exercise their right to vote with a number of votes equal to the number of their member States that are Parties to this Agreement. Such an organization shall not exercise its right to vote if any of its member States exercises its right, and vice versa.

Article 26

The Secretary-General of the United Nations shall be the Depositary of this Agreement.

Article 27

No reservations may be made to this Agreement.

Article 28

1. At any time after three years from the date on which this Agreement has entered into force for a Party, that Party may withdraw from this Agreement by giving written notification to the Depositary.

2. Any such withdrawal shall take effect upon expiry of one year from the date of receipt by the Depositary of the no-

제25조

1. 각 당사자는 이 조 제2항에 규정된 경우를 제외하고는 하나의 투표권을 가진다.

2. 지역경제통합기구는 자신의 권한 범위의 문제에서 이 협정의 당사자인 그 기구 회원국의 수와 같은 수만큼의 투표권을 행사한다. 기구 회원국 중 어느 한 국가라도 투표권을 행사하는 경우, 그러한 기구는 투표권을 행사하지 아니하며, 그 반대의 경우에서도 또한 같다.

제26조

국제연합 사무총장은 이 협정의 수탁자가 된다.

제27조

이 협정에 대해서는 어떤 유보도 할 수 없다.

제28조

1. 당사자는 이 협정이 자신에 대하여 발효한 날부터 3년 후에는 언제든지 수탁자에게 서면통고를 하여 이 협정에서 탈퇴할 수 있다.

2. 그러한 탈퇴는 수탁자가 탈퇴통고서를 접수한 날부터 1년이 경과한 날 또는 탈퇴통고서에 그보다 더 나중의 날짜가 명시

tification of withdrawal, or on such later date as may be specified in the notification of withdrawal.

3. Any Party that withdraws from the
Convention shall be considered as also
having withdrawn from this Agreement.

Article 29

The original of this Agreement, of which
the Arabic, Chinese, English, French,
Russian and Spanish texts are equally authentic, shall be deposited with the
Secretary—General of the United Nations.

DONE at Paris this twelfth day of December two thousand and fifteen.

IN WITNESS WHEREOF, the undersigned,
being duly authorized to that effect, have
signed this Agreement.

된 경우에는 그 나중의 날에 효력이 발생
한다.

3. 협약에서 탈퇴한 당사자는 이 협정에서도
탈퇴한 것으로 본다.

제 29 조

아랍어, 중국어, 영어, 프랑스어, 러시아어
및 스페인어본이 동등하게 정본인 이 협정
의 원본은 국제연합 사무총장에게 기탁된다.

2015년 12월 12일에 파리에서 작성되었다.

이상의 증거로, 정당하게 권한을 위임받은
아래의 서명자들이 이 협정에 서명하였다.

COP 주요 결정문

6. 제15차 코펜하겐(2009) — Copenhagen Accord

Report of the Conference of the Parties on its fifteenth session, held in Copenhagen from 7 to 19 December 2009

Decision 2/CP.15
FCCC/CP/2009/11/Add.1
30 March 2010

The Conference of the Parties

Takes note of the Copenhagen Accord of 18 December 2009.

Copenhagen Accord

The Heads of State, Heads of Government, Ministers, and other heads of the following delegations present at the United Nations Climate Change Conference 2009 in Copenhagen:[1]

Albania, Algeria, Armenia, Australia, Austria, Bahamas, Bangladesh, Belarus, Belgium, Benin, Bhutan, Bosnia and Herzegovina, Botswana, Brazil, Bulgaria, Burkina Faso, Cambodia, Canada, Central African Republic, Chile, China, Colombia, Congo, Costa Rica, Côte d'Ivoire, Croatia, Cyprus, Czech Republic, Democratic Republic of the Congo, Denmark, Djibouti, Eritrea, Estonia, Ethiopia, European Union, Fiji, Finland, France, Gabon, Georgia, Germany, Ghana, Greece, Guatemala, Guinea, Guyana, Hungary, Iceland, India, Indonesia, Ireland, Israel, Italy, Japan, Jordan, Kazakhstan, Kiribati, Lao People's Democratic Republic, Latvia, Lesotho, Liechtenstein, Lithuania, Luxembourg, Madagascar, Malawi, Maldives, Mali, Malta, Marshall Islands, Mauritania, Mexico, Monaco, Mongolia, Montenegro, Morocco, Namibia, Nepal, Netherlands, New Zealand, Norway, Palau, Panama, Papua New Guinea, Peru, Poland, Portugal, Republic of Korea, Republic of Moldova, Romania, Russian Federation, Rwanda, Samoa, San Marino, Senegal, Serbia, Sierra Leone, Singapore, Slovakia, Slovenia, South Africa, Spain, Swaziland, Sweden, Switzerland, the former Yugoslav Republic of Macedonia, Tonga,

---

1) Some Parties listed above stated in their communications to the secretariat specific understandings on the nature of the Accord and related matters, based on which they have agreed to be listed here. The full text of the letters received from Parties in relation to the Copenhagen Accord, including the specific understandings, can be found at <http://unfccc.int/meetings/items/5276.php>.

Trinidad and Tobago, Tunisia, United Arab Emirates, United Kingdom of Great Britain and Northern Ireland, United Republic of Tanzania, United States of America, Uruguay and Zambia,

In pursuit of the ultimate objective of the Convention as stated in its Article 2,

Being guided by the principles and provisions of the Convention,

Noting the results of work done by the two Ad hoc Working Groups,

Endorsing decision 1/CP.15 on the Ad hoc Working Group on Long-term Cooperative Action and decision 1/CMP.5 that requests the Ad hoc Working Group on Further Commitments of Annex I Parties under the Kyoto Protocol to continue its work,

Have agreed on this Copenhagen Accord which is operational immediately.

1. We underline that climate change is one of the greatest challenges of our time. We emphasise our strong political will to urgently combat climate change in accordance with the principle of common but differentiated responsibilities and respective capabilities. To achieve the ultimate objective of the Convention to stabilize greenhouse gas concentration in the atmosphere at a level that would prevent dangerous anthropogenic interference with the climate system, we shall, recognizing the scientific view that the increase in global temperature should be below 2 degrees Celsius, on the basis of equity and in the context of sustainable development, enhance our long-term cooperative action to combat climate change. We recognize the critical impacts of climate change and the potential impacts of response measures on countries particularly vulnerable to its adverse effects and stress the need to establish a comprehensive adaptation programme including international support.

2. We agree that deep cuts in global emissions are required according to science, and as documented by the IPCC Fourth Assessment Report with a view to reduce global emissions so as to hold the increase in global temperature below 2 degrees Celsius, and take action to meet this objective consistent with science and on the basis of equity. We should cooperate in achieving the peaking of global and national emissions as soon as possible, recognizing that the time frame for peaking will be longer in developing countries and bearing in mind that social and economic development and poverty eradication are the first and overriding priorities of developing countries and that a low-emission development strategy is indispensable to sustainable development.

3. Adaptation to the adverse effects of climate change and the potential impacts of

response measures is a challenge faced by all countries. Enhanced action and international cooperation on adaptation is urgently required to ensure the implementation of the Convention by enabling and supporting the implementation of adaptation actions aimed at reducing vulnerability and building resilience in developing countries, especially in those that are particularly vulnerable, especially least developed countries, small island developing States and Africa. We agree that developed countries shall provide adequate, predictable and sustainable financial resources, technology and capacity-building to support the implementation of adaptation action in developing countries.

4. Annex I Parties commit to implement individually or jointly the quantified economy-wide emissions targets for 2020, to be submitted in the format given in Appendix I by Annex I Parties to the secretariat by 31 January 2010 for compilation in an INF document. Annex I Parties that are Party to the Kyoto Protocol will thereby further strengthen the emissions reductions initiated by the Kyoto Protocol. Delivery of reductions and financing by developed countries will be measured, reported and verified in accordance with existing and any further guidelines adopted by the Conference of the Parties, and will ensure that accounting of such targets and finance is rigorous, robust and transparent.

5. Non-Annex I Parties to the Convention will implement mitigation actions, including those to be submitted to the secretariat by non-Annex I Parties in the format given in Appendix II by 31 January 2010, for compilation in an INF document, consistent with Article 4.1 and Article 4.7 and in the context of sustainable development. Least developed countries and small island developing States may undertake actions voluntarily and on the basis of support. Mitigation actions subsequently taken and envisaged by Non-Annex I Parties, including national inventory reports, shall be communicated through national communications consistent with Article 12.1(b) every two years on the basis of guidelines to be adopted by the Conference of the Parties. Those mitigation actions in national communications or otherwise communicated to the Secretariat will be added to the list in appendix II. Mitigation actions taken by Non-Annex I Parties will be subject to their domestic measurement, reporting and verification the result of which will be reported through their national communications every two years. Non-Annex I Parties will communicate information on the implementation of their actions through National Communications, with provisions for international consultations and analysis under clearly defined guidelines that will ensure that national sovereignty is respected. Nationally appropriate mitigation actions seeking international support will be recorded in a registry

along with relevant technology, finance and capacity building support. Those actions supported will be added to the list in appendix II. These supported nationally appropriate mitigation actions will be subject to international measurement, reporting and verification in accordance with guidelines adopted by the Conference of the Parties.

6. We recognize the crucial role of reducing emission from deforestation and forest degradation and the need to enhance removals of greenhouse gas emission by forests and agree on the need to provide positive incentives to such actions through the immediate establishment of a mechanism including REDD-plus, to enable the mobilization of financial resources from developed countries.

7. We decide to pursue various approaches, including opportunities to use markets, to enhance the cost-effectiveness of, and to promote mitigation actions. Developing countries, especially those with low emitting economies should be provided incentives to continue to develop on a low emission pathway.

8. Scaled up, new and additional, predictable and adequate funding as well as improved access shall be provided to developing countries, in accordance with the relevant provisions of the Convention, to enable and support enhanced action on mitigation, including substantial finance to reduce emissions from deforestation and forest degradation (REDD-plus), adaptation, technology development and transfer and capacity-building, for enhanced implementation of the Convention. The collective commitment by developed countries is to provide new and additional resources, including forestry and investments through international institutions, approaching USD 30 billion for the period 2010–2012 with balanced allocation between adaptation and mitigation. Funding for adaptation will be prioritized for the most vulnerable developing countries, such as the least developed countries, small island developing States and Africa. In the context of meaningful mitigation actions and transparency on implementation, developed countries commit to a goal of mobilizing jointly USD 100 billion dollars a year by 2020 to address the needs of developing countries. This funding will come from a wide variety of sources, public and private, bilateral and multilateral, including alternative sources of finance. New multilateral funding for adaptation will be delivered through effective and efficient fund arrangements, with a governance structure providing for equal representation of developed and developing countries. A significant portion of such funding should flow through the Copenhagen Green Climate Fund.

9. To this end, a High Level Panel will be established under the guidance of and accountable to the Conference of the Parties to study the contribution of the potential

sources of revenue, including alternative sources of finance, towards meeting this goal.

10. We decide that the Copenhagen Green Climate Fund shall be established as an operating entity of the financial mechanism of the Convention to support projects, programme, policies and other activities in developing countries related to mitigation including REDD-plus, adaptation, capacity-building, technology development and transfer.

11. In order to enhance action on development and transfer of technology we decide to establish a Technology Mechanism to accelerate technology development and transfer in support of action on adaptation and mitigation that will be guided by a country-driven approach and be based on national circumstances and priorities.

12. We call for an assessment of the implementation of this Accord to be completed by 2015, including in light of the Convention's ultimate objective. This would include consideration of strengthening the long-term goal referencing various matters presented by the science, including in relation to temperature rises of 1.5 degrees Celsius.

APPENDIX I

Quantified economy-wide emissions targets for 2020

Annex I Parties	Quantified economy-wide emissions targets for 2020	
	Emissions reduction in 2020	Base year

APPENDIX II

Nationally appropriate mitigation actions of developing country Parties

Non-Annex I	Actions

9th plenary meeting
18–19 December 2009

7. 제16차 칸쿤(2010) ― Cancun Agreements(COP)

Report of the Conference of the Parties on its sixteenth session, held in Cancun from 29 November to 10 December 2010

Decision 1/CP.16
FCCC/CP/2010/7/Add.1
15 March 2011

The Cancun Agreements: Outcome of the work of the Ad Hoc Working Group on Long-term Cooperative Action under the Convention

The Conference of the Parties,

Recalling its decision 1/CP.13 (the Bali Action Plan) and decision 1/CP.15,

Seeking to secure progress in a balanced manner, with the understanding that, through this decision, not all aspects of the work of the Ad Hoc Working Group on Long-term Cooperative Action under the Convention are concluded, and that nothing in this decision shall prejudge prospects for, or the content of, a legally binding outcome in the future,

Reaffirming the commitment to enable the full, effective and sustained implementation of the Convention through long-term cooperative action, now, up to and beyond 2012, in order to achieve the ultimate objective of the Convention,

Recalling the principles, provisions and commitments set forth in the Convention, in particular its Articles 3 and 4,

Recognizing that climate change represents an urgent and potentially irreversible threat to human societies and the planet, and thus requires to be urgently addressed by all Parties,

Affirming the legitimate needs of developing country Parties for the achievement of sustained economic growth and the eradication of poverty, so as to be able to deal with climate change,

Noting resolution 10/4 of the United Nations Human Rights Council on human rights and climate change, which recognizes that the adverse effects of climate change have a range of direct and indirect implications for the effective enjoyment of human rights and that the effects of climate change will be felt most acutely by those segments of the population that are already vulnerable owing to geography, gender, age, indigenous or minority status, or disability,

I. A shared vision for long-term cooperative action

1. *Affirms* that climate change is one of the greatest challenges of our time and that all Parties share a vision for long-term cooperative action in order to achieve the objective of the Convention under its Article 2, including through the achievement of a global goal, on the basis of equity and in accordance with common but differentiated responsibilities and respective capabilities; this vision is to guide the policies and actions of all Parties, while taking into full consideration the different circumstances of Parties in accordance with the principles and provisions of the Convention; the vision addresses mitigation, adaptation, finance, technology development and transfer, and capacity-building in a balanced, integrated and comprehensive manner to enhance and achieve the full, effective and sustained implementation of the Convention, now, up to and beyond 2012;

2. *Further affirms* that:

(a) Scaled-up overall mitigation efforts that allow for the achievement of desired stabilization levels are necessary, with developed country Parties showing leadership by undertaking ambitious emission reductions and providing technology, capacity-building and financial resources to developing country Parties, in accordance with the relevant provisions of the Convention;

(b) Adaptation must be addressed with the same priority as mitigation and requires appropriate institutional arrangements to enhance adaptation action and support;

(c) All Parties should cooperate, consistent with the principles of the Convention, through effective mechanisms, enhanced means and appropriate enabling environments, and enhance technology development and the transfer of technologies to developing country Parties to enable action on mitigation and adaptation;

(d) Mobilization and provision of scaled-up, new, additional, adequate and predictable financial resources is necessary to address the adaptation and mitigation needs of developing countries;

(e) Capacity-building is essential to enable developing country Parties to participate fully in, and to implement effectively, their commitments under the Convention; and that the goal is to enhance the capacity of developing country Parties in all areas;

3. *Recognizes* that warming of the climate system is unequivocal and that most of the observed increase in global average temperatures since the mid-twentieth century is very likely due to the observed increase in anthropogenic greenhouse gas concentrations, as assessed by the Intergovernmental Panel on Climate Change in its Fourth Assessment Report;

4. *Further recognizes* that deep cuts in global greenhouse gas emissions are required according to science, and as documented in the Fourth Assessment Report of the Inter-governmental Panel on Climate Change, with a view to reducing global greenhouse gas emissions so as to hold the increase in global average temperature below 2 °C above pre-industrial levels, and that Parties should take urgent action to meet this long-term goal, consistent with science and on the basis of equity; *also recognizes* the need to consider, in the context of the first review, as referred to in paragraph 138 below, strengthening the long-term global goal on the basis of the best available scientific knowledge, including in relation to a global average temperature rise of 1.5 °C;

5. *Agrees*, in the context of the long-term goal and the ultimate objective of the Convention and the Bali Action Plan, to work towards identifying a global goal for substantially reducing global emissions by 2050, and to consider it at the seventeenth session of the Conference of the Parties;

6. *Also agrees* that Parties should cooperate in achieving the peaking of global and national greenhouse gas emissions as soon as possible, recognizing that the time frame for peaking will be longer in developing countries, and bearing in mind that social and economic development and poverty eradication are the first and overriding priorities of developing countries and that a low-carbon development strategy is indispensable to sustainable development; in this context, *further agrees* to work towards identifying a time frame for global peaking of greenhouse gas emissions based on the best available scientific knowledge and equitable access to sustainable development, and to consider it at the seventeenth session of the Conference of the Parties;

7. *Recognizes* the need to engage a broad range of stakeholders at the global, regional, national and local levels, be they government, including subnational and local government, private business or civil society, including youth and persons with disability, and

that gender equality and the effective participation of women and indigenous peoples are important for effective action on all aspects of climate change;

8. *Emphasizes* that Parties should, in all climate change related actions, fully respect human rights;

9. *Confirms* that Parties, especially developing country Parties that would have to bear a disproportionate or abnormal burden under the long-term cooperative action under the Convention, should be given full consideration;

10. *Realizes* that addressing climate change requires a paradigm shift towards building a low-carbon society that offers substantial opportunities and ensures continued high growth and sustainable development, based on innovative technologies and more sustainable production and consumption and lifestyles, while ensuring a just transition of the workforce that creates decent work and quality jobs;

II. Enhanced action on adaptation

11. *Agrees* that adaptation is a challenge faced by all Parties, and that enhanced action and international cooperation on adaptation is urgently required to enable and support the implementation of adaptation actions aimed at reducing vulnerability and building resilience in developing country Parties, taking into account the urgent and immediate needs of those developing countries that are particularly vulnerable;

12. *Affirms* that enhanced action on adaptation should be undertaken in accordance with the Convention, should follow a country-driven, gender-sensitive, participatory and fully transparent approach, taking into consideration vulnerable groups, communities and ecosystems, and should be based on and guided by the best available science and, as appropriate, traditional and indigenous knowledge, with a view to integrating adaptation into relevant social, economic and environmental policies and actions, where appropriate;

13. *Decides* to hereby establish the Cancun Adaptation Framework encompassing the provisions laid out below, with the objective of enhancing action on adaptation, including through international cooperation and coherent consideration of matters relating to adaptation under the Convention;

14. *Invites* all Parties to enhance action on adaptation under the Cancun Adaptation Framework, taking into account their common but differentiated responsibilities and respective capabilities, and specific national and regional development priorities, objectives

and circumstances, by undertaking, inter alia, the following:

(a) Planning, prioritizing and implementing adaptation actions, including projects and programmes,[1] and actions identified in national and subnational adaptation plans and strategies, national adaptation programmes of action of the least developed countries, national communications, technology needs assessments and other relevant national planning documents;

(b) Impact, vulnerability and adaptation assessments, including assessments of financial needs as well as economic, social and environmental evaluation of adaptation options;

(c) Strengthening institutional capacities and enabling environments for adaptation, including for climate-resilient development and vulnerability reduction;

(d) Building resilience of socio-economic and ecological systems, including through economic diversification and sustainable management of natural resources;

(e) Enhancing climate change related disaster risk reduction strategies, taking into consideration the Hyogo Framework for Action,[2] where appropriate, early warning systems, risk assessment and management, and sharing and transfer mechanisms such as insurance, at the local, national, subregional and regional levels, as appropriate;

(f) Measures to enhance understanding, coordination and cooperation with regard to climate change induced displacement, migration and planned relocation, where appropriate, at the national, regional and international levels;

(g) Research, development, demonstration, diffusion, deployment and transfer of technologies, practices and processes, and capacity-building for adaptation, with a view to promoting access to technologies, in particular in developing country Parties;

(h) Strengthening data, information and knowledge systems, education and public awareness;

(i) Improving climate-related research and systematic observation for climate data collection, archiving, analysis and modelling in order to provide decision makers at the national and regional levels with improved climate-related data and information;

---

1) Including in the areas of water resources; health; agriculture and food security; infrastructure; socio-economic activities; terrestrial, freshwater and marine ecosystems; and coastal zones.
2) <http://www.unisdr.org/eng/hfa/hfa.htm>.

15. *Decides* to hereby establish a process to enable least developed country Parties to formulate and implement national adaptation plans, building upon their experience in preparing and implementing national adaptation programmes of action, as a means of identifying medium-and long-term adaptation needs and developing and implementing strategies and programmes to address those needs;

16. *Invites* other developing country Parties to employ the modalities formulated to support the above-mentioned national adaptation plans in the elaboration of their planning effort referred to in paragraph 14 (a) above;

17. *Requests* the Subsidiary Body for Implementation to elaborate modalities and guidelines for the provisions of paragraphs 15 and 16 above, for adoption by the Conference of the Parties at its seventeenth session;

18. *Requests* developed country Parties to provide developing country Parties, taking into account the needs of those that are particularly vulnerable, with long-term, scaled-up, predictable, new and additional finance, technology and capacity-building, consistent with relevant provisions, to implement urgent, short-, medium-and long-term adaptation actions, plans, programmes and projects at the local, national, subregional and regional levels, in and across different economic and social sectors and ecosystems, as well as to undertake the activities referred to in paragraphs 14–16 above and paragraphs 30, 32 and 33 below;

19. *Acknowledges* the need to strengthen, enhance and better utilize existing institutional arrangements and expertise under the Convention;

20. *Decides* to hereby establish an Adaptation Committee to promote the implementation of enhanced action on adaptation in a coherent manner under the Convention, inter alia, through the following functions:

(a) Providing technical support and guidance to the Parties, respecting the country-driven approach, with a view to facilitating the implementation of adaptation activities, including those listed in paragraphs 14 and 15 above, where appropriate;

(b) Strengthening, consolidating and enhancing the sharing of relevant information, knowledge, experience and good practices, at the local, national, regional and international levels, taking into account, as appropriate, traditional knowledge and practices;

(c) Promoting synergy and strengthening engagement with national, regional and international organizations, centres and networks, in order to enhance the implementation of adaptation actions, in particular in developing country Parties;

(d) Providing information and recommendations, drawing on adaptation good practices, for consideration by the Conference of the Parties when providing guidance on means to incentivize the implementation of adaptation actions, including finance, technology and capacity-building and other ways to enable climate-resilient development and reduce vulnerability, including to the operating entities of the financial mechanism of the Convention, as appropriate;

(e) Considering information communicated by Parties on their monitoring and review of adaptation actions, support provided and received, possible needs and gaps and other relevant information, including information communicated under the Convention, with a view to recommending what further actions may be required, as appropriate;

21. *Invites* Parties to submit to the secretariat, by 21 February 2011, views on the composition of, and modalities and procedures for, the Adaptation Committee, including on proposed linkages with other relevant institutional arrangements;

22. *Requests* the secretariat to compile these submissions into a miscellaneous document, to be made available by the fourteenth session of the Ad Hoc Working Group on Long-term Cooperative Action under the Convention, and to prepare a synthesis report based on those submissions by the fourteenth session of the Ad Hoc Working Group on Long-term Cooperative Action under the Convention;

23. *Requests* the Ad Hoc Working Group on Long-term Cooperative Action under the Convention, taking into account the above-mentioned submissions and synthesis report, to elaborate the composition of, and modalities and procedures for, the Adaptation Committee, for adoption by the Conference of the Parties at its seventeenth session;

24. *Also requests* the Ad Hoc Working Group on Long-term Cooperative Action under the Convention, in elaborating the above-mentioned modalities and procedures, to define, as appropriate, linkages with other relevant institutional arrangements under and outside the Convention, including at the national and regional levels;

25. *Recognizes* the need to strengthen international cooperation and expertise in order to understand and reduce loss and damage associated with the adverse effects of climate change, including impacts related to extreme weather events and slow onset events;[3]

---

3) Including sea level rise, increasing temperatures, ocean acidification, glacial retreat and related impacts, salinization, land and forest degradation, loss of biodiversity and desertification.

26. *Decides* to hereby establish a work programme in order to consider, including through workshops and expert meetings, as appropriate, approaches to address loss and damage associated with climate change impacts in developing countries that are particularly vulnerable to the adverse effects of climate change;

27. *Requests* the Subsidiary Body for Implementation to agree on activities to be undertaken under the above-mentioned work programme;

28. *Invites* Parties and relevant organizations to submit to the secretariat, by 21 February 2011, views and information on what elements should be included in the work programme, including the following:

(a) Possible development of a climate risk insurance facility to address impacts associated with severe weather events;

(b) Options for risk management and reduction, risk sharing and transfer mechanisms such as insurance, including options for micro-insurance, and resilience-building, including through economic diversification;

(c) Approaches for addressing rehabilitation measures associated with slow onset events;

(d) Engagement of stakeholders with relevant specialized expertise;

29. *Requests* the secretariat to compile these submissions into a miscellaneous document and to prepare a synthesis report based on those submissions, to be made available for consideration by the Subsidiary Body for Implementation at its thirty-fourth session, and with a view to making recommendations on loss and damage to the Conference of the Parties for its consideration at its eighteenth session;

30. *Invites* Parties to strengthen and, where necessary, establish regional centres and networks, in particular in developing countries, with support from developed country Parties and relevant organizations, as appropriate, and to facilitate and enhance national and regional adaptation actions, in a manner that is country-driven, encourages cooperation and coordination between regional stakeholders and improves the flow of information between the Convention process and national and regional activities;

31. *Notes* that an international centre to enhance adaptation research and coordination could also be established in a developing country;

32. *Invites* all Parties to strengthen and, where necessary, establish and/or designate

national-level institutional arrangements, with a view to enhancing work on the full range of adaptation actions, from planning to implementation;

33. *Decides* that all Parties should use existing channels to provide information, as appropriate, on support provided and received for adaptation actions in developing countries and on activities undertaken, including, inter alia, progress made, experiences, lessons learned, and challenges and gaps in the delivery of support, with a view to ensuring transparency and accountability and encouraging best practices;

34. *Invites* relevant multilateral, international, regional and national organizations, the public and private sectors, civil society and other relevant stakeholders to undertake and support enhanced action on adaptation at all levels, including under the Cancun Adaptation Framework, as appropriate, in a coherent and integrated manner, building on synergies among activities and processes, and to make information available on the progress made;

35. *Requests* the secretariat to support the implementation of the Cancun Adaptation Framework, including related institutional arrangements under the Convention, in accordance with its mandate and subject to the availability of resources;

Ⅲ. Enhanced action on mitigation

A. Nationally appropriate mitigation commitments or actions by developed country Parties

Emphasizing the need for deep cuts in global greenhouse gas emissions and early and urgent undertakings to accelerate and enhance the implementation of the Convention by all Parties, on the basis of equity and in accordance with their common but differentiated responsibilities and respective capabilities,

Acknowledging that the largest share of historical global emissions of greenhouse gases originated in developed countries and that, owing to this historical responsibility, developed country Parties must take the lead in combating climate change and the adverse effects thereof,

36. *Takes note* of quantified economy-wide emission reduction targets to be implemented by Parties included in Annex I to the Convention as communicated by them and contained in document FCCC/SB/2011/INF.1[4] (to be issued);

---

4) Parties' communications to the secretariat that are included in the information document are considered communications under the Convention.

37. *Urges* developed country Parties to increase the ambition of their economy-wide emission reduction targets, with a view to reducing their aggregate anthropogenic emissions of carbon dioxide and other greenhouse gases not controlled by the Montreal Protocol to a level consistent with the Fourth Assessment Report of the Intergovernmental Panel on Climate Change;

38. *Requests* the secretariat to organize workshops to clarify the assumptions and the conditions related to the attainment of these targets, including the use of carbon credits from the market-based mechanisms and land use, land-use change and forestry activities, and options and ways to increase their level of ambition;

39. *Also requests* the secretariat to prepare a technical paper based on Parties' submissions with the aim of facilitating understanding of the assumptions and conditions related to the attainment of their emission reduction targets and a comparison of the level of emission reduction efforts;

40. *Decides*, building on existing reporting and review guidelines, processes and experiences, to enhance reporting in the national communications of Parties included in Annex I to the Convention on mitigation targets and on the provision of financial, technological and capacity-building support to developing country Parties as follows:

(a) Developed countries should submit annual greenhouse gas inventories and inventory reports and biennial reports on their progress in achieving emission reductions, including information on mitigation actions to achieve their quantified economy-wide emission targets and emission reductions achieved, projected emissions and the provision of financial, technology and capacity-building support to developing country Parties;

(b) Developed countries shall submit supplementary information on the achievement of quantified economy-wide emission reductions;

(c) Developed countries shall improve the reporting of information on the provision of financial, technology and capacity-building support to developing country Parties;

41. *Also decides* to enhance the guidelines for the reporting of information in naional communications by Parties included in Annex I to the Convention, including the development of common reporting formats and methodology for finance, in order to ensure that information provided is complete, comparable, transparent and accurate;

42. *Further decides* to enhance guidelines for the review of information in national communications with respect to the following:

(a) Progress made in achieving emission reductions;

(b) Provision of financial, technology and capacity-building support to developing country Parties;

43. *Decides* that developed countries should establish national arrangements for the estimation of anthropogenic emissions by sources and removals by sinks of all greenhouse gases not controlled by the Montreal Protocol;

44. *Also decides* to establish a process for international assessment of emissions and removals related to quantified economy-wide emission reduction targets under the Subsidiary Body for Implementation, taking into account national circumstances, in a rigorous, robust and transparent manner, with a view to promoting comparability and building confidence;

45. *Further decides* that developed countries should develop low-carbon development strategies or plans;

46. *Decides* on the following work programme for the development of modalities and guidelines described above, building on existing reporting and review guidelines, processes and experiences:

(a) The revision of guidelines, as necessary, on the reporting of national communications, including the biennial report:

(i) The provision of financing, through enhanced common reporting formats, methodologies for finance and tracking of climate-related support;

(ii) Supplementary information on achievement of quantified economy-wide emission reduction targets;

(iii) Information on national inventory arrangements;

(b) The revision of guidelines for the review of national communications, including the biennial report, annual greenhouse gas inventories and national inventory systems;

(c) The establishment of guidelines for national inventory arrangements;

(d) Modalities and procedures for international assessment and review of emissions and removals related to quantified economy-wide emission reduction targets in accordance with paragraph 44 above, including the role of land use, land-use change and forestry, and carbon credits from market-based mechanisms, taking into account international experience;

47. *Invites* Parties to submit views on the items mentioned in paragraph 46 above, including with respect to the initial scheduling of the processes described in this section, by 28 March 2011;

B. Nationally appropriate mitigation actions by developing country Parties

Recognizing that developing country Parties are already contributing and will continue to contribute to a global mitigation effort in accordance with the principles and provisions of the Convention, and could enhance their mitigation actions, depending on provision of finance, technology and capacity-building support by developed country Parties,

Reaffirming that social and economic development and poverty eradication are the first and overriding priorities of developing country Parties, and that the share of global emissions originating in developing countries will grow to meet their social and development needs,

48. *Agrees* that developing country Parties will take nationally appropriate mitigation actions in the context of sustainable development, supported and enabled by technology, financing and capacity-building, aimed at achieving a deviation in emissions relative to 'business as usual' emissions in 2020;

49. *Takes note* of nationally appropriate mitigation actions to be implemented by Parties not included in Annex I to the Convention as communicated by them and contained in document FCCC/AWGLCA/2011/INF.1[5] (to be issued);

50. *Invites* developing countries that wish to voluntarily inform the Conference of the Parties of their intention to implement nationally appropriate mitigation actions in association with this decision to submit information on those actions to the secretariat;

51. *Requests* the secretariat to organize workshops to understand the diversity of mitigation actions submitted, underlying assumptions and any support needed for the implementation of these actions, noting different national circumstances and the respective capabilities of developing country Parties;

52. *Decides* that, in accordance with Article 4, paragraph 3, of the Convention, devel-

5) Parties' communications to the secretariat that are included in the information document are considered communications under the Convention.

oped country Parties shall provide enhanced financial, technological and capacity-building support for the preparation and implementation of nationally appropriate mitigation actions of developing country Parties   and for enhanced reporting by these Parties;

53. *Also decides* to set up a registry to record nationally appropriate mitigation actions seeking international support and to facilitate matching of finance, technology and capacity-building support for these actions;

54. *Invites* developing country Parties to submit to the secretariat information on nationally appropriate mitigation actions for which they are seeking support, along with estimated costs and emission reductions, and the anticipated time frame for implementation;

55. *Also invites* developed country Parties to submit to the secretariat information on support available and provided for nationally appropriate mitigation actions;

56. *Requests* the secretariat to record and regularly update in the registry the information provided by Parties on:

(a) Nationally appropriate mitigation actions seeking international support;

(b) Support available from developed country Parties for these actions;

(c) Support provided for nationally appropriate mitigation actions;

57. *Agrees* to develop modalities for the facilitation of support through the registry referred to in paragraph 53 above, including any functional relationship with the financial mechanism;

58. *Decides* to recognize nationally appropriate mitigation actions of developing countries in a separate section of the registry;

59. *Requests* the secretariat to record, and regularly update, in a separate section of the registry, information submitted by Parties on the following:

(a) Mitigation actions contained in document FCCC/AWGLCA/2011/INF.1;

(b) Additional mitigation actions submitted in association with paragraph 50 above;

(c) Once support has been provided, internationally supported mitigation actions and associated support;

60. *Decides* to enhance reporting in national communications, including inventories,

from Parties not included in Annex I to the Convention on mitigation actions and their effects, and support received, with additional flexibility to be given to the least developed country Parties and small island developing States:

(a) The content and frequency of national communications from Parties not included in Annex I to the Convention will not be more onerous than that for Parties included in Annex I to the Convention;

(b) Parties not included in Annex I to the Convention should submit their national communications to the Conference of the Parties, in accordance with Article 12, paragraph 1, of the Convention, every four years or in accordance with any further decisions on frequency by the Conference of the Parties, taking into account a differentiated timetable and the prompt provision of financial resources to cover the agreed full costs incurred by Parties not included in Annex I to the Convention in preparing their national communications;

(c) Developing countries, consistent with their capabilities and the level of support provided for reporting, should also submit biennial update reports containing updates of national greenhouse gas inventories, including a national inventory report and information on mitigation actions, needs and support received;

61. *Also decides* that internationally supported mitigation actions will be measured, reported and verified domestically and will be subject to international measurement, reporting and verification in accordance with guidelines to be developed under the Convention;

62. *Further decides* that domestically supported mitigation actions will be measured, reported and verified domestically in accordance with general guidelines to be developed under the Convention;

63. *Decides* to conduct international consultations and analysis of biennial reports under the Subsidiary Body for Implementation, in a manner that is non-intrusive, non-punitive and respectful of national sovereignty; the international consultations and analysis will aim to increase transparency of mitigation actions and their effects, through analysis by technical experts in consultation with the Party concerned and through a facilitative sharing of views, and will result in a summary report;

64. *Also decides* that information considered should include the national greenhouse gas inventory report, information on mitigation actions, including a description, analysis

of the impacts and associated methodologies and assumptions, progress in implementation and information on domestic measurement, reporting and verification, and support received; discussion about the appropriateness of such domestic policies and measures is not part of the process; discussions should be intended to provide transparency of information related to unsupported actions;

65. *Encourages* developing countries to develop low-carbon development strategies or plans in the context of sustainable development;

66. *Agrees* on a work programme for the development of modalities and guidelines for: facilitation of support to nationally appropriate mitigation actions through a registry; measurement, reporting and verification of supported actions and corresponding support; biennial reports as part of national communications from Parties not included in Annex I to the Convention; domestic verification of mitigation actions undertaken with domestic resources; and international consultations and analysis;

67. *Invites* Parties to submit views on the items mentioned in paragraph 66 above, including with respect to the initial scheduling of the processes described in this section, by 28 March 2011;

C. Policy approaches and positive incentives on issues relating to reducing emissions from deforestation and forest degradation in developing countries; and the role of conservation, sustainable management of forests and enhancement of forest carbon stocks in developing countries

Affirming that, in the context of the provision of adequate and predictable support to developing country Parties, Parties should collectively aim to slow, halt and reverse forest cover and carbon loss, in accordance with national circumstances, consistent with the ultimate objective of the Convention, as stated in Article 2,

Also affirming the need to promote broad country participation in all phases described in paragraph 73 below, including through the provision of support that takes into account existing capacities,

68. *Encourages* all Parties to find effective ways to reduce the human pressure on forests that results in greenhouse gas emissions, including actions to address drivers of deforestation;

69. *Affirms* that the implementation of the activities referred to in paragraph 70 be-

low should be carried out in accordance with appendix I to this decision, and that the safeguards referred to in paragraph 2 of appendix I to this decision should be promoted and supported;

70. *Encourages* developing country Parties to contribute to mitigation actions in the forest sector by undertaking the following activities, as deemed appropriate by each Party and in accordance with their respective capabilities and national circumstances:

(a) Reducing emissions from deforestation;

(b) Reducing emissions from forest degradation;

(c) Conservation of forest carbon stocks;

(d) Sustainable management of forests;

(e) Enhancement of forest carbon stocks;

71. *Requests* developing country Parties aiming to undertake the activities referred to in paragraph 70 above, in the context of the provision of adequate and predictable support, including financial resources and technical and technological support to developing country Parties, in accordance with national circumstances and respective capabilities, to develop the following elements:

(a) A national strategy or action plan;

(b) A national forest reference emission level and/or forest reference level[6] or, if appropriate, as an interim measure, subnational forest reference emission levels and/or forest reference levels, in accordance with national circumstances, and with provisions contained in decision 4/CP.15, and with any further elaboration of those provisions adopted by the Conference of the Parties;

(c) A robust and transparent national forest monitoring system for the monitoring and reporting of the activities referred to in paragraph 70 above, with, if appropriate, subnational monitoring and reporting as an interim measure,[7] in accordance with national circumstances, and with the provisions contained in decision 4/CP.15, and with

---

6) In accordance with national circumstances, national forest reference emission levels and/or forest reference levels could be a combination of subnational forest reference emissions levels and/or forest reference levels.

7) Including monitoring and reporting of emissions displacement at the national level, if appropriate, and reporting on how displacement of emissions is being addressed, and on the means to integrate subnational monitoring systems into a national monitoring system.

any further elaboration of those provisions agreed by the Conference of the Parties;

(d) A system for providing information on how the safeguards referred to in appendix I to this decision are being addressed and respected throughout the implementation of the activities referred to in paragraph 70 above, while respecting sovereignty;

72. *Also requests* developing country Parties, when developing and implementing their national strategies or action plans, to address, inter alia, the drivers of deforestation and forest degradation, land tenure issues, forest governance issues, gender considerations and the safeguards identified in paragraph 2 of appendix I to this decision, ensuring the full and effective participation of relevant stakeholders, inter alia indigenous peoples and local communities;

73. *Decides* that the activities undertaken by Parties referred to in paragraph 70 above should be implemented in phases, beginning with the development of national strategies or action plans, policies and measures, and capacity-building, followed by the implementation of national policies and measures and national strategies or action plans that could involve further capacity-building, technology development and transfer and results-based demonstration activities, and evolving into results-based actions that should be fully measured, reported and verified;

74. *Recognizes* that the implementation of the activities referred to in paragraph 70 above, including the choice of a starting phase as referred to in paragraph 73 above, depends on the specific national circumstances, capacities and capabilities of each developing country Party and the level of support received;

75. *Requests* the Subsidiary Body for Scientific and Technological Advice to develop a work programme on the matters referred to in appendix II to this decision;

76. *Urges* Parties, in particular developed country Parties, to support, through multilateral and bilateral channels, the development of national strategies or action plans, policies and measures and capacity-building, followed by the implementation of national policies and measures and national strategies or action plans that could involve further capacity-building, technology development and transfer and results-based demonstration activities, including consideration of the safeguards referred to in paragraph 2 of appendix I to this decision, taking into account the relevant provisions on finance including those relating to reporting on support;

77. *Requests* the Ad Hoc Working Group on Long-term Cooperative Action under the Convention to explore financing options for the full implementation of the results-based actions[8] referred to in paragraph 73 above and to report on progress made, including any recommendations for draft decisions on this matter, to the Conference of the Parties at its seventeenth session;

78. *Also requests* Parties to ensure coordination of the activities referred to in paragraph 70 above, including of the related support, particularly at the national level;

79. *Invites* relevant international organizations and stakeholders to contribute to the activities referred to in paragraphs 70 and 78 above;

D. Various approaches, including opportunities for using markets, to enhance the cost-effectiveness of, and to promote, mitigation actions, bearing in mind different circumstances of developed and developing countries

Acknowledging the need to maintain consistency with the principles of the Convention,

Emphasizing the importance of contributing to sustainable development, including through technology transfer and other co-benefits,

Recognizing the importance of enhancing sustainable lifestyles and patterns of production and consumption,

Aware of the need to provide incentives in support of low-emission development strategies,

80. *Decides* to consider the establishment, at the seventeenth session of the Conference of the Parties, of one or more market-based mechanisms to enhance the cost-effectiveness of, and to promote, mitigation actions, taking into account the following:

(a) Ensuring voluntary participation of Parties, supported by the promotion of fair and equitable access for all Parties;

(b) Complementing other means of support for nationally appropriate mitigation actions by developing country Parties;

(c) Stimulating mitigation across broad segments of the economy;

---

8) These actions require national monitoring systems.

(d) Safeguarding environmental integrity;

(e) Ensuring a net decrease and/or avoidance of global greenhouse gas emissions;

(f) Assisting developed country Parties to meet part of their mitigation targets, while ensuring that the use of such a mechanism or mechanisms is supplemental to domestic mitigation efforts;

(g) Ensuring good governance and robust market functioning and regulation;

81. *Requests* the Ad Hoc Working Group on Long-term Cooperative Action under the Convention to elaborate the mechanism or mechanisms referred to in paragraph 80 above, with a view to recommending a draft decision or decisions to the Conference of the Parties for consideration at its seventeenth session;

82. *Invites* Parties and accredited observer organizations to submit to the secretariat, by 21 February 2011, their views on the matters referred to in paragraph 81 above;

83. *Undertakes*, in developing and implementing the mechanism or mechanisms referred to in paragraph 80 above, to maintain and build upon existing mechanisms, including those established under the Kyoto Protocol;

84. *Decides* to consider the establishment, at the seventeenth session of the Conference of the Parties, of one or more non-market-based mechanisms to enhance the cost-effectiveness of, and to promote, mitigation actions;

85. *Requests* the Ad Hoc Working Group on Long-term Cooperative Action under the Convention to elaborate the mechanism or mechanisms referred to in paragraph 84 above, with a view to recommending a draft decision or decisions to the Conference of the Parties for consideration at its seventeenth session;

86. *Invites* Parties and accredited observer organizations to submit to the secretariat, by 21 February 2011, their views on the matters referred to in paragraph 85 above;

87. *Also invites* Parties and accredited observer organizations to submit to the secretariat, by 21 February 2011, information on the evaluation of various approaches in enhancing the cost-effectiveness of, and promoting, mitigation actions, including activities implemented jointly under Article 4, paragraph 2(a), of the Convention and any other relevant activities, for synthesis by the secretariat;

E. Economic and social consequences of response measures

Reaffirming the importance of the objective of the Convention, and the relevant principles and provisions of the Convention related to economic and social consequences of response measures, in particular its Articles 2, 3 and 4,

Recognizing that the implementation of response measures to mitigate climate change taken by a Party may result in negative economic and social consequences for other Parties, and the need to take into consideration in the implementation of the commitments of the Convention the situation of Parties, particularly developing country Parties, with economies that are vulnerable to the adverse impact of the implementation of measures to respond to climate change, referred to in Article 4, paragraphs 8, 9 and 10, of the Convention,

Affirming that responses to climate change should be coordinated with social and economic development in an integrated manner, with a view to avoiding adverse impacts on the latter, taking fully into account the legitimate priority needs of developing country Parties for the achievement of sustained economic growth and the eradication of poverty, and the consequences for vulnerable groups, in particular women and children,

Recognizing the importance of avoiding or minimizing negative impacts of response measures on social and economic sectors, promoting a just transition of the workforce, the creation of decent work and quality jobs in accordance with nationally defined development priorities and strategies, and contributing to building new capacity for both production and service-related jobs in all sectors, promoting economic growth and sustainable development,

Taking note of relevant provisions of the United Nations Declaration on the Rights of Indigenous Peoples,

88. *Urges* Parties, in the implementation of measures to mitigate climate change, to take into consideration the economic and social impacts of response measures and the needs of Parties, in particular developing country Parties, impacted by response measures, consistent with relevant provisions of the Convention;

89. *Also urges* developed country Parties to strive to implement policies and measures to respond to climate change in such a way as to avoid negative social and economic consequences for developing country Parties, taking into account Article 3 of the Convention, and to assist these Parties to address such consequences by providing support, including financial resources, transfer of technology and capacity-building, in ac-

cordance with Article 4 of the Convention, to build up the resilience of societies and economies negatively affected by response measures;

90. *Reaffirms* that the Parties should cooperate to promote a supportive and open international economic system that would lead to sustainable economic growth and development in all Parties, particularly developing country Parties, thus enabling them better to address the problems of climate change; measures taken to combat climate change, including unilateral ones, should not constitute a means of arbitrary or unjustifiable discrimination or a disguised restriction on international trade;

91. *Agrees* that information relating to response measures should be considered in a structured manner in order to enhance the implementation of Article 4, paragraph 1(g) and (h), of the Convention, recognizing the needs of developing country Parties identified in Article 4, paragraphs 8, 9 and 10;

92. *Decides* that Parties should cooperate fully to enhance understanding of the economic and social consequences of response measures, taking into account the need for information from those affected, and evidence of actual impacts, and of both positive and negative effects; and *further decides* to consider how existing channels, such as national communications, including the possible submission of supplementary information, as considered by the Subsidiary Body for Implementation, could be improved and built upon;

93. *Further decides* to provide a forum on the impact of the implementation of response measures, and to that end requests the Chairs of the Subsidiary Body for Scientific and Technological Advice and the Subsidiary Body for Implementation to convene such a forum at the thirty-fourth and thirty-fifth sessions of these bodies, with the objective of developing a work programme under the subsidiary bodies to address these impacts, with a view to adopting, at the seventeenth session of the Conference of the Parties, modalities for the operationalization of the work programme and a possible forum on response measures;

94. *Invites* Parties and relevant intergovernmental organizations to submit to the secretariat, by 28 March 2011, their views on the issues referred to in paragraph 93 above for consideration by the Subsidiary Body for Scientific and Technological Advice and the Subsidiary Body for Implementation at their thirty-fourth sessions;

IV. Finance, technology and capacity-building

A. Finance

95. *Takes note* of the collective commitment by developed countries to provide new and additional resources, including forestry and investments through international institutions, approaching USD 30 billion for the period 2010–2012, with a balanced allocation between adaptation and mitigation; funding for adaptation will be prioritized for the most vulnerable developing countries, such as the least developed countries, small island developing States and Africa;

96. *Invites*, in order to enhance transparency, developed country Parties to submit to the secretariat for compilation into an information document, by May 2011, 2012 and 2013, information on the resources provided to fulfil the commitment referred to in paragraph 95 above, including ways in which developing country Parties access these resources;

97. *Decides* that, in accordance with the relevant provisions of the Convention, scaled-up, new and additional, predictable and adequate funding shall be provided to developing country Parties, taking into account the urgent and immediate needs of developing countries that are particularly vulnerable to the adverse effects of climate change;

98. *Recognizes* that developed country Parties commit, in the context of meaningful mitigation actions and transparency on implementation, to a goal of mobilizing jointly USD 100 billion per year by 2020 to address the needs of developing countries;

99. *Agrees* that, in accordance with paragraph 1(e) of the Bali Action Plan, funds provided to developing country Parties may come from a wide variety of sources, public and private, bilateral and multilateral, including alternative sources;

100. *Decides* that a significant share of new multilateral funding for adaptation should flow through the Green Climate Fund, referred to in paragraph 102 below;

101. *Takes note* of the relevant reports on the financing needs and options for the mobilization of resources to address the needs of developing country Parties with regard to climate change adaptation and mitigation, including the report of the High-level Advisory Group on Climate Change Financing;

102. *Decides* to establish a Green Climate Fund, to be designated as an operating entity of the financial mechanism of the Convention under Article 11, with arrangements

to be concluded between the Conference of the Parties and the Green Climate Fund to ensure that it is accountable to and functions under the guidance of the Conference of the Parties, to support projects, programmes, policies and other activities in developing country Parties using thematic funding windows;

103. *Also decides* that the Fund shall be governed by a Board of 24 members, comprising an equal number of members from developing and developed country Parties; representation from developing country Parties shall include representatives of relevant United Nations regional groupings and representatives of small island developing States and the least developed countries; each Board member shall have an alternate member; with alternate members entitled to participate in the meetings of the board only through the principal member, without the right to vote, unless they are serving as the member; during the absence of the member from all or part of a meeting of the Board, his or her alternate shall serve as the member;

104. *Further decides* that the Green Climate Fund shall have a trustee; the trustee for the Green Climate Fund shall have the administrative competence to manage the financial assets of the Green Climate Fund, maintain appropriate financial records and prepare financial statements and other reports required by the Board of the Green Climate Fund, in accordance with internationally accepted fiduciary standards;

105. *Decides* that the trustee shall administer the assets of the Green Climate Fund only for the purpose of, and in accordance with, the relevant decisions of the Green Climate Fund Board; the trustee shall hold the assets of the Green Climate Fund separate and apart from the assets of the trustee, but may commingle them for administrative and investment purposes with other assets maintained by the trustee; and the trustee shall establish and maintain separate records and accounts to identify the assets of the Green Climate Fund;

106. *Decides* that the trustee shall be accountable to the Green Climate Fund Board for the performance of its fiduciary responsibilities;

107. *Invites* the World Bank to serve as the interim trustee for the Green Climate Fund, subject to a review three years after operationalization of the Fund;

108. *Decides* that the operation of the Fund shall be supported by an independent secretariat;

109. *Also decides* that the Green Climate Fund shall be designed by a Transitional

Committee in accordance with the terms of reference contained in appendix III to this decision; the Transitional Committee shall have 40 members, with 15 members from developed country Parties and 25 members from developing country Parties as follows:

(a) Seven members from Africa;

(b) Seven members from Asia;

(c) Seven members from Group of Latin America and the Caribbean;

(d) Two members from small island developing States;

(e) Two members from the least developed countries;

110. *Invites* the Executive Secretary of the secretariat, in consultation with the President of the Conference of the Parties, to convene the initial meeting of the Transitional Committee, with members having the necessary experience and skills, notably in the area of finance and climate change; the meetings of the Transitional Committee will be open to observers;

111. *Requests* the secretariat, in consultation with the President of the Conference of the Parties, to make arrangements enabling relevant United Nations agencies, international financial institutions and multilateral development banks, along with the secretariat and the Global Environment Facility, to second staff to support the work of the Transitional Committee for the design phase of the Green Climate Fund;

112. *Decides* to establish a Standing Committee under the Conference of the Parties to assist the Conference of the Parties in exercising its functions with respect to the financial mechanism of the Convention in terms of improving coherence and coordination in the delivery of climate change financing, rationalization of the financial mechanism, mobilization of financial resources and measurement, reporting and verification of support provided to developing country Parties; Parties agree to further define the roles and functions of this Standing Committee;

B. Technology development and transfer

Recalling the commitments under the Convention, in particular Article 4, paragraphs 1, 3, 5, 7, 8 and 9,

Confirming the importance of promoting and enhancing national and international cooperative action on the development and transfer of environmentally sound technologies to developing country Parties to support action on mitigation and adaptation now, up to and beyond 2012, in order to achieve the ultimate objective of the Convention,

Recognizing that an early and rapid reduction in emissions and the urgent need to adapt to the adverse impacts of climate change require large-scale diffusion and transfer of, or access to, environmentally sound technologies,

Stressing the need for effective mechanisms, enhanced means, appropriate enabling environments and the removal of obstacles to the scaling up of the development and transfer of technology to developing country Parties,

113. *Decides* that the objective of enhanced action on technology development and transfer is to support action on mitigation and adaptation in order to achieve the full implementation of the Convention;

114. *Also decides* that, in pursuit of this objective, technology needs must be nationally determined, based on national circumstances and priorities;

115. *Further decides* to accelerate action consistent with international obligations, at different stages of the technology cycle, including research and development, demonstration, deployment, diffusion and transfer of technology (hereinafter referred in this decision as technology development and transfer) in support of action on mitigation and adaptation;

116. *Encourages* Parties, in the context of Article 4, paragraphs 1(c) and 5, of the Convention and consistent with their respective capabilities and national circumstances and priorities, to undertake domestic actions identified through country-driven approaches, to engage in bilateral and multilateral cooperative activities on technology development and transfer and to increase private and public research, development and demonstration in relation to technologies for mitigation and adaptation;

117. *Decides* to establish a Technology Mechanism to facilitate the implementation of actions for achieving the objective referred to in paragraphs 113–115 above, under the guidance of and accountable to the Conference of the Parties, which will consist of the following components:

(a) A Technology Executive Committee, to undertake the functions contained in paragraph 121 below;

(b) A Climate Technology Centre and Network, to undertake the functions contained in paragraph 123 below;

118. *Also decides* that the Technology Executive Committee and the Climate Technology Centre and Network, consistent with their respective functions, should facilitate the effective implementation of the Technology Mechanism, under the guidance of the Conference of the Parties;

119. *Further decides* that the Technology Executive Committee shall further implement the framework for meaningful and effective actions to enhance the implementation of Article 4, paragraph 5, of the Convention adopted by decision 4/CP.7 and enhanced by decision 3/CP.13;

120. *Decides* that priority areas that could be considered under the Convention may include:

(a) Development and enhancement of the endogenous capacities and technologies of developing country Parties, including cooperative research, development and demonstration programmes;

(b) Deployment and diffusion of environmentally sound technologies and know-how in developing country Parties;

(c) Increased public and private investment in technology development, deployment, diffusion and transfer;

(d) Deployment of soft and hard technologies for the implementation of adaptation and mitigation actions;

(e) Improved climate change observation systems and related information management;

(f) Strengthening of national systems of innovation and technology innovation centres;

(g) Development and implementation of national technology plans for mitigation and adaptation;

121. *Also decides* that the functions of the Technology Executive Committee shall be to:

(a) Provide an overview of technological needs and analysis of policy and technical issues related to the development and transfer of technologies for mitigation and adaptation;

(b) Consider and recommend actions to promote technology development and transfer, in order to accelerate action on mitigation and adaptation;

(c) Recommend guidance on policies and programme priorities related to technology development and transfer with special consideration given to the least developed country Parties;

(d) Promote and facilitate collaboration on the development and transfer of technologies for mitigation and adaptation between governments, the private sector, non-profit organizations and academic and research communities;

(e) Recommend actions to address the barriers to technology development and transfer in order to enable enhanced action on mitigation and adaptation;

(f) Seek cooperation with relevant international technology initiatives, stakeholders and organizations, and promote coherence and cooperation across technology activities, including activities under and outside of the Convention;

(g) Catalyse the development and use of technology road maps or action plans at the international, regional and national levels through cooperation between relevant stakeholders, particularly governments and relevant organizations or bodies, including the development of best practice guidelines as facilitative tools for action on mitigation and adaptation;

122. *Further decides* that the Technology Executive Committee shall have the mandate and composition as contained in appendix IV to this decision;

123. *Decides* that the Climate Technology Centre shall facilitate a network of national, regional, sectoral and international technology networks, organizations and initiatives with a view to engaging the participants of the Network effectively in the following functions:

(a) At the request of a developing country Party:

(i) Providing advice and support related to the identification of technology needs and the implementation of environmentally sound technologies, practices and processes;

(ii) Facilitating the provision of information, training and support for programmes to build or strengthen capacity of developing countries to identify technology options, make technology choices and operate, maintain and adapt technology;

(iii) Facilitating prompt action on the deployment of existing technology in developing country Parties based on identified needs;

(b) Stimulating and encouraging, through collaboration with the private sector, public institutions, academia and research institutions, the development and transfer of existing and emerging environmentally sound technologies, as well as opportunities for North–South, South–South and triangular technology cooperation;

(c) Facilitating a network of national, regional, sectoral and international technology centres, networks, organization and initiatives with a view to:

(i) Enhancing cooperation with national, regional and international technology centres and relevant national institutions;

(ii) Facilitating international partnerships among public and private stakeholders to accelerate the innovation and diffusion of environmentally sound technologies to developing country Parties;

(iii) Providing, at the request of a developing country Party, in-country technical assistance and training to support identified technology actions in developing country Parties;

(iv) Stimulating the establishment of twinning centre arrangements to promote North–South, South–South and triangular partnerships, with a view to encouraging cooperative research and development;

(v) Identifying, disseminating and assisting with developing analytical tools, policies and best practices for country-driven planning to support the dissemination of environmentally sound technologies;

(d) Performing other such activities as may be necessary to carry out its functions;

124. *Also decides* to terminate the mandate of the Expert Group on Technology Transfer at the conclusion of the sixteenth session of the Conference of the Parties;

125. *Further decides* that the Technology Executive Committee shall convene its first meeting as soon as practicable following the election of its members and shall elaborate its modalities and procedures taking into account the need to achieve coherence and

maintain interactions with other relevant institutional arrangements under and outside of the Convention, for consideration by the Conference of the Parties at its seventeenth session;

126. *Decides* that the Technology Executive Committee and the Climate Technology Centre and Network shall report, on an interim basis[9] and without prejudice to the relationship between the Technology Executive Committee and the Climate Technology Centre and Network as referred to in paragraph 128 (a) below to the Conference of the Parties, through the subsidiary bodies, on their respective activities and the performance of their respective functions;

127. *Also decides* that the Climate Technology Centre and Network and the Technology Executive Committee shall relate so as to promote coherence and synergy;

Work programme for the Ad Hoc Working Group on Long-term Cooperative Action under the Convention in 2011 on technology development and transfer

128. *Underlines* the importance of continued dialogue among Parties in 2011 through the Ad Hoc Working Group on Long-term Cooperative Action under the Convention, including on the following matters, with a view to the Conference of the Parties taking a decision at its seventeenth session, in order to make the Technology Mechanism fully operational in 2012:

(a) The relationship between the Technology Executive Committee and the Climate Technology Centre and Network, and their reporting lines;

(b) The governance structure of and terms of reference for the Climate Technology Centre and Network and how the Climate Technology Centre will relate to the Network, drawing upon the results of the workshop referred to in paragraph 129 below;

(c) The procedure for calls for proposals and the criteria to be used to evaluate and select the host of the Climate Technology Centre and Network;

(d) The potential links between the Technology Mechanism and the financial mechanism;

(e) Consideration of additional functions for the Technology Executive Committee and the Climate Technology Centre and Network;

129. *Requests* the Ad Hoc Working Group on Long-term Cooperative Action under

---

9) Until there is a decision on the issues contained in paragraph 128 (a) below.

the Convention to convene an expert workshop, in conjunction with one of its sessions in 2011, on the matters contained in paragraph 128 above, drawing upon the preliminary work undertaken by the Expert Group on Technology Transfer, and to report on the results of this workshop at that session;

C. Capacity-building

Reaffirming that capacity-building is essential to enable developing country Parties to participate fully in addressing the challenges of climate change, and to implement effectively their commitments under the Convention,

Recalling the provisions related to capacity-building for developing country Parties contained in relevant decisions adopted by the Conference of the Parties, especially decision 2/CP.7,

Taking into account that the scope of capacity-building and related needs as contained in the annex to decision 2/CP.7 and the key factors identified in decision 2/CP.10 remain valid,

Acknowledging that capacity-building is cross-cutting in nature and an integral part of enhanced action on mitigation, adaptation, technology development and transfer, and access to financial resources,

Also acknowledging that, in addition, there may be specific capacity-building activities that require support to enable developing countries to undertake the enhanced implementation of the Convention,

Reaffirming that capacity-building should be a continuous, progressive and iterative process that is participatory, country-driven and consistent with national priorities and circumstances,

130. *Decides* that capacity-building support to developing country Parties should be enhanced with a view to strengthening endogenous capacities at the subnational, national or regional levels, as appropriate, taking into account gender aspects, to contribute to the achievement of the full, effective and sustained implementation of the Convention, by, inter alia:

(a) Strengthening relevant institutions at various levels, including focal points and national coordinating bodies and organizations;

(b) Strengthening networks for the generation, sharing and management of information and knowledge, including through North–South, South–South and triangular cooperation;

(c) Strengthening climate change communication, education, training and public awareness at all levels;

(d) Strengthening integrated approaches and the participation of various stakeholders in relevant social, economic and environmental policies and actions;

(e) Supporting existing and emerging capacity-building needs identified in the areas of mitigation, adaptation, technology development and transfer, and access to financial resources;

131. *Also decides* that financial resources for enhanced action on capacity-building in developing country Parties should be provided by Parties included in Annex II to the Convention and other Parties in a position to do so through the current and any future operating entities of the financial mechanism, as well as through various bilateral, regional and other multilateral channels, as appropriate;

132. *Encourages* developed country Parties to continue to report through their national communications, in accordance with the "Guidelines for the preparation of national communications by Parties included in Annex I to the Convention, Part II: UNFCCC reporting guidelines on national communications", on the support they have provided for capacity-building in developing country Parties;

133. *Invites* developed country Parties in a position to do so to provide information, hrough annual submissions to the secretariat and other appropriate channels, on the support they have provided for capacity-building in developing country Parties;

134. *Encourages* developing country Parties to continue to report through their national communications, in accordance with the "Guidelines for the preparation of national communications from Parties not included in Annex I to the Convention", on progress made in enhancing their capacity to address climate change, including on the use of the support received;

135. *Invites* developing country Parties in a position to do so to provide information, through annual submissions to the secretariat and other appropriate channels, on progress made in enhancing their capacity to address climate change, including on the use of the support received;

136. *Requests* the Ad Hoc Working Group on Long-term Cooperative Action under the Convention to consider ways to further enhance the monitoring and review of the effectiveness of capacity-building, for consideration by the Conference of the Parties at its seventeenth session;

137. *Also requests* the Ad Hoc Working Group on Long-term Cooperative Action under the Convention to further elaborate the modalities regarding institutional arrangements for capacity-building, for consideration by the Conference of the Parties at its seventeenth session;

V. Review

138. *Decides* to periodically review the adequacy of the long-term global goal referred to in paragraph 4 above, in the light of the ultimate objective of the Convention, and overall progress towards achieving it, in accordance with the relevant principles and provisions of the Convention;

139. Also decides that:

(a) This review should be guided by the principles of equity, and common but differentiated responsibilities and respective capabilities and take into account, inter alia:

(i) The best available scientific knowledge, including the assessment reports of the Intergovernmental Panel on Climate Change;

(ii) Observed impacts of climate change;

(iii) An assessment of the overall aggregated effect of the steps taken by Parties in order to achieve the ultimate objective of the Convention;

(iv) Consideration of strengthening the long-term global goal, referencing various matters presented by the science, including in relation to temperature rises of 1.5 °C;

(b) The first review should start in 2013 and should be concluded by 2015;

(c) The Conference of the Parties shall take appropriate action based on the review;

140. *Requests* the Ad Hoc Working Group on Long-term Cooperative Action under the Convention to further define the scope of this review and develop its modalities, including the required inputs, with a view to their adoption by the Conference of the

Parties at its seventeenth session;

VI. Other matters

Parties included in Annex I to the Convention undergoing the process of transition to a market economy

Recalling Article 4, paragraph 6, of the Convention and relevant decisions of the Conference of the Parties, especially decisions 3/CP.7 and 3/CP.13 relating to Parties included in Annex I to the Convention undergoing the process of transition to a market economy,

Noting that Parties included in Annex I to the Convention undergoing the process of transition to a market economy are not included in Annex II to the Convention and as such are not subject to the provisions of Article 4, paragraphs 3 and 4, of the Convention,

Recalling that Article 4, paragraph 6, of the Convention provides that a certain degree of flexibility shall be allowed by the Conference of the Parties to Parties included in Annex I to the Convention undergoing the process of transition to a market economy,

Taking note of the submissions from Parties contained in document FCCC/AWGLCA/2010/MISC.6/Add.2,

141. *Requests* the Ad Hoc Working Group on Long-term Cooperative Action under the Convention to continue consideration of these issues with a view to promoting access by Parties included in Annex I to the Convention undergoing the process of transition to a market economy to technology, capacity-building and finance in order to enhance their ability to develop low-emission economies;

Parties included in Annex I to the Convention whose special circumstances are recognized by the Conference of the Parties

Recalling decision 26/CP.7 that amended the list in Annex II to the Convention by deleting the name of Turkey,

Recalling decision 26/CP.7 that invited Parties to recognize the special circumstances of Turkey, which place Turkey in a situation different from that of other Parties included in Annex I to the Convention,

Recognizing that Turkey is in a situation different from that of other Parties included in Annex I to the Convention,

Noting that Turkey is not included in Annex II to the Convention and as such is not subject to the commitments of Article 4, paragraphs 3–5, of the Convention and that Turkey is eligible for support under Article 4, paragraph 5, of the Convention,

Taking note of the submission from Turkey contained in document FCCC/AWGLCA/2010/MISC.8,

142. *Requests* the Ad Hoc Working Group on Long-term Cooperative Action under the Convention to continue consideration of these issues with a view to promoting access by Turkey to finance, technology and capacity-building in order to enhance its ability to better implement the Convention;

Ⅶ. Extension of the Ad Hoc Working Group on Long-term Cooperative Action under the Convention

143. *Decides* to extend the Ad Hoc Working Group on Long-term Cooperative Action under the Convention for one year, in order for it to continue its work with a view to carrying out the undertakings contained in this decision and present the results to the Conference of the Parties for consideration at its seventeenth session;

144. *Requests* the Ad Hoc Working Group on Long-term Cooperative Action under the Convention to continue its work drawing on the documents under its consideration;

145. *Also requests* the Ad Hoc Working Group on Long-term Cooperative Action under the Convention to continue discussing legal options with the aim of completing an agreed outcome based on decision 1/CP.13 (Bali Action Plan), the work done at the sixteenth session of the Conference of the Parties and proposals made by Parties under Article 17 of the Convention;

146. *Further requests* the secretariat to make the necessary arrangements in accordance with any guidance from the Bureau of the Conference of the Parties;

147. *Mandates* the host country of the next session of the Conference of the Parties to undertake inclusive and transparent consultations in order to facilitate the work towards the success of that session.

Appendix I

Guidance and safeguards for policy approaches and positive incentives on issues relating to reducing emissions from deforestation and forest degradation in developing countries; and the role of conservation, sustainable management of forests and enhancement of forest carbon stocks in developing countries

1. The activities referred to in paragraph 70 of this decision should:

(a) Contribute to the achievement of the objective set out in Article 2 of the Convention;

(b) Contribute to the fulfilment of the commitments set out in Article 4, paragraph 3, of the Convention;

(c) Be country-driven and be considered options available to Parties;

(d) Be consistent with the objective of environmental integrity and take into account the multiple functions of forests and other ecosystems;

(e) Be undertaken in accordance with national development priorities, objectives and circumstances and capabilities and should respect sovereignty;

(f) Be consistent with Parties' national sustainable development needs and goals;

(g) Be implemented in the context of sustainable development and reducing poverty, while responding to climate change;

(h) Be consistent with the adaptation needs of the country;

(i) Be supported by adequate and predictable financial and technology support, including support for capacity-building;

(j) Be results-based;

(k) Promote sustainable management of forests;

2. When undertaking the activities referred to in paragraph 70 of this decision, the following safeguards should be promoted and supported:

(a) That actions complement or are consistent with the objectives of national forest programmes and relevant international conventions and agreements;

(b) Transparent and effective national forest governance structures, taking into account national legislation and sovereignty;

(c) Respect for the knowledge and rights of indigenous peoples and members of local communities, by taking into account relevant international obligations, national circumstances and laws, and noting that the United Nations General Assembly has adopted the United Nations Declaration on the Rights of Indigenous Peoples;

(d) The full and effective participation of relevant stakeholders, in particular indigenous peoples and local communities, in the actions referred to in paragraphs 70 and 72 of this decision;

(e) That actions are consistent with the conservation of natural forests and biological diversity, ensuring that the actions referred to in paragraph 70 of this decision are not used for the conversion of natural forests, but are instead used to incentivize the protection and conservation of natural forests and their ecosystem services, and to enhance other social and environmental benefits;[1]

(f) Actions to address the risks of reversals;

(g) Actions to reduce displacement of emissions.

---

1) Taking into account the need for sustainable livelihoods of indigenous peoples and local communities and their interdependence on forests in most countries, reflected in the United Nations Declaration on the Rights of Indigenous Peoples, as well as the International Mother Earth Day.

Appendix II

Work programme of the Subsidiary Body for Scientific and Technological Advice on policy approaches and positive incentives on issues relating to reducing emissions from deforestation and forest degradation in developing countries; and the role of conservation, sustainable management of forests and enhancement of forest carbon stocks in developing countries

In the development of its work programme, the Subsidiary Body for Scientific and Technological Advice is requested to:

(a) Identify land use, land-use change and forestry activities in developing countries, in particular those that are linked to the drivers of deforestation and forest degradation, identify the associated methodological issues to estimate emissions and removals resulting from these activities, and assess the potential contribution of these activities to the mitigation of climate change, and report on the findings and outcomes of this work to the Conference of the Parties (COP) at its eighteenth session on the outcomes of the work referred to in this paragraph;

(b) Develop modalities relating to paragraphs 71 (b) and (c) and guidance relating to paragraph 71 (d) of this decision, for consideration by the COP at its seventeenth session;

(c) Develop, as necessary, modalities for measuring, reporting and verifying anthropogenic forest-related emissions by sources and removals by sinks, forest carbon stocks, and forest carbon stock and forest-area changes resulting from the implementation of the activities referred to in paragraph 70 of this decision, consistent with any guidance on measuring, reporting and verifying nationally appropriate mitigation actions by developing country Parties agreed by the COP, taking into account methodological guidance in accordance with decision 4/CP.15, for consideration by the COP at its seventeenth session.

Appendix III

Terms of reference for the design of the Green Climate Fund

1. The Transitional Committee shall develop and recommend to the Conference of the Parties for its approval at its seventeenth session operational documents that address, inter alia:

(a) The legal and institutional arrangements for the establishment and operationalization of the Green Climate Fund;

(b) The rules of procedure of the Green Climate Fund Board and other governance issues related to the Board;

(c) Methods to manage the large scale of financial resources from a number of sources and deliver through a variety of financial instruments, funding windows and access modalities, including direct access, with the objective of achieving a balanced allocation between adaptation and mitigation;

(d) The financial instruments that the Fund can use to achieve its priorities;

(e) Methods to enhance complementarity between the Fund's activities and those of other bilateral, regional and multilateral funding mechanisms and institutions;

(f) The role of the Fund's secretariat and the procedure for selecting and/or establishing the secretariat;

(g) A mechanism to ensure periodic independent evaluation of the Fund's performance;

(h) Mechanisms to ensure financial accountability and to evaluate the performance of activities supported by the Fund, in order to ensure the application of environmental and social safeguards as well as internationally accepted fiduciary standards and sound financial management to the Fund's activities;

(i) Mechanisms to ensure the provision of appropriate expert and technical advice, including from relevant thematic bodies established under the Convention;

(j) Mechanisms to ensure stakeholder input and participation.

2. In the conduct of its work, the Transitional Committee shall:

(a) Convene its first meeting by March 2011;

(b) Encourage input from all Parties and from relevant international organizations and observers;

(c) Take into account the findings contained in relevant reports.

Appendix IV

Composition and mandate of the Technology Executive Committee

1. The Technology Executive Committee shall comprise 20 expert members, elected by the Conference of the Parties (COP), serving in their personal capacity and nominated by Parties with the aim of achieving a fair and balanced representation, as follows:

(a) Nine members from Parties included in Annex I to the Convention (Annex I Parties);

(b) Three members from each of the three regions of the Parties not included in Annex I to the Convention (non-Annex I Parties), namely Africa, Asia and the Pacific, and Latin America and the Caribbean, one member from a small island developing State and one member from a least developed country Party.

2. Decisions will be taken according to the rule of consensus.

3. Parties are encouraged to nominate senior experts to the Technology Executive Committee, with a view to achieving, within the membership, an appropriate balance of technical, legal, policy, social development and financial expertise relevant to the development and transfer of technology for adaptation and mitigation, taking into account the need to achieve gender balance in accordance with decision 36/CP.7.

4. Members shall serve for a term of two years and shall be eligible to serve a maximum of two consecutive terms of office. The following rules shall apply:

(a) Half of the members shall be elected initially for a term of three years and half of the members shall be elected for a term of two years;

(b) Thereafter, the COP shall elect every year a member for a term of two years;

(c) The members shall remain in office until their successors are elected.

5. The Technology Executive Committee shall elect annually a chair and a vice-chair from among its members for a term of one year each, with one being a member from an Annex I Party and the other being a member from a non-Annex I Party. The positions of chair and vice-chair shall alternate annually between a member from an Annex I Party and a member from a non-Annex I Party.

6. If the chair is temporarily unable to fulfil the obligations of the office, the

vice-chair shall serve as chair. In the absence of the chair and vice-chair at a particular meeting, any other member designated by the Technology Executive Committee shall temporarily serve as the chair of that meeting.

7. If the chair or vice-chair is unable to complete the term of office, the Technology Executive Committee shall elect a replacement to complete the term of office, taking into account paragraph 5 above.

8. If a member of the Technology Executive Committee resigns or is otherwise unable to complete the assigned term of office or to perform the functions of that office, the Technology Executive Committee may decide, bearing in mind the proximity of the next session of the COP, to appoint another member from the same constituency to replace said member for the remainder of that member's mandate, in which case the appointment shall count as one term.

9. The Technology Executive Committee, in performing its functions, should draw upon outside expertise, including the UNFCCC roster of experts and the Climate Technology Centre and Network, to provide advice, including as expert advisers at its meetings.

10. The Technology Executive Committee should seek input from intergovernmental and international organizations and the private sector and may seek input from civil society in undertaking its work. It may invite advisers drawn from relevant intergovernmental and international organizations as well as the private sector and civil society to participate in its meetings as expert advisers on specific issues as they arise.

11. The meetings of the Technology Executive Committee shall be open to attendance by accredited observer organizations, except where otherwise decided by the Technology Executive Committee.

12. The secretariat shall support and facilitate the work of the Technology Executive Committee.

9th plenary meeting
10–11 December 2010

7-1. 제16차 칸쿤(2010) — Cancun Agreements(CMP)

Report of the Conference of the Parties on its sixteenth session, held in Cancun from 29 November to 10 December 2010

Decision 1/CMP.6
FCCC/KP/CMP/2010/12/Add.1
15 March 2011

The Cancun Agreements: Outcome of the work of the Ad Hoc Working Group on Further Commitments for Annex I Parties under the Kyoto Protocol at its fifteenth session

The Conference of the Parties serving as the meeting of the Parties to the Kyoto Protocol,

Recalling Article 3, paragraph 9, of the Kyoto Protocol,

Also recalling Article 20, paragraph 2, and Article 21, paragraph 7, of the Kyoto Protocol,

Further recalling decisions 1/CMP.1 and 1/CMP.5,

Recognizing that Parties included in Annex I (Annex I Parties) should continue to take the lead in combating climate change,

Also recognizing that the contribution of Working Group III to the Fourth Assessment Report of the Intergovernmental Panel on Climate Change, *Climate Change 2007: Mitigation of Climate Change*, indicates that achieving the lowest levels assessed by the Intergovernmental Panel on Climate Change to date and its corresponding potential damage limitation would require Annex I Parties as a group to reduce emissions in a range of 25–40 per cent below 1990 levels by 2020, through means that may be available to these Parties to reach their emission reduction targets,

Noting the reports of the Ad Hoc Working Group on Further Commitments for Annex I Parties under the Kyoto Protocol from its sessions to date and the oral report by the Chair to the Conference of the Parties serving as the meeting of the Parties to the Kyoto Protocol at its sixth session,

Welcoming the progress achieved by the Ad Hoc Working Group on Further Commitments for Annex I Parties under the Kyoto Protocol on its work pursuant to decisions 1/CMP.1 and 1/CMP.5,

Cognizant of decision 1/CP.16 (Outcome of the work of the Ad Hoc Working Group on Long-term Cooperative Action under the Convention),

1. *Agrees* that the Ad Hoc Working Group on Further Commitments for Annex I Parties under the Kyoto Protocol shall aim to complete its work pursuant to decision 1/CMP.1 and have its results adopted by the Conference of the Parties serving as the meeting of the Parties to the Kyoto Protocol as early as possible and in time to ensure that there is no gap between the first and second commitment periods;

2. *Requests* the Ad Hoc Working Group on Further Commitments for Annex I Parties under the Kyoto Protocol to continue its work referred to in paragraph 1 above on the proposals contained in document FCCC/KP/AWG/2010/CRP.4/Rev.4;

3. *Takes note* of quantified economy-wide emission reduction targets to be implemented by Annex I Parties as communicated by them and contained in document FCCC/SB/2011/INF.1;[1][2]

4. *Urges* Annex I Parties to raise the level of ambition of the emission reductions to be achieved by them individually or jointly, with a view to reducing their aggregate level of emissions of greenhouse gases in accordance with the range indicated by Working Group III to the Fourth Assessment Report of the Intergovernmental Panel on Climate Change, *Climate Change 2007: Mitigation of Climate Change*, and taking into account the quantitative implications of the use of land use, land-use change and forestry activities, emissions trading and project-based mechanisms and the carry-over of units from the first to the second commitment period;

5. *Agrees* that further work is needed to convert emission reduction targets to quantified economy-wide limitation or reduction commitments;

6. *Also agrees* that:

(a) In the second commitment period the base year shall be 1990, or the base year

---

1) The content of the table in this information document is shown without prejudice to the position of the Parties or to the right of Parties under Article 21, paragraph 7, of the Kyoto Protocol.

2) Document to be issued.

or period determined in accordance with Article 3, paragraph 5, of the Kyoto Protocol, for the purpose of calculating assigned amounts; in addition, a reference year may be used by a Party on an optional basis for its own purposes to express its quantified emission limitation and reduction objectives as a percentage of emissions of that year, that is not internationally binding under the Kyoto Protocol, in addition to the listing of its quantified emission limitation and reduction objectives in relation to the base year;

(b) Emissions trading and the project-based mechanisms under the Kyoto Protocol shall continue to be available to Annex I Parties as a means to meet their quantified emission limitation and reduction objectives in accordance with relevant decisions of the Conference of the Parties serving as the meeting of the Parties to the Kyoto Protocol as may be further improved through decisions to be adopted based on the draft text contained in chapter III of document FCCC/KP/AWG/2010/CRP.4/Rev.4;

(c) Measures to reduce greenhouse gas emissions and to enhance removals resulting from anthropogenic land use, land-use change and forestry activities shall continue to be available to Annex I Parties as a means to reach their quantified emission limitation and reduction objectives, in accordance with decision 2/CMP.6;

(d) The global warming potentials used to calculate the carbon dioxide equivalence of anthropogenic emissions by sources and removals by sinks of greenhouse gases listed in Annex A for the second commitment period shall be those provided by the Intergovernmental Panel on Climate Change and agreed upon by the Conference of the Parties serving as the meeting of the Parties to the Kyoto Protocol together with other methodological issues based on the draft text contained in chapter IV of document FCCC/KP/AWG/2010/CRP.4/Rev.4;

(e) Further work on the consideration of information on potential environmental, economic and social consequences, including spillover effects, of tools, policies, measures and methodologies available to Annex I Parties shall continue on the basis of proposals contained in chapter V of document FCCC/KP/AWG/2010/CRP.4/Rev.4.

10ᵗʰ plenary meeting
10-11 December 2010

Decision 2/CMP.6

The Cancun Agreements: Land use, land-use change and forestry

The Conference of the Parties serving as the meeting of the Parties to the Kyoto Protocol,

Affirming that the implementation of land use, land-use change and forestry activities included under the provisions of the Kyoto Protocol shall be consistent with the objectives and principles of, and any decisions taken under, the Convention and its Kyoto Protocol,

1. *Affirms* that the principles contained in paragraph 1 of decision 16/CMP.1 continue to govern the treatment of land use, land-use change and forestry activities;

2. *Agrees* that the definitions of forest, afforestation, reforestation, deforestation, revegetation, forest management, cropland management and grazing land management shall be the same as in the first commitment period under the Kyoto Protocol;

3. *Requests* the Ad Hoc Working Group on Further Commitments for Annex I Parties under the Kyoto Protocol to consider, in time for possible inclusion in the second commitment period of the Kyoto Protocol, if appropriate, whether a cap should be applied to emissions and removals from forest management and how extraordinary occurrences (called force majeure) whose severity is beyond the control of, and not materially influenced by, a Party can be addressed;

4. *Also requests* each Annex I Party to submit to the secretariat, by 28 February 2011, information on the forest management reference level[1] inscribed in appendix I to this decision, including any update to replace the value, in accordance with the guide-

---

1) The forest management reference levels inscribed in appendix I to this decision were set transparently, taking into account the following: (a) removals or emissions from forest management as shown in greenhouse gas inventories and relevant historical data; (b) age-class structure; (c) forest management activities already undertaken; (d) projected forest management activities under a 'business as usual' scenario; (e) continuity with the treatment of forest management in the first commitment period; (f) the need to exclude removals from accounting in accordance with decision 16/CMP.1, paragraph 1. Points (c), (d) and (e) above were applied where relevant. The forest management reference levels also took into account the need for consistency with the inclusion of carbon pools. Reference levels including and excluding 'force majeure' should be provided.

lines outlined in part I of appendix II to this decision;

5. *Decides* that each submission referred to in paragraph 4 above shall be subject to a technical assessment by a review team in accordance with the guidelines outlined in part II of appendix II to this decision, and that outcomes of the technical assessment will be considered by the Conference of the Parties serving as the meeting of the Parties to the Kyoto Protocol at its next session;

6. *Requests* the secretariat, subject to the availability of funds, to organize the technical assessments referred to in paragraph 5 above;

7. *Also requests* the Ad Hoc Working Group on Further Commitments for Annex I Parties under the Kyoto Protocol to continue its consideration of definitions, modalities, rules and guidelines relating to land use, land-use change and forestry activities under the Kyoto Protocol for application in the second commitment period.

Appendix I

Reference levels submitted by Annex I Parties to the Kyoto Protocol

Party	Reference level (Mt CO_2eq/year)
Australia	−9.16
Austria	−2.12
Belarus	−24.93
Belgium	−3.40
Bulgaria	−10.08
Canada	−105.40
Croatia	−
Cyprus[a]	−0.16
Czech Republic	−3.86
Denmark	0.18
Estonia	−1.97
European Union (27)	−283.20[a]
Finland	−13.70
France	−66.98
Germany	−2.07
Greece	−1.38
Hungary	−0.50
Iceland	−
Ireland	−0.07
Italy	−15.61
Japan	0.00
Latvia	−12.93
Liechtenstein	−
Lithuania	−11.48
Luxembourg	−0.26
Malta[a]	−0.05
Monaco	−
Netherlands	−1.69
New Zealand	17.05
Norway	−14.20
Poland	−34.67
Portugal	−0.92
Romania	−29.43
Russian Federation	−89.10
Slovakia	−0.51
Slovenia	−2.73
Spain	−41.53
Sweden	−21.84
Switzerland	0.48
Ukraine	−28.5[b]
United Kingdom of Great Britain and Northern Ireland	−3.44

a   The European Union total includes Cyprus and Malta. Cyprus and Malta are member States of the European Union but are not Parties to the Convention that are also Parties to the Kyoto Protocol with a commitment inscribed in Annex B to the Kyoto Protocol.

b   As per the submission from Ukraine received by the secretariat on 10 December 2010, this number is based on the assumption of a 50/50 per cent split between managed and unmanaged forests and will be updated as soon as possible on the basis of the most recent information.

Note: Parties have made different assumptions in the construction of the reference levels proposed in the table above. These assumptions can be found in Parties' submissions at <http://unfccc.int/meetings/ad_hoc_working_groups/kp/items/4907.php>.

Appendix II

Guidelines for the submission and review of information on forest management reference levels/baselines

1.   Each Party included in Annex I shall include in its submission transparent, complete, consistent, comparable and accurate information required under part I of these guidelines, for the purpose of allowing a technical assessment, as specified in part II, of the data, methodologies and procedures used in the construction of reference levels as specified in appendix I above to facilitate consideration of the forest management reference level.

Part I: Guidelines for submissions of information on forest management reference levels
  Objectives

2. The objectives of the submission are:

(a) To provide information consistent with the general reporting principles set out by the Convention and elaborated by the Intergovernmental Panel on Climate Change (IPCC)[1] on how the elements contained in footnote 1 in paragraph 4 of this decision were taken into account by Parties in the construction of forest management reference levels, and to provide any additional relevant information;

(b) To document the information that was used by Parties in constructing forest management reference levels in a comprehensive and transparent way;

(c) To provide transparent, complete, consistent, comparable and accurate methodological information used at the time of the construction of forest management reference levels.

3. Parties shall provide submissions in accordance with the following guidelines:

General description

4. Provide a general description of the construction of the forest management reference levels consistent with footnote 1 in paragraph 4 of this decision.

5. Provide a description on how each element contained in footnote 1 in paragraph

---

1) UNFCCC Annex I Reporting Guidelines, IPCC *Good Practice Guidance for Land Use, Land-Use Change and Forestry.*

4 of this decision was taken into account in the construction of the forest management reference level.

Pools and gases

6. Identify pools and gases which have been included in the reference level and explain the reasons for omitting a pool from the reference level construction.

7. Explain consistency between the pools included in the reference level.

Approaches, methods and models used

8. Provide a description of approaches, methods and models, including assumptions, used in the construction of the forest management reference level, referring, where relevant, to the most recently submitted national inventory report.

Description of construction of reference levels

9. Provide a description of how each of the following elements were considered or treated in the construction of the forest management reference level, taking into account the principles in decision 16/CMP.1:

(a) Area under forest management;

(b) Emissions and removals from forest management and the relationship between forest management and forest land remaining forest land as shown in greenhouse gas inventories and relevant historical data, including information provided under Article 3, paragraph 3, and, if applicable, Article 3, paragraph 4, on forest management of the Kyoto Protocol and under forest land remaining forest land under the Convention;

(c) Forest characteristics, including age-class structure, increments, rotation length and other relevant information, including information on forest management activities under 'business as usual';

(d) Historical and assumed harvesting rates;

(e) Harvested wood products;

(f) Disturbances in the context of force majeure;

(g) Factoring out in accordance with paragraph 1 (h) (i) and (ii) of decision 16/CMP.1.

10. Provide a description of any other relevant elements considered or treated in the

construction of the forest management reference level, including any additional information related to footnote 1 in paragraph 4 of this decision.

Policies included

11. Provide a description of the domestic policies adopted and implemented no later than December 2009 and considered in the construction of the forest management reference level and explain how these polices have been considered in the construction of the reference level.

12. Provide confirmation that the construction of the forest management reference level neither includes assumptions about changes to domestic policies adopted and implemented after December 2009 nor includes new domestic policies.

Part II: Guidelines for review of submissions of information on forest management reference levels

Objectives of review

13. The objectives of the review are:

(a) To assess whether Parties have provided transparent, complete, consistent, comparable and accurate information on how the elements contained in footnote 1 in paragraph 4 of this decision were taken into account in the construction of forest management reference levels;

(b) To ascertain whether the construction of the forest management reference level is consistent with the information and descriptions used by the Party;

(c) To provide, as appropriate, technical recommendations to the Annex I Party;

(d) To provide a technical assessment to support consideration by the Conference of the Parties serving as the meeting of the Parties to the Kyoto Protocol at its seventh session of the forest management reference levels to be used during the second commitment period of the Kyoto Protocol;

(e) To assess whether Parties have provided transparent, complete, consistent, comparable and accurate methodological information to facilitate reviews of methodological consistency.

Scope of the review

14. A technical assessment of the data, methodologies, assumptions and procedures used in the construction of the forest management reference levels of Annex I Parties to determine whether they are consistent with the guidelines in part I of this appendix.

15. The review team will assess the following issues:

(a) Whether the Party has identified pools and gases included in the forest management reference level and explained the reasons for omitting a pool or a gas from the forest management reference level and whether the coverage of pools in the forest management reference level is consistent;

(b) The description of approaches, methods and models used in the construction of reference levels;

(c) How each element in paragraphs 9 and 10 above is considered, including justification for why any particular element was not considered;

(d) Whether the forest management reference level value is consistent with the information and descriptions provided by the Party;

(e) Whether the information was provided by the Party in a transparent manner;

(f) Whether a description is provided of domestic policies included in accordance with the provisions contained in paragraph 11 above that were used in the construction of the reference level and how these policies were used in the construction of the reference level;

(g) Whether confirmation has been provided that the construction of the forest management reference level does not include assumptions about changes to domestic policies in accordance with paragraph 12 above.

16. As part of the technical assessment, the review process may provide technical recommendations to the Annex I Party on the construction of its forest management reference level. This may include a recommendation to make a technical revision to elements used in its construction.

17. Review teams shall refrain from making any judgment on domestic policies taken into account in the construction of the reference level.

Review procedures

General procedures

18. Review teams will meet in a single location to perform a centralized review of all forest management reference level submissions.

19. Each submission will be assigned to a review team responsible for performing the technical assessment in accordance with procedures and time frames established in these guidelines.

20. Each review team will provide a thorough and comprehensive assessment of the forest management reference level submission and will under its collective responsibility prepare a report.

21. The review process will be coordinated by the secretariat. Review teams will be composed of land use, land-use change and forestry review experts selected from the roster of experts. Participating experts will serve in their personal capacity and will be neither nationals of the Party under review nor funded by that Party.

22. Review teams will work under the same rules as those set out in paragraphs 9 and 10 of the annex to decision 22/CMP.1.

Composition of the review teams

23. Review teams should be made up of at least three land use, land-use change and forestry experts. The secretariat shall ensure that in any review team one co-lead reviewer shall be from an Annex I Party and one co-lead reviewer shall be from a non-Annex I Party. The secretariat will select the members of the review team with a view to achieving a balance between experts from Annex I Parties and non-Annex I Parties.

Timing

24. In order to facilitate the secretariat's work, each Party should confirm to the secretariat, by the end of February 2011, its active experts on the land use, land-use change and forestry roster of experts who will be able to participate in the review of forest management reference levels in 2011.

25. The secretariat should forward all relevant information to the review teams in

good time before the start of the review.

26. Prior to the review, the review team should identify any preliminary questions requiring clarification by the Party, as appropriate.

27. The review should take place no later than by the end of May 2011 and be conducted according to the indicative timings set out in paragraphs 28 to 32 below. The Party being reviewed may interact with the review team during the review of its submission in order to respond to questions and to provide additional information as requested by the review team.

28. The review team may seek any additional clarification from the Party no later than one week following the review. This may include technical recommendations to the Party on the construction of its reference level. The Party is to provide any required clarifications to the review team no later than five weeks following the request and may also submit a revised reference level in response to the technical recommendations of the review team.

29. The review team will prepare a draft report and make it available to the Party no later than eight weeks following the review. The report should include a short summary.

30. The Party will have three weeks to respond to the draft report of the review team.

31. If the Party does not agree with the findings in the draft report, in responding to the Party's comments the review team will seek advice from a small group of experienced reviewers to be convened by the secretariat, which will consider comparability across Parties.

32. The review team will prepare a final report within three weeks following the Party's response and the report will be sent to the secretariat for publication on the UNFCCC website. The final report will contain the technical assessment, technical recommendations, if appropriate, the responses by the Party and, where provided, the advice of the small group of experienced reviewers convened by the secretariat.

33. The secretariat will prepare a synthesis report of key conclusions of the forest management reference level review process, including comments by Parties, for consideration at the Conference of the Parties serving as the meeting of the Parties to the Kyoto Protocol at its seventh session. The synthesis report will be made publicly available and will be published on the UNFCCC website.

10th plenary meeting
10–11 December 2010

8. 제17차 더반(2011) — Durban Platform

Report of the Conference of the Parties on its seventeenth session, held in Durban from 28 November to 11 December 2011

Decision 1/CP.17
FCCC/CP/2011/9/Add.1
15 March 2012

Establishment of an Ad Hoc Working Group on the Durban Platform for Enhanced Action

The Conference of the Parties,

Recognizing that climate change represents an urgent and potentially irreversible threat to human societies and the planet and thus requires to be urgently addressed by all Parties, and acknowledging that the global nature of climate change calls for the widest possible cooperation by all countries and their participation in an effective and appropriate international response, with a view to accelerating the reduction of global greenhouse gas emissions,

Noting with grave concern the significant gap between the aggregate effect of Parties' mitigation pledges in terms of global annual emissions of greenhouse gases by 2020 and aggregate emission pathways consistent with having a likely chance of holding the increase in global average temperature below 2 °C or 1.5 °C above pre-industrial levels,

Recognizing that fulfilling the ultimate objective of the Convention will require strengthening of the multilateral, rules-based regime under the Convention,

Noting decision 1/CMP.7,

Also noting decision 2/CP.17,

1. *Decides* to extend the Ad Hoc Working Group on Long-term Cooperative Action under the Convention for one year in order for it to continue its work and reach the agreed outcome pursuant to decision 1/CP.13 (Bali Action Plan) through decisions

adopted by the sixteenth, seventeenth and eighteenth sessions of the Conference of the Parties, at which time the Ad Hoc Working Group on Long-term Cooperative Action under the Convention shall be terminated;

2. *Also decides* to launch a process to develop a protocol, another legal instrument or an agreed outcome with legal force under the Convention applicable to all Parties, through a subsidiary body under the Convention hereby established and to be known as the Ad Hoc Working Group on the Durban Platform for Enhanced Action;

3. *Further decides* that the Ad Hoc Working Group on the Durban Platform for Enhanced Action shall start its work as a matter of urgency in the first half of 2012 and shall report to future sessions of the Conference of the Parties on the progress of its work;

4. *Decides* that the Ad Hoc Working Group on the Durban Platform for Enhanced Action shall complete its work as early as possible but no later than 2015 in order to adopt this protocol, another legal instrument or an agreed outcome with legal force at the twenty-first session of the Conference of the Parties and for it to come into effect and be implemented from 2020;

5. *Also decides* that the Ad Hoc Working Group on the Durban Platform for Enhanced Action shall plan its work in the first half of 2012, including, inter alia, on mitigation, adaptation, finance, technology development and transfer, transparency of action and support, and capacity-building, drawing upon submissions from Parties and relevant technical, social and economic information and expertise;

6. *Further decides* that the process shall raise the level of ambition and shall be informed, inter alia, by the Fifth Assessment Report of the Intergovernmental Panel on Climate Change, the outcomes of the 2013–2015 review and the work of the subsidiary bodies;

7. *Decides* to launch a workplan on enhancing mitigation ambition to identify and to explore options for a range of actions that can close the ambition gap with a view to ensuring the highest possible mitigation efforts by all Parties;

8. *Requests* Parties and observer organizations to submit by 28 February 2012 their views on options and ways for further increasing the level of ambition and decides to hold an in-session workshop at the first negotiating session in 2012 to consider options and ways for increasing ambition and possible further actions.

10th plenary meeting
11 December 2011

9. 제18차 도하(2012) — Doha Amendment

Report of the Conference of the Parties serving as the meeting of the Parties to the Kyoto Protocol on its eighth session, held in Doha from 26 November to 8 December 2012

Decision 1/CMP.8

FCCC/KP/CMP/2012/13/Add.1

28 February 2013

Amendment to the Kyoto Protocol pursuant to its Article 3, paragraph 9 (the Doha Amendment)

The Conference of the Parties serving as the meeting of the Parties to the Kyoto Protocol,

Recalling Article 3, paragraph 9, Article 20, paragraph 2, and Article 21, paragraph 7, of the Kyoto Protocol,

Recalling also decisions 1/CMP.1 and 1/CMP.7,

Recalling further decision 1/CP.17,

Emphasizing the role of the Kyoto Protocol in the mitigation efforts by Parties included in Annex I,

Welcoming the decision by a number of Parties included in Annex I to inscribe quantified emission limitation and reduction commitments for the second commitment period in the third column of Annex B,

Recognizing the urgent need for Parties to deposit their instruments of acceptance without delay in order to ensure the prompt entry into force of the amendment to the Kyoto Protocol contained in annex I to this decision,

Desiring to facilitate the broad participation of Parties included in Annex I in the second commitment period,

Recognizing also the need for continued smooth implementation of the Kyoto Protocol, including its mechanisms under Articles 6, 12 and 17, pending the entry into force of the amendment for the second commitment period,

Taking note of the declarations set out in annex II to this decision,

Taking note also of decision 1/CP.18,

Noting the importance of the work under the Ad Hoc Working Group on the Durban Platform for Enhanced Action to adopt a protocol, another legal instrument or an agreed outcome with legal force as soon as possible but no later than 2015, to come into effect and be implemented from 2020, as well as the workplan on enhancing mitigation ambition with a view to ensuring the highest possible mitigation efforts by all Parties, pursuant to decision 1/CP.17,

I.

1. *Adopts*, in accordance with Articles 20 and 21 of the Kyoto Protocol, the amendment set out in annex I to this decision;

2. *Requests* the secretariat to communicate the adopted amendment to the Depositary for circulation to all Parties for acceptance, in accordance with Articles 20 and 21 of the Kyoto Protocol;

3. *Calls* on all Parties to deposit as soon as possible with the Depositary their instruments of acceptance in respect of the amendment pursuant to Article 20 of the Kyoto Protocol with a view to expedite its entry into force;

4. *Reaffirms* that the second commitment period will begin on 1 January 2013 and decides that it will end on 31 December 2020;

II.

5. *Recognizes* that Parties may provisionally apply the amendment pending its entry into force in accordance with Articles 20 and 21 of the Kyoto Protocol, and decides that Parties will provide notification of any such provisional application to the Depositary;

6. *Decides* also that Parties that do not provisionally apply the amendment under paragraph 5 will implement their commitments and other responsibilities in relation to the second commitment period, in a manner consistent with their national legislation or domestic processes, as of 1 January 2013 and pending the entry into force of the amendment in accordance with Articles 20 and 21 of the Kyoto Protocol;

III.

7. *Decides* that each Party included in Annex I will revisit its quantified emission limitation and reduction commitment for the second commitment period at the latest by 2014. In order to increase the ambition of its commitment, such Party may decrease the percentage inscribed in the third column of Annex B of its quantified emission limitation and reduction commitment, in line with an aggregate reduction of greenhouse gas emissions not controlled by the Montreal Protocol by Parties included in Annex I of at least 25 to 40 per cent below 1990 levels by 2020;

8. *Decides also* that in order to ensure that an increase in ambition referred to in Article 3, paragraphs 1 ter and 1 quater, is effective, the Party concerned shall either adjust the calculation of its assigned amount or cancel, upon the establishment of its assigned amount, a number of assigned amount units (AAUs) equivalent to the decrease in its quantified emission limitation and reduction commitment inscribed in the third column in Annex B as contained in annex I to this decision through transferring these units to a cancellation account established in its national registry for this purpose, and communicating such adjustment of the calculation or transfer to the secretariat;

9. *Requests* each Party with a quantified emission limitation and reduction commitment inscribed in the third column of Annex B as contained in annex I to this decision to submit to the secretariat, by 30 April 2014, information relating to its intention to increase the ambition of its commitment, including progress made towards achieving its quantified emission limitation and reduction commitment, the most recently updated projections for greenhouse gas emissions until the end of the second commitment period, and the potential for increasing ambition;

10. *Decides further* that the information submitted by Parties included in Annex I in accordance with paragraph 9 above shall be considered by Parties at a high level ministerial round table to be held during the first sessional period in 2014, and requests the secretariat to prepare a report on the round table for consideration by the Conference of the Parties serving as the meeting of the Parties to the Kyoto Protocol at its tenth session;

11. *Takes note* of the estimated budgetary implications of the activities to be undertaken by the secretariat pursuant to the provisions contained in paragraph 10 above and requests that the actions of the secretariat called for in in paragraph 10 above be undertaken subject to the availability of financial resources;

IV.

12. *Clarifies* that, for the second commitment period, starting from 1 January 2013, Parties not included in Annex I continue to be able to participate in ongoing project activities under Article 12 of the Kyoto Protocol and in any project activities to be registered after 31 December 2012 in accordance with the provisions of the annex to decision 3/CMP.1;

13. *Clarifies also* that for the purposes of the second commitment period, from 1 January 2013 onwards, a Party included in Annex I may continue to participate in ongoing project activities under Article 12 and in any project activities to be registered after 31 December 2012, but only a Party with a quantified emission limitation and reduction commitment inscribed in the third column of Annex B as contained in annex I to this decision shall be eligible to transfer and acquire certified emission reductions (CERs) in accordance with decision 3/CMP.1 and with paragraph 15 below;

14. *Decides* that a Party referred to in paragraphs 15 and 16 below shall be eligible to use CERs to contribute to compliance with part of its commitment under Article 3 of the Kyoto Protocol for the second commitment period upon the entry into force for that Party of the amendment contained in annex I to this decision and upon that Party meeting the requirements set out in paragraph 31 of the annex to decision 3/CMP.1;

15. *Decides*, with respect to joint implementation under Article 6 and emissions trading under Article 17 of the Kyoto Protocol, that:

(a) As of 1 January 2013, only a Party with a commitment inscribed in the third column of Annex B as contained in annex I to this decision whose eligibility has been established in accordance with the provisions of paragraph 3 of the annex to decision 11/CMP.1 in the first commitment period, shall be eligible to transfer and acquire CERs, AAUs, emission reduction units (ERUs) and removal units (RMUs) valid for the second commitment period under Article 17 of the Kyoto Protocol, subject to the provisions of paragraph 3(b) of the annex to decision 11/CMP.1;

(b) Paragraph 2(b) of the annex to decision 11/CMP.1 shall apply to such Party only upon calculation and recording of its assigned amount for the second commitment period;

16. *Requests* the Subsidiary Body for Implementation to consider modalities for expediting the continued issuance, transfer and acquisition of ERUs under Article 6 for the second commitment period with respect to Parties referred to in paragraph 15 above and

modalities for expediting the establishment of eligibility of Parties referred to in paragraph 15 above whose eligibility has not been established in the first commitment period;

17. *Decides* that the provisions of the second sentence of paragraph 31(e) of the annex to decision 3/CMP.1, the second sentence of subparagraph 21(e) of the annex to decision 9/CMP.1 and the second sentence of paragraph 2(e) of the annex to decision 11/CMP.1 shall be extended to apply to the second commitment period;

18. *Decides also* with regard to paragraphs 6–10 of the annex to decision 11/CMP.1 that for the purposes of the second commitment period:

(a) They shall apply to each Party referred to in paragraphs 15 and 16 above only upon calculation and recording of its assigned amount for the second commitment period;

(b) Any references to Article 3, paragraphs 7 and 8, of the Kyoto Protocol shall be read as references to Article 3, paragraphs 7 bis, 8 and 8 bis, of the Kyoto Protocol;

(c) The reference to "five times its most recently reviewed inventory" in paragraph 6 of the annex to decision 11/CMP.1 shall be read as "eight times its most recently reviewed inventory";

19. *Decides further* that paragraph 23 of the annex to decision 13/CMP.1 shall not apply for the purposes of the second commitment period;

V.

20. *Decides* that the share of proceeds to assist developing country Parties that are particularly vulnerable to the adverse effects of climate change to meet the costs of adaptation referred to in Article 12, paragraph 8, of the Kyoto Protocol and decision 17/CP.7, paragraph 15(a), shall be maintained at 2 per cent of the CERs issued for project activities;

21. *Decides also* that for the second commitment period, the Adaptation Fund shall be further augmented through a 2 per cent share of the proceeds levied on the first international transfers of AAUs and the issuance of ERUs for Article 6 projects immediately upon the conversion to ERUs of AAUs or RMUs previously held by Parties;

22. *Reaffirms* that in accordance with decision 17/CP.7, clean development mechanism project activities in least developed country Parties shall continue to be exempt from the share of proceeds to assist with the costs of adaptation;

VI.

23. *Decides* that each Party included in Annex I with a commitment inscribed in the third column of Annex B as contained in annex I to this decision shall establish a previous period surplus reserve account in its national registry;

24. *Decides also* that where the emissions of a Party referred to in paragraph 23 above in a commitment period are less than its assigned amount under Article 3, the difference shall, on request of that Party, be carried over to the subsequent commitment period, as follows:

(a) Any ERUs or CERs held in that Party's national registry that have not been retired for that commitment period or cancelled may be carried over to the subsequent commitment period, up to a maximum for each unit type of 2.5 per cent of the assigned amount calculated pursuant to Article 3, paragraphs 7 and 8;

(b) Any AAUs held in that Party's national registry that have not been retired for that commitment period or cancelled shall be added to the assigned amount for that Party for the second commitment period. That part of a Party's assigned amount consisting of AAUs held in that Party's national registry that has not been retired for that commitment period or cancelled shall be transferred to its previous period surplus reserve account for the subsequent commitment period, to be established in its national registry;

25. *Decides further* that units in a Party's previous period surplus reserve account may be used for retirement during the additional period for fulfilling commitments of the second commitment period up to the extent by which emissions during the second commitment period exceed the assigned amount for that commitment period, as defined in Article 3, paragraphs 7 bis, 8 and 8 bis, of the Kyoto Protocol;

26. *Decides* that units may be transferred and acquired between previous period surplus reserve accounts. A Party referred to in paragraph 23 above may acquire units from other Parties' previous period surplus reserve accounts into its previous period surplus reserve account up to 2 per cent of its assigned amount for the first commitment period pursuant to Article 3, paragraph 7 and 8;

VII.

27. *Takes note* of decision 2/CMP.8 on the implications of the implementation of decisions 2/CMP.7 to 5/CMP.7 on the previous decisions of the Conference of the Parties serving as the meeting of the Parties to the Kyoto Protocol on methodological issues re-

lated to the Kyoto Protocol, including those relating to Articles 5, 7 and 8;

28. *Requests* the Subsidiary Body for Scientific and Technological Advice to take into account the provisions of this decision in its work pursuant to decision 2/CMP.8;

29. *Requests also* the secretariat and the relevant bodies under the Kyoto Protocol to take all necessary measures to facilitate the implementation of this decision;

30. *Decides* that the Ad Hoc Working Group on Further Commitments for Annex I Parties under the Kyoto Protocol has fulfilled the mandate set out in decision 1/CMP.1 and that its work is hereby concluded.

Annex I

Doha amendment to the Kyoto Protocol
Article 1: Amendment

A. Annex B to the Kyoto Protocol

The following table shall replace the table in Annex B to the Protocol:

1	2	3	4	5	6
Party	Quantified emission limitation or reduction commitment (2008–2012) (percentage of base year or period)	Quantified emission limitation or reduction commitment (2013–2020) (percentage of base year or period)	Reference year[1]	Quantified emission limitation or reduction commitment (2013–2020) (expressed as percentage of reference year)[1]	Pledges for the reduction of greenhouse gas emissions by 2020 (percentage of reference year)
Australia	108	99.5	2000	98	–5 to –15% or –25%
Austria	92	80[4]	NA	NA	
Belarus[5]*		88	1990	NA	–8%
Belgium	92	80[4]	NA	NA	
Bulgaria*	92	80[4]	NA	NA	
Croatia*	95	80[6]	NA	NA	–20%/–30%
Cyprus		80[4]	NA	NA	
Czech Republic*	92	80[4]	NA	NA	
Denmark	92	80[4]	NA	NA	
Estonia*	92	80[4]	NA	NA	
European Union	92	80[4]	1990	NA	–20%/–30%
Finland	92	80[4]	NA	NA	
France	92	80[4]	NA	NA	
Germany	92	80[4]	NA	NA	
Greece	92	80[4]	NA	NA	
Hungary*	94	80[4]	NA	NA	
Iceland	110	80[8]	NA	NA	
Ireland	92	80[4]	NA	NA	
Italy	92	80[4]	NA	NA	
Kazakhstan*		95	1990	95	–7%
Latvia*	92	80[4]	NA	NA	
Liechtenstein	92	84	1990	84	–20%/–30%

1	2	3	4	5	6
Party	Quantified emission limitation or reduction commitment (2008–2012) (percentage of base year or period)	Quantified emission limitation or reduction commitment (2013–2020) (percentage of base year or period)	Reference year[1]	Quantified emission limitation or reduction commitment (2013–2020) (expressed as percentage of reference year)[1]	Pledges for the reduction of greenhouse gas emissions by 2020 (percentage of reference year)[2]
Lithuania*	92	80[4]	NA	NA	
Luxembourg	92	80[4]	NA	NA	
Malta		80[4]	NA	NA	
Monaco	92	78	1990	78	−30%
Netherlands	92	80[4]	NA	NA	
Norway	101	84	1990	84	−30% to −40%[10]
Poland*	94	80[4]	NA	NA	
Portugal	92	80[4]	NA	NA	
Romania*	92	80[4]	NA	NA	
Slovakia*	92	80[4]	NA	NA	
Slovenia*	92	80[4]	NA	NA	
Spain	92	80[4]	NA	NA	
Sweden	92	80[4]	NA	NA	
Switzerland	92	84.2	1990	NA	−20% to −30%[11]
Ukraine*	100	76[12]	1990	NA	−20%
United Kingdom of Great Britain and Northern Ireland	92	80[4]	NA	NA	

Party	Quantified emission limitation or reduction commitment (2008–2012) (percentage of base year or period)
Canada[13]	94
Japan[14]	94
New Zealand[15]	100
Russian Federation[16]*	100

Abbreviation: NA = not applicable.
* Countries that are undergoing the process of transition to a market economy.
All footnotes below, except for footnotes 1, 2 and 5, have been provided through communications from the respective Parties.

1   A reference year may be used by a Party on an optional basis for its own purposes to express its quantified emission limitation or reduction commitment (QELRC) as a percentage of emissions of that year, that is not internationally binding under the Kyoto Protocol, in addition to the listing of its QELRC(s) in relation to the base year in the second and third columns of this table, which are internationally legally binding.

2   Further information on these pledges can be found in documents FCCC/SB/ 2011/INF.1/Rev.1 and FCCC/KP/AWG/2012/MISC.1, Add.1 and Add.2.

3   Australia's QELRC under the second commitment period of the Kyoto Protocol is consistent with the achievement of Australia's unconditional 2020 target of 5 per cent below 2000 levels. Australia retains the option later to move up within its 2020 target of 5 to 15, or 25 per cent below 2000 levels, subject to certain conditions being met. This reference retains the status of these pledges as made under the Cancun Agreements and does not amount to a new legally binding commitment under this Protocol or its associated rules and modalities.

4   The QELRCs for the European Union and its member States for a second commitment period under the Kyoto Protocol are based on the understanding that these will be fulfilled jointly with the European Union and its member States, in accordance with Article 4 of the Kyoto Protocol. The QELRCs are without prejudice to the subsequent notification by the European Union and its member States of an agreement to fulfil their commitments jointly in accordance with the provisions of the Kyoto Protocol.

5   Added to Annex B by an amendment adopted pursuant to decision 10/CMP.2. This amendment has not yet entered into force.

6   Croatia's QELRC for a second commitment period under the Kyoto Protocol is based on the understanding that it will fulfil this QELRC jointly with the European Union and its member States, in accordance with Article 4 of the Kyoto Protocol. As a consequence, Croatia's accession to the European Union shall not affect its participation in such joint fulfilment agreement pursuant to Article 4 or its QELRC.

7   As part of a global and comprehensive agreement for the period beyond 2012, the European Union reiterates its conditional offer to move to a 30 per cent reduction by 2020 compared to 1990 levels, provided that other developed countries commit themselves to comparable emission reductions and developing countries contribute adequately according to their responsibilities and respective capabilities.

8   The QELRC for Iceland for a second commitment period under the Kyoto Protocol is based on the understanding that it will be fulfilled jointly with the European Union and its member States, in accordance with Article 4 of the Kyoto Protocol.

9   The QELRC presented in column three refers to a reduction target of 20 per cent by 2020 compared to 1990 levels. Liechtenstein would consider a higher reduction target of up to 30 per cent by 2020 compared to 1990 levels under the condition that other developed countries commit themselves to comparable emission reductions and that economically more advanced developing countries contribute adequately according to their responsibilities and respective capabilities.

10   Norway's QELRC of 84 is consistent with its target of 30 per cent reduction of emissions by

2020, compared to 1990. If it can contribute to a global and comprehensive agreement where major emitting Parties agree on emission reductions in line with the 2° C target, Norway will move to a level of 40 per cent reduction for 2020 based on 1990 levels. This reference retains the status of the pledge made under the Cancun Agreements and does not amount to a new legally binding commitment under this Protocol.

11 The QELRC presented in the third column of this table refers to a reduction target of 20 per cent by 2020 compared to 1990 levels. Switzerland would consider a higher reduction target up to 30 per cent by 2020 compared to 1990 levels subject to comparable emission reduction commitments from other developed countries and adequate contribution from developing countries according to their responsibilities and capabilities in line with the 2° C target. This reference retains the status of the pledge made under the Cancun Agreements and does not amount to a new legally binding commitment under this Protocol or its associated rules and modalities.

12 Should be full carry-over and there is no acceptance of any cancellation or any limitation on use of this legitimately acquired sovereign property.

13 On 15 December 2011, the Depositary received written notification of Canada's withdrawal from the Kyoto Protocol. This action will become effective for Canada on 15 December 2012.

14 In a communication dated 10 December 2010, Japan indicated that it does not have any intention to be under obligation of the second commitment period of the Kyoto Protocol after 2012.

15 New Zealand remains a Party to the Kyoto Protocol. It will be taking a quantified economy-wide emission reduction target under the United Nations Framework Convention on Climate Change in the period 2013 to 2020.

16 In a communication dated 8 December 2010 that was received by the secretariat on 9 December 2010, the Russian Federation indicated that it does not intend to assume a quantitative emission limitation or reduction commitment for the second commitment period.

B. Annex A to the Kyoto Protocol

The following list shall replace the list under the heading "Greenhouse gases" in Annex A to the Protocol:

Greenhouse gases
Carbon dioxide (CO_2)
Methane (CH_4)
Nitrous oxide (N_2O)
Hydrofluorocarbons (HFCs)
Perfluorocarbons (PFCs)
Sulphur hexafluoride (SF_6)
Nitrogen trifluoride (NF_3)[1]

---

1) Applies only from the beginning of the second commitment period.

C. Article 3, paragraph 1 bis

The following paragraph shall be inserted after paragraph 1 of Article 3 of the Protocol:

1 bis. The Parties included in Annex 1 shall, individually or jointly, ensure that their aggregate anthropogenic carbon dioxide equivalent emissions of the greenhouse gases listed in Annex A do not exceed their assigned amounts, calculated pursuant to their quantified emission limitation and reduction commitments inscribed in the third column of the table contained in Annex B and in accordance with the provisions of this Article, with a view to reducing their overall emissions of such gases by at least 18 per cent below 1990 levels in the commitment period 2013 to 2020.

D. Article 3, paragraph 1 ter

The following paragraph shall be inserted after paragraph 1 bis of Article 3 of the Protocol:

1 ter. A Party included in Annex B may propose an adjustment to decrease the percentage inscribed in the third column of Annex B of its quantified emission limitation and reduction commitment inscribed in the third column of the table contained in Annex B. A proposal for such an adjustment shall be communicated to the Parties by the secretariat at least three months before the meeting of the Conference of the Parties serving as the meeting of the Parties to this Protocol at which it is proposed for adoption.

E. Article 3, paragraph 1 quater

The following paragraph shall be inserted after paragraph 1 ter of Article 3 of the Protocol:

1 quater. An adjustment proposed by a Party included in Annex I to increase the ambition of its quantified emission limitation and reduction commitment in accordance with Article 3, paragraph 1 ter, above shall be considered adopted by the Conference of the Parties serving as the meeting of the Parties to this Protocol unless more than three-fourths of the Parties present and voting object to its adoption. The adopted adjustment shall be communicated by the secretariat to the Depositary, who shall circulate it to all Parties, and shall enter into force on 1 January of the year fol-

lowing the communication by the Depositary. Such adjustments shall be binding upon Parties.

F. Article 3, paragraph 7 bis

The following paragraphs shall be inserted after paragraph 7 of Article 3 of the Protocol:

7 bis. In the second quantified emission limitation and reduction commitment period, from 2013 to 2020, the assigned amount for each Party included in Annex I shall be equal to the percentage inscribed for it in the third column of the table contained in Annex B of its aggregate anthropogenic carbon dioxide equivalent emissions of the greenhouse gases listed in Annex A in 1990, or the base year or period determined in accordance with paragraph 5 above, multiplied by eight. Those Parties included in Annex I for whom land-use change and forestry constituted a net source of greenhouse gas emissions in 1990 shall include in their 1990 emissions base year or period the aggregate anthropogenic carbon dioxide equivalent emissions by sources minus removals by sinks in 1990 from land-use change for the purposes of calculating their assigned amount.

G. Article 3, paragraph 7 ter

The following paragraph shall be inserted after paragraph 7 bis of Article 3 of the Protocol:

7 ter. Any positive difference between the assigned amount of the second commitment period for a Party included in the Annex I and average annual emissions for the first three years of the preceding commitment period multiplied by eight shall be transferred to the cancellation account of that Party.

H. Article 3, paragraph 8

In paragraph 8 of Article 3 of the Protocol, the words:

calculation referred to in paragraph 7 above

shall be substituted by:

calculations referred to in paragraphs 7 and 7 bis above

I. Article 3, paragraph 8 bis

The following paragraph shall be inserted after paragraph 8 of Article 3 of the Protocol:

8 bis. Any Party included in Annex I may use 1995 or 2000 as its base year for nitrogen trifluoride for the purposes of the calculation referred to in paragraph 7 bis above.

J. Article 3, paragraphs 12 bis and ter

The following paragraphs shall be inserted after paragraph 12 of Article 3 of the Protocol:

12 bis. Any units generated from market-based mechanisms to be established under the Convention or its instruments may be used by Parties included in Annex I to assist them in achieving compliance with their quantified emission limitation and reduction commitments under Article 3. Any such units which a Party acquires from another Party to the Convention shall be added to the assigned amount for the acquiring Party and subtracted from the quantity of units held by the transferring Party.

12 ter. The Conference of the Parties serving as the meeting of the Parties to this Protocol shall ensure that, where units from approved activities under market-based mechanisms referred to in paragraph 12 bis above are used by Parties included in Annex I to assist them in achieving compliance with their quantified emission limitation and reduction commitments under Article 3, a share of these units is used to cover administrative expenses, as well as to assist developing country Parties that are particularly vulnerable to the adverse effects of climate change to meet the costs of adaptation if these units are acquired under Article 17.

K. Article 4, paragraph 2

The following words shall be added to the end of the first sentence of paragraph 2 of Article 4 of the Protocol:

, or on the date of deposit of their instruments of acceptance of any amendment to Annex B pursuant to Article 3, paragraph 9

L. Article 4, paragraph 3

In paragraph 3 of Article 4 of the Protocol, the words:

, paragraph 7

shall be substituted by:

to which it relates

Article 2: Entry into force

This amendment shall enter into force in accordance with Articles 20 and 21 of the Kyoto Protocol.

Annex II

Political declarations relating to assigned amount units carried over from the first commitment period of the Kyoto Protocol

Australia

1. Australia will not purchase AAUs carried over from the first commitment period. Australia will adhere to arrangements in other countries relating to the transfer of AAUs under any arrangement that Australia may have linking our emissions trading scheme with any other scheme. Imported AAUs will continue to be ineligible for surrender for compliance by liable entities in Australia's emissions trading scheme.

European Union and its 27 member States

European Union legislation on Climate-Energy Package for the implementation of its emission reduction objectives for the period 2013-2020 does not allow the use of surplus AAUs carried over from the first commitment period to meet these objectives.

Japan

The Government of Japan will not purchase AAUs carried over from the first commitment period.

Liechtenstein

Liechtenstein will not acquire and use surplus assigned amount units carried over from the first commitment period to comply with its commitments in the second commitment period.

Monaco

Monaco will not purchase carried over AAUs from the first commitment period under the Kyoto Protocol.

Norway

Norway will not purchase carried over AAUs from the first commitment period under the Kyoto Protocol.

Switzerland

Under the Swiss domestic legislation applicable during the second commitment period, Switzerland will not use carried-over AAUs transferred from other Parties for compliance under Article 3 of the Kyoto Protocol for the second commitment period. Switzerland will adhere to arrangements in other countries relating to the transfer of AAUs under any arrangement that Switzerland may have linking our emissions trading scheme with any other emissions trading schemes.

9th *plenary meeting*
8 December 2012

10. 제21차 파리(2015) — Adoption of the Paris Agreement

FCCC/CP/2015/L.9/Rev.1
12 December 2015

ADOPTION OF THE PARIS AGREEMENT

Proposal by the President
Draft decision -/CP.21

The Conference of the Parties,

Recalling decision 1/CP.17 on the establishment of the Ad Hoc Working Group on the Durban Platform for Enhanced Action,

Also recalling Articles 2, 3 and 4 of the Convention,

Further recalling relevant decisions of the Conference of the Parties, including decisions 1/CP.16, 2/CP.18, 1/CP.19 and 1/CP.20,

Welcoming the adoption of United Nations General Assembly resolution A/RES/70/1, "Transforming our world: the 2030 Agenda for Sustainable Development", in particular its goal 13, and the adoption of the Addis Ababa Action Agenda of the third International Conference on Financing for Development and the adoption of the Sendai Framework for Disaster Risk Reduction,

Recognizing that climate change represents an urgent and potentially irreversible threat to human societies and the planet and thus requires the widest possible cooperation by all countries, and their participation in an effective and appropriate international response, with a view to accelerating the reduction of global greenhouse gas emissions,

Also recognizing that deep reductions in global emissions will be required in order to achieve the ultimate objective of the Convention and emphasizing the need for urgency in addressing climate change,

Acknowledging that climate change is a common concern of humankind, Parties should, when taking action to address climate change, respect, promote and consider their respective obligations on human rights, the right to health, the rights of indigenous peoples, local communities, migrants, children, persons with disabilities and people in vulnerable situations and the right to development, as well as gender equality, empowerment of women and intergenerational equity,

Also acknowledging the specific needs and concerns of developing country Parties arising from the impact of the implementation of response measures and, in this regard, decisions 5/CP.7, 1/CP.10, 1/CP.16 and 8/CP.17,

Emphasizing with serious concern the urgent need to address the significant gap between the aggregate effect of Parties' mitigation pledges in terms of global annual emissions of greenhouse gases by 2020 and aggregate emission pathways consistent with holding the increase in the global average temperature to well below 2 °C above pre-industrial levels and pursuing efforts to limit the temperature increase to 1.5 °C above pre-industrial levels,

Also emphasizing that enhanced pre-2020 ambition can lay a solid foundation for enhanced post-2020 ambition,

Stressing the urgency of accelerating the implementation of the Convention and its Kyoto Protocol in order to enhance pre-2020 ambition,

Recognizing the urgent need to enhance the provision of finance, technology and capacity-building support by developed country Parties, in a predictable manner, to enable enhanced pre-2020 action by developing country Parties,

Emphasizing the enduring benefits of ambitious and early action, including major reductions in the cost of future mitigation and adaptation efforts,

Acknowledging the need to promote universal access to sustainable energy in developing countries, in particular in Africa, through the enhanced deployment of renewable energy,

Agreeing to uphold and promote regional and international cooperation in order to mobilize stronger and more ambitious climate action by all Parties and non-Party stakeholders, including civil society, the private sector, financial institutions, cities and other subnational authorities, local communities and indigenous peoples,

I. ADOPTION

1. *Decides* to adopt the Paris Agreement under the United Nations Framework

Convention on Climate Change (hereinafter referred to as "the Agreement") as contained in the annex;

2. *Requests* the Secretary-General of the United Nations to be the Depositary of the Agreement and to have it open for signature in New York, United States of America, from 22 April 2016 to 21 April 2017;

3. *Invites* the Secretary-General to convene a high-level signature ceremony for the Agreement on 22 April 2016;

4. *Also invites* all Parties to the Convention to sign the Agreement at the ceremony to be convened by the Secretary-General, or at their earliest opportunity, and to deposit their respective instruments of ratification, acceptance, approval or accession, where appropriate, as soon as possible;

5. *Recognizes* that Parties to the Convention may provisionally apply all of the provisions of the Agreement pending its entry into force, and *requests* Parties to provide notification of any such provisional application to the Depositary;

6. *Notes* that the work of the Ad Hoc Working Group on the Durban Platform for Enhanced Action, in accordance with decision 1/CP.17, paragraph 4, has been completed;

7. *Decides* to establish the Ad Hoc Working Group on the Paris Agreement under the same arrangement, mutatis mutandis, as those concerning the election of officers to the Bureau of the Ad Hoc Working Group on the Durban Platform for Enhanced Action;[1]

8. *Also decides* that the Ad Hoc Working Group on the Paris Agreement shall prepare for the entry into force of the Agreement and for the convening of the first session of the Conference of the Parties serving as the meeting of the Parties to the Paris Agreement;

9. *Further decides* to oversee the implementation of the work programme resulting from the relevant requests contained in this decision;

10. *Requests* the Ad Hoc Working Group on the Paris Agreement to report regularly to the Conference of the Parties on the progress of its work and to complete its work by the first session of the Conference of the Parties serving as the meeting of the Parties to the Paris Agreement;

---

1) Endorsed by decision 2/CP.18, paragraph 2.

11. *Decides* that the Ad Hoc Working Group on the Paris Agreement shall hold its sessions starting in 2016 in conjunction with the sessions of the Convention subsidiary bodies and shall prepare draft decisions to be recommended through the Conference of the Parties to the Conference of the Parties serving as the meeting of the Parties to the Paris Agreement for consideration and adoption at its first session;

II. INTENDED NATIONALLY DETERMINED CONTRIBUTIONS

12. *Welcomes* the intended nationally determined contributions that have been communicated by Parties in accordance with decision 1/CP.19, paragraph 2(b);

13. *Reiterates* its invitation to all Parties that have not yet done so to communicate to the secretariat their intended nationally determined contributions towards achieving the objective of the Convention as set out in its Article 2 as soon as possible and well in advance of the twenty-second session of the Conference of the Parties (November 2016) and in a manner that facilitates the clarity, transparency and understanding of the intended nationally determined contributions;

14. *Requests* the secretariat to continue to publish the intended nationally determined contributions communicated by Parties on the UNFCCC website;

15. *Reiterates* its call to developed country Parties, the operating entities of the Financial Mechanism and any other organizations in a position to do so to provide support for the preparation and communication of the intended nationally determined contributions of Parties that may need such support;

16. *Takes note* of the synthesis report on the aggregate effect of intended nationally determined contributions communicated by Parties by 1 October 2015, contained in document FCCC/CP/2015/7;

17. *Notes* with concern that the estimated aggregate greenhouse gas emission levels in 2025 and 2030 resulting from the intended nationally determined contributions do not fall within least-cost 2 $^\circ$C scenarios but rather lead to a projected level of 55 gigatonnes in 2030, and *also notes* that much greater emission reduction efforts will be required than those associated with the intended nationally determined contributions in order to hold the increase in the global average temperature to below 2 $^\circ$C above pre-industrial levels by reducing emissions to 40 gigatonnes or to 1.5 $^\circ$C above pre-industrial levels by reducing to a level to be identified in the special report referred to in paragraph 21 below;

18. *Also notes, in this context,* the adaptation needs expressed by many developing country Parties in their intended nationally determined contributions;

19. *Requests* the secretariat to update the synthesis report referred to in paragraph 16 above so as to cover all the information in the intended nationally determined contributions communicated by Parties pursuant to decision 1/CP.20 by 4 April 2016 and to make it available by 2 May 2016;

20. *Decides* to convene a facilitative dialogue among Parties in 2018 to take stock of the collective efforts of Parties in relation to progress towards the long-term goal referred to in Article 4, paragraph 1, of the Agreement and to inform the preparation of nationally determined contributions pursuant to Article 4, paragraph 8, of the Agreement;

21. *Invites* the Intergovernmental Panel on Climate Change to provide a special report in 2018 on the impacts of global warming of 1.5 °C above pre-industrial levels and related global greenhouse gas emission pathways;

III. DECISIONS TO GIVE EFFECT TO THE AGREEMENT
MITIGATION

22. *Invites* Parties to communicate their first nationally determined contribution no later than when the Party submits its respective instrument of ratification, accession, or approval of the Paris Agreement. If a Party has communicated an intended nationally determined contribution prior to joining the Agreement, that Party shall be considered to have satisfied this provision unless that Party decides otherwise;

23. *Urges* those Parties whose intended nationally determined contribution pursuant to decision 1/CP.20 contains a time frame up to 2025 to communicate by 2020 a new nationally determined contribution and to do so every five years thereafter pursuant to Article 4, paragraph 9, of the Agreement;

24. *Requests* those Parties whose intended nationally determined contribution pursuant to decision 1/CP.20 contains a time frame up to 2030 to communicate or update by 2020 these contributions and to do so every five years thereafter pursuant to Article 4, paragraph 9, of the Agreement;

25. *Decides* that Parties shall submit to the secretariat their nationally determined contributions referred to in Article 4 of the Agreement at least 9 to 12 months in advance of the relevant meeting of the Conference of the Parties serving as the meeting of the

Parties to the Paris Agreement with a view to facilitating the clarity, transparency and understanding of these contributions, including through a synthesis report prepared by the secretariat;

26. *Requests* the Ad Hoc Working Group on the Paris Agreement to develop further guidance on features of the nationally determined contributions for consideration and adoption by the Conference of the Parties serving as the meeting of the Parties to the Paris Agreement at its first session;

27. *Agrees* that the information to be provided by Parties communicating their nationally determined contributions, in order to facilitate clarity, transparency and understanding, may include, as appropriate, inter alia, quantifiable information on the reference point (including, as appropriate, a base year), time frames and/or periods for implementation, scope and coverage, planning processes, assumptions and methodological approaches including those for estimating and accounting for anthropogenic greenhouse gas emissions and, as appropriate, removals, and how the Party considers that its nationally determined contribution is fair and ambitious, in the light of its national circumstances, and how it contributes towards achieving the objective of the Convention as set out in its Article 2;

28. *Requests* the Ad Hoc Working Group on the Paris Agreement to develop further guidance for the information to be provided by Parties in order to facilitate clarity, transparency and understanding of nationally determined contributions for consideration and adoption by the Conference of the Parties serving as the meeting of the Parties to the Paris Agreement at its first session;

29. *Also requests* the Subsidiary Body for Implementation to develop modalities and procedures for the operation and use of the public registry referred to in Article 4, paragraph 12, of the Agreement, for consideration and adoption by the Conference of the Parties serving as the meeting of the Parties to the Paris Agreement at its first session;

30. *Further requests* the secretariat to make available an interim public registry in the first half of 2016 for the recording of nationally determined contributions submitted in accordance with Article 4 of the Agreement, pending the adoption by the Conference of the Parties serving as the meeting of the Parties to the Paris Agreement of the modalities and procedures referred to in paragraph 29 above;

31. *Requests* the Ad Hoc Working Group on the Paris Agreement to elaborate, drawing from approaches established under the Convention and its related legal instruments

as appropriate, guidance for accounting for Parties' nationally determined contributions, as referred to in Article 4, paragraph 13, of the Agreement, for consideration and adoption by the Conference of the Parties serving as the meeting of the Parties to the Paris Agreement at its first session, which ensures that:

(a) Parties account for anthropogenic emissions and removals in accordance with methodologies and common metrics assessed by the Intergovernmental Panel on Climate Change and adopted by the Conference of the Parties serving as the meeting of the Parties to the Paris Agreement;

(b) Parties ensure methodological consistency, including on baselines, between the communication and implementation of nationally determined contributions;

(c) Parties strive to include all categories of anthropogenic emissions or removals in their nationally determined contributions and, once a source, sink or activity is included, continue to include it;

(d) Parties shall provide an explanation of why any categories of anthropogenic emissions or removals are excluded;

32. *Decides* that Parties shall apply the guidance mentioned in paragraph 31 above to the second and subsequent nationally determined contributions and that Parties may elect to apply such guidance to their first nationally determined contribution;

33. *Also decides* that the Forum on the Impact of the Implementation of response measures, under the subsidiary bodies, shall continue, and shall serve the Agreement;

34. *Further decides* that the Subsidiary Body for Scientific and Technological Advice and the Subsidiary Body for Implementation shall recommend, for consideration and adoption by the Conference of the Parties serving as the meeting of the Parties to the Paris Agreement at its first session, the modalities, work programme and functions of the Forum on the Impact of the Implementation of response measures to address the effects of the implementation of response measures under the Agreement by enhancing cooperation amongst Parties on understanding the impacts of mitigation actions under the Agreement and the exchange of information, experiences, and best practices amongst Parties to raise their resilience to these impacts;*

---

* Paragraph 35 has been deleted, and subsequent paragraph numbering and cross references to other paragraphs within the document will be amended at a later stage.

36. *Invites* Parties to communicate, by 2020, to the secretariat mid-century, long-term low greenhouse gas emission development strategies in accordance with Article 4, paragraph 19, of the Agreement, and *requests* the secretariat to publish on the UNFCCC website Parties' low greenhouse gas emission development strategies as communicated;

37. *Requests* the Subsidiary Body for Scientific and Technological Advice to develop and recommend the guidance referred to under Article 6, paragraph 2, of the Agreement for adoption by the Conference of the Parties serving as the meeting of the Parties to the Paris Agreement at its first session, including guidance to ensure that double counting is avoided on the basis of a corresponding adjustment by Parties for both anthropogenic emissions by sources and removals by sinks covered by their nationally determined contributions under the Agreement;

38. *Recommends* that the Conference of the Parties serving as the meeting of the Parties to the Paris Agreement adopt rules, modalities and procedures for the mechanism established by Article 6, paragraph 4, of the Agreement on the basis of:

(a) Voluntary participation authorized by each Party involved;

(b) Real, measurable, and long-term benefits related to the mitigation of climate change;

(c) Specific scopes of activities;

(d) Reductions in emissions that are additional to any that would otherwise occur;

(e) Verification and certification of emission reductions resulting from mitigation activities by designated operational entities;

(f) Experience gained with and lessons learned from existing mechanisms and approaches adopted under the Convention and its related legal instruments;

39. *Requests* the Subsidiary Body for Scientific and Technological Advice to develop and recommend rules, modalities and procedures for the mechanism referred to in paragraph 38 above for consideration and adoption by the Conference of the Parties serving as the meeting of the Parties to the Paris Agreement at its first session;

40. *Also requests* the Subsidiary Body for Scientific and Technological Advice to undertake a work programme under the framework for non-market approaches to sustainable development referred to in Article 6, paragraph 8, of the Agreement, with the objective of considering how to enhance linkages and create synergy between, inter alia,

mitigation, adaptation, finance, technology transfer and capacity-building, and how to facilitate the implementation and coordination of non-market approaches;

41. *Further requests* the Subsidiary Body for Scientific and Technological Advice to recommend a draft decision on the work programme referred to in paragraph 40 above, taking into account the views of Parties, for consideration and adoption by the Conference of the Parties serving as the meeting of the Parties to the Paris Agreement at its first session;

ADAPTATION

42. *Requests* the Adaptation Committee and the Least Developed Countries Expert Group to jointly develop modalities to recognize the adaptation efforts of developing country Parties, as referred to in Article 7, paragraph 3, of the Agreement, and make recommendations for consideration and adoption by the Conference of the Parties serving as the meeting of the Parties to the Paris Agreement at its first session;

43. *Also requests* the Adaptation Committee, taking into account its mandate and its second three-year workplan, and with a view to preparing recommendations for consideration and adoption by the Conference of the Parties serving as the meeting of the Parties to the Paris Agreement at its first session:

(a) To review, in 2017, the work of adaptation-related institutional arrangements under the Convention, with a view to identifying ways to enhance the coherence of their work, as appropriate, in order to respond adequately to the needs of Parties;

(b) To consider methodologies for assessing adaptation needs with a view to assisting developing countries, without placing an undue burden on them;

44. *Invites* all relevant United Nations agencies and international, regional and national financial institutions to provide information to Parties through the secretariat on how their development assistance and climate finance programmes incorporate climate-proofing and climate resilience measures;

45. *Requests* Parties to strengthen regional cooperation on adaptation where appropriate and, where necessary, establish regional centres and networks, in particular in developing countries, taking into account decision 1/CP.16, paragraph 13;

46. *Also requests* the Adaptation Committee and the Least Developed Countries Expert Group, in collaboration with the Standing Committee on Finance and other relevant in-

stitutions, to develop methodologies, and make recommendations for consideration and adoption by the Conference of the Parties serving as the meeting of the Parties to the Paris Agreement at its first session on:

(a) Taking the necessary steps to facilitate the mobilization of support for adaptation in developing countries in the context of the limit to global average temperature increase referred to in Article 2 of the Agreement;

(b) Reviewing the adequacy and effectiveness of adaptation and support referred to in Article 7, paragraph 14(c), of the Agreement;

47. *Further requests* the Green Climate Fund to expedite support for the least developed countries and other developing country Parties for the formulation of national adaptation plans, consistent with decisions 1/CP.16 and 5/CP.17, and for the subsequent implementation of policies, projects and programmes identified by them;

LOSS AND DAMAGE

48. *Decides* on the continuation of the Warsaw International Mechanism for Loss and Damage associated with Climate Change Impacts, following the review in 2016;

49. *Requests* the Executive Committee of the Warsaw International Mechanism to establish a clearinghouse for risk transfer that serves as a repository for information on insurance and risk transfer, in order to facilitate the efforts of Parties to develop and implement comprehensive risk management strategies;

50. *Also requests* the Executive Committee of the Warsaw International Mechanism to establish, according to its procedures and mandate, a task force to complement, draw upon the work of and involve, as appropriate, existing bodies and expert groups under the Convention including the Adaptation Committee and the Least Developed Countries Expert Group, as well as relevant organizations and expert bodies outside the Convention, to develop recommendations for integrated approaches to avert, minimize and address displacement related to the adverse impacts of climate change;

51. *Further requests* the Executive Committee of the Warsaw International Mechanism to initiate its work, at its next meeting, to operationalize the provisions referred to in paragraphs 49 and 50 above, and to report on progress thereon in its annual report;

52. *Agrees* that Article 8 of the Agreement does not involve or provide a basis for any liability or compensation;

FINANCE

53. *Decides* that, in the implementation of the Agreement, financial resources provided to developing countries should enhance the implementation of their policies, strategies, regulations and action plans and their climate change actions with respect to both mitigation and adaptation to contribute to the achievement of the purpose of the Agreement as defined in Article 2;

54. *Also decides* that, in accordance with Article 9, paragraph 3, of the Agreement, developed countries intend to continue their existing collective mobilization goal through 2025 in the context of meaningful mitigation actions and transparency on implementation; prior to 2025 the Conference of the Parties serving as the meeting of the Parties to the Paris Agreement shall set a new collective quantified goal from a floor of USD 100 billion per year, taking into account the needs and priorities of developing countries;

55. *Recognizes* the importance of adequate and predictable financial resources, including for results-based payments, as appropriate, for the implementation of policy approaches and positive incentives for reducing emissions from deforestation and forest degradation, and the role of conservation, sustainable management of forests and enhancement of forest carbon stocks; as well as alternative policy approaches, such as joint mitigation and adaptation approaches for the integral and sustainable management of forests; while reaffirming the importance of non-carbon benefits associated with such approaches; encouraging the coordination of support from, inter alia, public and private, bilateral and multilateral sources, such as the Green Climate Fund, and alternative sources in accordance with relevant decisions by the Conference of the Parties;

56. *Decides* to initiate, at its twenty-second session, a process to identify the information to be provided by Parties, in accordance with Article 9, paragraph 5, of the Agreement with the view to providing a recommendation for consideration and adoption by the Conference of the Parties serving as the meeting of the Parties to the Paris Agreement at its first session;

57. *Also decides* to ensure that the provision of information in accordance with Article 9, paragraph 7 of the Agreement shall be undertaken in accordance with modalities, procedures and guidelines referred to in paragraph 96 below;

58. *Requests* Subsidiary Body for Scientific and Technological Advice to develop modalities for the accounting of financial resources provided and mobilized through public

interventions in accordance with Article 9, paragraph 7, of the Agreement for consideration by the Conference of the Parties at its twenty-fourth session (November 2018), with the view to making a recommendation for consideration and adoption by the Conference of the Parties serving as the meeting of the Parties to the Paris Agreement at its first session;

59. *Decides* that the Green Climate Fund and the Global Environment Facility, the entities entrusted with the operation of the Financial Mechanism of the Convention, as well as the Least Developed Countries Fund and the Special Climate Change Fund, administered by the Global Environment Facility, shall serve the Agreement;

60. *Recognizes* that the Adaptation Fund may serve the Agreement, subject to relevant decisions by the Conference of the Parties serving as the meeting of the Parties to the Kyoto Protocol and the Conference of the Parties serving as the meeting of the Parties to the Paris Agreement;

61. *Invites* the Conference of the Parties serving as the meeting of the Parties to the Kyoto Protocol to consider the issue referred to in paragraph 60 above and make a recommendation to the Conference of the Parties serving as the meeting of the Parties to the Paris Agreement at its first session;

62. *Recommends* that the Conference of the Parties serving as the meeting of the Parties to the Paris Agreement shall provide guidance to the entities entrusted with the operation of the Financial Mechanism of the Convention on the policies, programme priorities and eligibility criteria related to the Agreement for transmission by the Conference of the Parties;

63. *Decides* that the guidance to the entities entrusted with the operations of the Financial Mechanism of the Convention in relevant decisions of the Conference of the Parties, including those agreed before adoption of the Agreement, shall apply mutatis mutandis;

64. *Also decides* that the Standing Committee on Finance shall serve the Agreement in line with its functions and responsibilities established under the Conference of the Parties;

65. *Urges* the institutions serving the Agreement to enhance the coordination and delivery of resources to support country-driven strategies through simplified and efficient application and approval procedures, and through continued readiness support to devel-

oping country Parties, including the least developed countries and small island develop-ing States, as appropriate;

TECHNOLOGY DEVELOPMENT AND TRANSFER

66. *Takes note of* the interim report of the Technology Executive Committee on guid-ance on enhanced implementation of the results of technology needs assessments as re-ferred to in document FCCC/SB/2015/INF.3;

67. *Decides* to strengthen the Technology Mechanism and requests the Technology Executive Committee and the Climate Technology Centre and Network, in supporting the implementation of the Agreement, to undertake further work relating to, inter alia:

(a) Technology research, development and demonstration;

(b) The development and enhancement of endogenous capacities and technologies;

68. *Requests* the Subsidiary Body for Scientific and Technological Advice to initiate, at its forty-fourth session (May 2016), the elaboration of the technology framework estab-lished under Article 10, paragraph 4, of the Agreement and to report on its findings to the Conference of the Parties, with a view to the Conference of the Parties making a rec-ommendation on the framework to the Conference of the Parties serving as the meeting of the Parties to the Paris Agreement for consideration and adoption at its first session, taking into consideration that the framework should facilitate, inter alia:

(a) The undertaking and updating of technology needs assessments, as well as the *enhanced* implementation of their results, particularly technology action plans and project ideas, through the preparation of bankable projects;

(b) The provision of enhanced financial and technical support for the im-plementation of the results of the technology needs assessments;

(c) The assessment of technologies that are ready for transfer;

(d) The enhancement of enabling environments for and the addressing of barriers to the development and transfer of socially and environmentally sound technologies;

69. *Decides* that the Technology Executive Committee and the Climate Technology Centre and Network shall report to the Conference of the Parties serving as the meeting of the Parties to the Paris Agreement, through the subsidiary bodies, on their activities to support the implementation of the Agreement;

70. *Also decides* to undertake a periodic assessment of the effectiveness of and the adequacy of the support provided to the Technology Mechanism in supporting the implementation of the Agreement on matters relating to technology development and transfer;

71. *Requests* the Subsidiary Body for Implementation to initiate, at its forty-fourth session , the elaboration of the scope of and modalities for the periodic assessment referred to in paragraph 70 above, taking into account the review of the Climate Technology Centre and Network as referred to in decision 2/CP.17, annex VII, paragraph 20 and the modalities for the global stocktake referred to in Article 14 of the Agreement, for consideration and adoption by the Conference of the Parties at its twenty-fifth session (November 2019);

CAPACITY-BUILDING

72. *Decides* to establish the Paris Committee on Capacity-building whose aim will be to address gaps and needs, both current and emerging, in implementing capacity-building in developing country Parties and further enhancing capacity-building efforts, including with regard to coherence and coordination in capacity-building activities under the Convention;

73. *Also decides* that the Paris Committee on Capacity-building will manage and oversee the work plan mentioned in paragraph 74 below;

74. *Further decides* to launch a work plan for the period 2016–2020 with the following activities:

(a) Assessing how to increase synergies through cooperation and avoid duplication among existing bodies established under the Convention that implement capacity-building activities, including through collaborating with institutions under and outside the Convention;

(b) Identifying capacity gaps and needs and recommending ways to address them;

(c) Promoting the development and dissemination of tools and methodologies for the implementation of capacity-building;

(d) Fostering global, regional, national and subnational cooperation;

(e) Identifying and collecting good practices, challenges, experiences, and lessons learned from work on capacity-building by bodies established under the Convention;

(f) Exploring how developing country Parties can take ownership of building and maintaining capacity over time and space;

(g) Identifying opportunities to strengthen capacity at the national, regional, and subnational level;

(h) Fostering dialogue, coordination, collaboration and coherence among relevant processes and initiatives under the Convention, including through exchanging information on capacity-building activities and strategies of bodies established under the Convention;

(i) Providing guidance to the secretariat on the maintenance and further development of the web-based capacity-building portal;

75. *Decides* that the Paris Committee on Capacity-building will annually focus on an area or theme related to enhanced technical exchange on capacity-building, with the purpose of maintaining up-to-date knowledge on the successes and challenges in building capacity effectively in a particular area;

76. *Requests* the Subsidiary Body for Implementation to organize annual in-session meetings of the Paris Committee on Capacity-building;

77. *Also requests* the Subsidiary Body for Implementation to develop the terms of reference for the Paris Committee on Capacity-building, in the context of the third comprehensive review of the implementation of the capacity-building framework, also taking into account paragraphs 75, 76, 77 and 78 above and paragraphs 82 and 83 below, with a view to recommending a draft decision on this matter for consideration and adoption by the Conference of the Parties at its twenty-second session;

78. *Invites* Parties to submit their views on the membership of the Paris Committee on Capacity-building by 9 March 2016;[2]

79. *Requests* the secretariat to compile the submissions referred to in paragraph 78 above into a miscellaneous document for consideration by the Subsidiary Body for Implementation at its forty-fourth session;

80. *Decides* that the inputs to the Paris Committee on Capacity-building will include, inter alia, submissions, the outcome of the third comprehensive review of the implementation of the capacity-building framework, the secretariat's annual synthesis report on the implementation of the framework for capacity-building in developing countries,

---

2)   Parties should submit their views via the submissions portal at <http://www.unfccc.int/5900>.

the secretariat's compilation and synthesis report on capacity-building work of bodies established under the Convention and its Kyoto Protocol, and reports on the Durban Forum and the capacity-building portal;

81. *Requests* the Paris Committee on Capacity-building to prepare annual technical progress reports on its work, and to make these reports available at the sessions of the Subsidiary Body for Implementation coinciding with the sessions of the Conference of the Parties;

82. *Also requests* the Conference of the Parties at its twenty-fifth session (November 2019), to review the progress, need for extension, the effectiveness and enhancement of the Paris Committee on Capacity-building and to take any action it considers appropriate, with a view to making recommendations to the Conference of the Parties serving as the meeting of the Parties to the Paris Agreement at its first session on enhancing institutional arrangements for capacity-building consistent with Article 11, paragraph 5, of the Agreement;

83. *Calls upon* all Parties to ensure that education, training and public awareness, as reflected in Article 6 of the Convention and in Article 12 of the Agreement are adequately considered in their contribution to capacity-building;

84. *Invites* the Conference of the Parties serving as the meeting of the Parties to the Paris Agreement at its first session to explore ways of enhancing the implementation of training, public awareness, public participation and public access to information so as to enhance actions under the Agreement;

TRANSPARENCY OF ACTION AND SUPPORT

85. *Decides* to establish a Capacity-building Initiative for Transparency in order to build institutional and technical capacity, both pre- and post-2020. This initiative will support developing country Parties, upon request, in meeting enhanced transparency requirements as defined in Article 13 of the Agreement in a timely manner;

86. *Also decides* that the Capacity-building Initiative for Transparency will aim:

(a) To strengthen national institutions for transparency-related activities in line with national priorities;

(b) To provide relevant tools, training and assistance for meeting the provisions stipulated in Article 13 of the Agreement;

(c) To assist in the improvement of transparency over time;

87. *Urges and requests* the Global Environment Facility to make arrangements to support the establishment and operation of the Capacity-building Initiative for Transparency as a priority reporting-related need, including through voluntary contributions to support developing countries in the sixth replenishment of the Global Environment Facility and future replenishment cycles, to complement existing support under the Global Environment Facility;

88. *Decides* to assess the implementation of the Capacity-building Initiative for Transparency in the context of the seventh review of the financial mechanism;

89. *Requests* that the Global Environment Facility, as an operating entity of the financial mechanism include in its annual report to the Conference of the Parties the progress of work in the design, development and implementation of the Capacity-building Initiative for Transparency referred to in paragraph 85 above starting in 2016;

90. *Decides* that, in accordance with Article 13, paragraph 2, of the Agreement, developing countries shall be provided flexibility in the implementation of the provisions of that Article, including in the scope, frequency and level of detail of reporting, and in the scope of review, and that the scope of review could provide for in-country reviews to be optional, while such flexibilities shall be reflected in the development of modalities, procedures and guidelines referred to in paragraph 92 below;

91. *Also decides* that all Parties, except for the least developed country Parties and small island developing States, shall submit the information referred to in Article 13, paragraphs 7, 8, 9 and 10, as appropriate, no less frequently than on a biennial basis, and that the least developed country Parties and small island developing States may submit this information at their discretion;

92. *Requests* the Ad Hoc Working Group on the Paris Agreement to develop recommendations for modalities, procedures and guidelines in accordance with Article 13, paragraph 13, of the Agreement, and to define the year of their first and subsequent review and update, as appropriate, at regular intervals, for consideration by the Conference of the Parties, at its twenty-fourth session, with a view to forwarding them to the Conference of the Parties serving as the meeting of the Parties to the Paris Agreement for adoption at its first session;

93. *Also requests* the Ad Hoc Working Group on the Paris Agreement in developing

the recommendations for the modalities, procedures and guidelines referred to in paragraph 92 above to take into account, inter alia:

(a) The importance of facilitating improved reporting and transparency over time;

(b) The need to provide flexibility to those developing country Parties that need it in the light of their capacities;

(c) The need to promote transparency, accuracy, completeness, consistency, and comparability;

(d) The need to avoid duplication as well as undue burden on Parties and the secretariat;

(e) The need to ensure that Parties maintain at least the frequency and quality of reporting in accordance with their respective obligations under the Convention;

(f) The need to ensure that double counting is avoided;

(g) The need to ensure environmental integrity;

94. *Further requests* the Ad Hoc Working Group on the Paris Agreement, when developing the modalities, procedures and guidelines referred to in paragraph 92 above, to draw on the experiences from and take into account other on-going relevant processes under the Convention;

95. *Requests* the Ad Hoc Working Group on the Paris Agreement, when developing modalities, procedures and guidelines referred to in paragraph 92 above, to consider, inter alia:

(a) The types of flexibility available to those developing countries that need it on the basis of their capacities;

(b) The consistency between the methodology communicated in the nationally determined contribution and the methodology for reporting on progress made towards achieving individual Parties' respective nationally determined contribution;

(c) That Parties report information on adaptation action and planning including, if appropriate, their national adaptation plans, with a view to collectively exchanging information and sharing lessons learned;

(d) Support provided, enhancing delivery of support for both adaptation and mitigation through, inter alia, the common tabular formats for reporting support, and taking into account issues considered by the Subsidiary Body for Scientific and Technological Advice on methodologies for reporting on financial information, and enhancing the reporting by developing countries on support received, including the use, impact and estimated results thereof;

(e) Information in the biennial assessments and other reports of the Standing Committee on Finance and other relevant bodies under the Convention;

(f) Information on the social and economic impact of response measures;

96. *Also requests* the Ad Hoc Working Group on the Paris Agreement, when developing recommendations for modalities, procedures and guidelines referred to in paragraph 92 above, to enhance the transparency of support provided in accordance with Article 9 of the Agreement;

97. *Further requests* the Ad Hoc Working Group on the Paris Agreement to report on the progress of work on the modalities, procedures and guidelines referred to in paragraph 92 above to future sessions of the Conference of the Parties, and that this work be concluded no later than 2018;

98. *Decides* that the modalities, procedures and guidelines developed under paragraph 92 above, shall be applied upon the entry into force of the Paris Agreement;

99. *Also decides* that the modalities, procedures and guidelines of this transparency framework shall build upon and eventually supersede the measurement, reporting and verification system established by decision 1/CP.16, paragraphs 40 to 47 and 60 to 64, and decision 2/CP.17, paragraphs 12 to 62, immediately following the submission of the final biennial reports and biennial update reports;

GLOBAL STOCKTAKE

100. *Requests* the Ad Hoc Working Group on the Paris Agreement to identify the sources of input for the global stocktake referred to in Article 14 of the Agreement and to report to the Conference of the Parties, with a view to the Conference of the Parties making a recommendation to the Conference of the Parties serving as the meeting of the Parties to the Paris Agreement for consideration and adoption at its first session, including, but not limited to:

(a) Information on:

(i) The overall effect of the nationally determined contributions communicated by Parties;

(ii) The state of adaptation efforts, support, experiences and priorities from the communications referred to in Article 7, paragraphs 10 and 11, of the Agreement, and reports referred to in Article 13, paragraph 7, of the Agreement;

(iii) The mobilization and provision of support;

(b) The latest reports of the Intergovernmental Panel on Climate Change;

(c) Reports of the subsidiary bodies;

101. *Also requests* the Subsidiary Body for Scientific and Technological Advice to provide advice on how the assessments of the Intergovernmental Panel on Climate Change can inform the global stocktake of the implementation of the Agreement pursuant to its Article 14 of the Agreement and to report on this matter to the Ad Hoc Working Group on the Paris Agreement at its second session;

102. *Further requests* the Ad Hoc Working Group on the Paris Agreement to develop modalities for the global stocktake referred to in Article 14 of the Agreement and to report to the Conference of the Parties, with a view to making a recommendation to the Conference of the Parties serving as the meeting of the Parties to the Paris Agreement for consideration and adoption at its first session;

FACILITATING IMPLEMENTATION AND COMPLIANCE

103. *Decides* that the committee referred to in Article 15, paragraph 2, of the Agreement shall consist of 12 members with recognized competence in relevant scientific, technical, socio-economic or legal fields, to be elected by the Conference of the Parties serving as the meeting of the Parties to the Paris Agreement on the basis of equitable geographical representation, with two members each from the five regional groups of the United Nations and one member each from the small island developing States and the least developed countries, while taking into account the goal of gender balance;

104. *Requests* the Ad Hoc Working Group on the Paris Agreement to develop the modalities and procedures for the effective operation of the committee referred to in Article 15, paragraph 2, of the Agreement, with a view to the Ad Hoc Working Group on the Paris Agreement completing its work on such modalities and procedures for consideration and adoption by the Conference of the Parties serving as the meeting of the

Parties to the Paris Agreement at its first session;

FINAL CLAUSES

105. *Also requests* the secretariat, solely for the purposes of Article 21 of the Agreement, to make available on its website on the date of adoption of the Agreement as well as in the report of the Conference of the Parties at its twenty-first session, information on the most up-to-date total and per cent of greenhouse gas emissions communicated by Parties to the Convention in their national communications, greenhouse gas inventory reports, biennial reports or biennial update reports;

Ⅳ. ENHANCED ACTION PRIOR TO 2020

106. *Resolves* to ensure the highest possible mitigation efforts in the pre-2020 period, including by:

(a) Urging all Parties to the Kyoto Protocol that have not already done so to ratify and implement the Doha Amendment to the Kyoto Protocol;

(b) Urging all Parties that have not already done so to make and implement a mitigation pledge under the Cancun Agreements;

(c) Reiterating its resolve, as set out in decision 1/CP.19, paragraphs 3 and 4, to accelerate the full implementation of the decisions constituting the agreed outcome pursuant to decision 1/CP.13 and enhance ambition in the pre-2020 period in order to ensure the highest possible mitigation efforts under the Convention by all Parties;

(d) Inviting developing country Parties that have not submitted their first biennial update reports to do so as soon as possible;

(e) Urging all Parties to participate in the existing measurement, reporting and verification processes under the Cancun Agreements, in a timely manner, with a view to demonstrating progress made in the implementation of their mitigation pledges;

107. *Encourages* Parties to promote the voluntary cancellation by Party and non-Party stakeholders, without double counting of units issued under the Kyoto Protocol, including certified emission reductions that are valid for the second commitment period;

108. *Urges* host and purchasing Parties to report transparently on internationally transferred mitigation outcomes, including outcomes used to meet international pledges, and

emission units issued under the Kyoto Protocol with a view to promoting environmental integrity and avoiding double counting;

109. *Recognizes* the social, economic and environmental value of voluntary mitigation actions and their co-benefits for adaptation, health and sustainable development;

110. *Resolves* to strengthen, in the period 2016–2020, the existing technical examination process on mitigation as defined in decision 1/CP.19, paragraph 5(a), and decision 1/CP.20, paragraph 19, taking into account the latest scientific knowledge, including by:

(a) Encouraging Parties, Convention bodies and international organizations to engage in this process, including, as appropriate, in cooperation with relevant non-Party stakeholders, to share their experiences and suggestions, including from regional events, and to cooperate in facilitating the implementation of policies, practices and actions identified during this process in accordance with national sustainable development priorities;

(b) Striving to improve, in consultation with Parties, access to and participation in this process by developing country Party and non-Party experts;

(c) Requesting the Technology Executive Committee and the Climate Technology Centre and Network in accordance with their respective mandates:

(i) To engage in the technical expert meetings and enhance their efforts to facilitate and support Parties in scaling up the implementation of policies, practices and actions identified during this process;

(ii) To provide regular updates during the technical expert meetings on the progress made in facilitating the implementation of policies, practices and actions previously identified during this process;

(iii) To include information on their activities under this process in their joint annual report to the Conference of the Parties;

(d) Encouraging Parties to make effective use of the Climate Technology Centre and Network to obtain assistance to develop economically, environmentally and socially viable project proposals in the high mitigation potential areas identified in this process;

111. *Encourages* the operating entities of the Financial Mechanism of the Convention to engage in the technical expert meetings and to inform participants of their contribution to facilitating progress in the implementation of policies, practices and actions identified

during the technical examination process;

112. *Requests* the secretariat to organize the process referred to in paragraph 110 above and disseminate its results, including by:

(a) Organizing, in consultation with the Technology Executive Committee and relevant expert organizations, regular technical expert meetings focusing on specific policies, practices and actions representing best practices and with the potential to be scalable and replicable;

(b) Updating, on an annual basis, following the meetings referred to in paragraph 112(a) above and in time to serve as input to the summary for policymakers referred to in paragraph 112(c) below, a technical paper on the mitigation benefits and co-benefits of policies, practices and actions for enhancing mitigation ambition, as well as on options for supporting their implementation, information on which should be made available in a user-friendly online format;

(c) Preparing, in consultation with the champions referred to in paragraph 122 below, a summary for policymakers, with information on specific policies, practices and actions representing best practices and with the potential to be scalable and replicable, and on options to support their implementation, as well as on relevant collaborative initiatives, and publishing the summary at least two months in advance of each session of the Conference of the Parties as input for the high-level event referred to in paragraph 121 below;

113. *Decides* that the process referred to in paragraph 110 above should be organized jointly by the Subsidiary Body for Implementation and the Subsidiary Body for Scientific and Technological Advice and should take place on an ongoing basis until 2020;

114. *Also decides* to conduct in 2017 an assessment of the process referred to in paragraph 110 above so as to improve its effectiveness;

115. *Resolves* to enhance the provision of urgent and adequate finance, technology and capacity-building support by developed country Parties in order to enhance the level of ambition of pre-2020 action by Parties, and in this regard *strongly urges* developed country Parties to scale up their level of financial support, with a concrete roadmap to achieve the goal of jointly providing USD 100 billion annually by 2020 for mitigation and adaptation while significantly increasing adaptation finance from current levels and to further provide appropriate technology and capacity-building support;

116. *Decides* to conduct a facilitative dialogue in conjunction with the twenty-second session of the Conference of the Parties to assess the progress in implementing decision 1/CP.19, paragraphs 3 and 4, and identify relevant opportunities to enhance the provision of financial resources, including for technology development and transfer and capacity-building support, with a view to identifying ways to enhance the ambition of mitigation efforts by all Parties, including identifying relevant opportunities to enhance the provision and mobilization of support and enabling environments;

117. *Acknowledges* with appreciation the results of the Lima-Paris Action Agenda, which build on the climate summit convened on 23 September 2014 by the Secretary-General of the United Nations;

118. *Welcomes* the efforts of non-Party stakeholders to scale up their climate actions, and *encourages* the registration of those actions in the Non-State Actor Zone for Climate Action platform;[3]

119. *Encourages* Parties to work closely with non-Party stakeholders to catalyse efforts to strengthen mitigation and adaptation action;

120. *Also encourages* non-Party stakeholders to increase their engagement in the processes referred to in paragraph 110 above and paragraph 125 below;

121. *Agrees* to convene, pursuant to decision 1/CP.20, paragraph 21, building on the Lima-Paris Action Agenda and in conjunction with each session of the Conference of the Parties during the period 2016–2020, a high-level event that:

(a) Further strengthens high-level engagement on the implementation of policy options and actions arising from the processes referred to in paragraph 110 above and paragraph 125 below, drawing on the summary for policymakers referred to in paragraph 112(c) above;

(b) Provides an opportunity for announcing new or strengthened voluntary efforts, initiatives and coalitions, including the implementation of policies, practices and actions arising from the processes referred to in paragraph 110 above and paragraph 125 below and presented in the summary for policymakers referred to in paragraph 112(c) above;

(c) Takes stock of related progress and recognizes new or strengthened voluntary efforts, initiatives and coalitions;

---

3) <http://climateaction.unfccc.int/>.

(d) Provides meaningful and regular opportunities for the effective high-level engagement of dignitaries of Parties, international organizations, international cooperative initiatives and non-Party stakeholders;

122. *Decides* that two high-level champions shall be appointed to act on behalf of the President of the Conference of the Parties to facilitate through strengthened high-level engagement in the period 2016–2020 the successful execution of existing efforts and the scaling-up and introduction of new or strengthened voluntary efforts, initiatives and coalitions, including by:

(a) Working with the Executive Secretary and the current and incoming Presidents of the Conference of the Parties to coordinate the annual high-level event referred to in paragraph 121 above;

(b) Engaging with interested Parties and non-Party stakeholders, including to further the voluntary initiatives of the Lima-Paris Action Agenda;

(c) Providing guidance to the secretariat on the organization of technical expert meetings referred to in paragraph 112(a) above and paragraph 130(a) below;

123. *Also decides* that the high-level champions referred to in paragraph 122 above should normally serve for a term of two years, with their terms overlapping for a full year to ensure continuity, such that:

(a) The President of the Conference of the Parties of the twenty-first session should appoint one champion, who should serve for one year from the date of the appointment until the last day of the Conference of the Parties at its twenty-second session;

(b) The President of the Conference of the Parties of the twenty-second session should appoint one champion who should serve for two years from the date of the appointment until the last day of the Conference of the Parties at its twenty-third session (November 2017);

(c) Thereafter, each subsequent President of the Conference of the Parties should appoint one champion who should serve for two years and succeed the previously appointed champion whose term has ended;

124. *Invites* all interested Parties and relevant organizations to provide support for the work of the champions referred to in paragraph 122 above;

125. *Decides* to launch, in the period 2016-2020, a technical examination process on adaptation;

126. *Also decides* that the technical examination process on adaptation referred to in paragraph 125 above will endeavour to identify concrete opportunities for strengthening resilience, reducing vulnerabilities and increasing the understanding and implementation of adaptation actions;

127. *Further decides* that the technical examination process referred to in paragraph 125 above should be organized jointly by the Subsidiary Body for Implementation and the Subsidiary Body for Scientific and Technological Advice, and conducted by the Adaptation Committee;

128. *Decides* that the process referred to in paragraph 125 above will be pursued by:

(a) Facilitating the sharing of good practices, experiences and lessons learned;

(b) Identifying actions that could significantly enhance the implementation of adaptation actions, including actions that could enhance economic diversification and have mitigation co-benefits;

(c) Promoting cooperative action on adaptation;

(d) Identifying opportunities to strengthen enabling environments and enhance the provision of support for adaptation in the context of specific policies, practices and actions;

129. *Also decides* that the technical examination process on adaptation referred to in paragraph 125 above will take into account the process, modalities, outputs, outcomes and lessons learned from the technical examination process on mitigation referred to in paragraph 110 above;

130. *Requests* the secretariat to support the technical examination process referred to in paragraph 125 above by:

(a) Organizing regular technical expert meetings focusing on specific policies, strategies and actions;

(b) Preparing annually, on the basis of the meetings referred to in paragraph 130(a) above and in time to serve as an input to the summary for policymakers referred to in paragraph 112(c) above, a technical paper on opportunities to enhance adaptation action, as well as options to support their implementation, information on which should be made available in a user-friendly online format;

131. *Decides* that in conducting the process referred to in paragraph 125 above, the Adaptation Committee will engage with and explore ways to take into account, synergize with and build on the existing arrangements for adaptation-related work programmes, bodies and institutions under the Convention so as to ensure coherence and maximum value;

132. *Also decides* to conduct, in conjunction with the assessment referred to in paragraph 120 above, an assessment of the process referred to in paragraph 125 above, so as to improve its effectiveness;

133. *Invites* Parties and observer organizations to submit information on the opportunities referred to in paragraph 126 above by 3 February 2016;

V. NON-PARTY STAKEHOLDERS

134. *Welcomes* the efforts of all non-Party stakeholders to address and respond to climate change, including those of civil society, the private sector, financial institutions, cities and other subnational authorities;

135. *Invites* the non-Party stakeholders referred to in paragraph 134 above to scale up their efforts and support actions to reduce emissions and/or to build resilience and decrease vulnerability to the adverse effects of climate change and demonstrate these efforts via the Non-State Actor Zone for Climate Action platform[4] referred to in paragraph 118 above;

136. *Recognizes* the need to strengthen knowledge, technologies, practices and efforts of local communities and indigenous peoples related to addressing and responding to climate change, and *establishes* a platform for the exchange of experiences and sharing of best practices on mitigation and adaptation in a holistic and integrated manner;

137. *Also recognizes* the important role of providing incentives for emission reduction activities, including tools such as domestic policies and carbon pricing;

---

4) <http://climateaction.unfccc.int/>.

VI. ADMINISTRATIVE AND BUDGETARY MATTERS

138. *Takes note* of the estimated budgetary implications of the activities to be undertaken by the secretariat referred to in this decision and requests that the actions of the secretariat called for in this decision be undertaken subject to the availability of financial resources;

139. *Emphasizes* the urgency of making additional resources available for the implementation of the relevant actions, including actions referred to in this decision, and the implementation of the work programme referred to in paragraph 9 above;

140. *Urges* Parties to make voluntary contributions for the timely implementation of this decision.

박덕영

연세대학교 법과대학 졸업
연세대학교 대학원 법학석사, 법학박사
영국 University of Cambridge 법학석사 (L.L.M)
영국 University of Edinburgh 박사과정 마침
교육부 국비유학시험 합격
(현) 연세대학교 법학전문대학원 교수
　　　대한국제법학회 부회장
　　　한국국제경제법학회 회장
　　　산업통상자원부 통상교섭민간자문위원
　　　대한민국 국회 입법자문위원
　　　법제처 정부입법자문위원
　　　연세대 SSK 기후변화와 국제법연구센터장
　　　연세대 외교통상학 연계전공, UIC JCL 책임교수

『EU란 무엇인가』, 『알기쉬운 국제중재』, 『국제법 기본조약집』, 『국제경제법 기본조약집』,
『국제투자법과 환경문제』, 『중국의 기후변화대응과 외교협상』, 『일본의 환경외교』, 『국제환경법』,
『국제환경법 주요판례』, 『국제투자법』, 『국제경제법의 쟁점』
Legal Issues on Climate Change and International Trade Law, Springer, 2016 외
국제통상법, 국제환경법 분야 국내외 저서와 논문 다수

기후변화 국제조약집

초판발행　　　2017년 6월 30일

편저자　　　박덕영
발행인　　　안종만

편 집　　　문선미
기획/마케팅　　　조성호
표지디자인　　　권효진
제 작　　　우인도·고철민

펴낸곳　　　(주) **박영사**
　　　　　서울특별시 종로구 새문안로3길 36, 1601
　　　　　등록 1959. 3. 11. 제3070-1959-1호(倫)

전 화　　　02)733-6771
f a x　　　02)736-4818
e-mail　　　pys@pybook.co.kr
homepage　　　www.pybook.co.kr
ISBN　　　979-11-303-3070-9　93360